Sites of Violence and Memory in Modern Spain

Sites of Violence and Memory in Modern Spain

From the Spanish Civil War to the Present Day

Edited by
Antonio Míguez Macho

BLOOMSBURY ACADEMIC
LONDON • NEW YORK • OXFORD • NEW DELHI • SYDNEY

BLOOMSBURY ACADEMIC
Bloomsbury Publishing Plc
50 Bedford Square, London, WC1B 3DP, UK
1385 Broadway, New York, NY 10018, USA
29 Earlsfort Terrace, Dublin 2, Ireland

BLOOMSBURY, BLOOMSBURY ACADEMIC and the Diana logo are trademarks of Bloomsbury Publishing Plc

First published in Great Britain 2021
Paperback edition first published 2023

Copyright © Antonio Míguez Macho, 2021

Antonio Míguez Macho has asserted his right under the Copyright, Designs and Patents Act, 1988, to be identified as Editor of this work.

Cover image: Ruins of the Theatre Vilagarcía (Vilagarcía de Arousa, Galicia-Spain) © nomesevoces.net

All rights reserved. No part of this publication may be reproduced or transmitted in any form or by any means, electronic or mechanical, including photocopying, recording, or any information storage or retrieval system, without prior permission in writing from the publishers.

Bloomsbury Publishing Plc does not have any control over, or responsibility for, any third-party websites referred to or in this book. All internet addresses given in this book were correct at the time of going to press. The author and publisher regret any inconvenience caused if addresses have changed or sites have ceased to exist, but can accept no responsibility for any such changes.

Every effort has been made to trace copyright holders and to obtain their permissions for the use of copyright material. The publisher apologizes for any errors or omissions and would be grateful if notified of any corrections that should be incorporated in future reprints or editions of this book.

A catalogue record for this book is available from the British Library.

Library of Congress Cataloging-in-Publication Data
Names: Mi′guez Macho, Antonio, editor.
Title: Sites of violence and memory in modern Spain : from the Spanish Civil War to the present day / edited by Antonio Mi′guez Macho.
Description: London ; New York : Bloomsbury Academic, 2021. | Includes bibliographical references and index. |
Identifiers: LCCN 2021017363 (print) | LCCN 2021017364 (ebook) | ISBN 9781350199200 (hardback) | ISBN 9781350199217 (ebook) | ISBN 9781350199224 (epub)
Subjects: LCSH: Political violence–Spain–Historiography. | Collective memory–Spain. | Historic sites–Spain. | Spain–History–Civil War, 1936-1939–Historiography. | Spain–History–1939-1975–Historiography.
Classification: LCC DP269.A56 S58 2021 (print) | LCC DP269.A56 (ebook) | DDC 946.08–dc23
LC record available at https://lccn.loc.gov/2021017363
LC ebook record available at https://lccn.loc.gov/2021017364

ISBN:	HB:	978-1-3501-9920-0
	PB:	978-1-3501-9924-8
	ePDF:	978-1-3501-9921-7
	eBook:	978-1-3501-9922-4

Typeset by Integra Software Services Pvt. Ltd.

To find out more about our authors and books visit www.bloomsbury.com and sign up for our newsletters.

Contents

List of Illustrations	viii
List of Map	x
List of Table	xi
List of Contributors	xii

1 'Where forgetting resides … '. Twentieth-century sites of violence and present-day sites of memory: A global vision from the Spanish case *Antonio Míguez Macho* 1
   - The era of justification 1
   - The era of denunciation 8
   - The era of memory 11
   - So that forgetting does not triumph: What we have done with this work 16
   - Notes 20

Part 1   Sites of Sentencing and Death

2 Civil government buildings: Hearts of rebel violence during the Spanish Civil War. The case of Granada *Miguel Ángel Del Arco Blanco* 27
   - The coup d'etat and civil governments 29
   - The civil government building and surrounding silence 33
   - The civil government and its men in the summer of 1936 34
   - Notes 41

3 The staging of 'formal' violence: Sentencing sites *Conchi López Sánchez* 47
   - The distorted use of military justice: The *inventio* – legal legitimacy of the coup 48
   - Spaces of legal domination: Maritime jurisdiction and land jurisdiction 53
   - Military trials sites and the legal spectacle 60
   - Notes 61

4	Memory and forgetting of the 'paseos': Places and accounts *Xabier Buxeiro Alonso*	65
	Paseos in history: Definition and typology	66
	Paseos in memory: Absences and tributes	71
	Paseos and memory policies	77
	Notes	79

Part 2   Sites of Confinement and Denial

5	Francoist concentration camps: Spaces of imprisonment and forced labour *Rafael García Ferreira*	85
	An overview on the concentration camps systems	85
	Spanish concentration camps	87
	A Francoist concentration camp: The case of Lavacolla	92
	Memory and forgetting of the Francoist concentration system	96
	The punishment of the defeated	99
	Notes	101
6	Imprisoned in everyday life: Sites of violence and social control in Franco's Spain (1936–1950) *Claudio Hernández Burgos*	105
	The dictatorship, space and violence	107
	Controlled spaces, spaces of struggle, redefined spaces	112
	Post-war communities as spaces of social control	117
	Notes	118
7	Memory alephs: The symbolization of violence through places where 'Nothing Ever Happens' *Aldara Cidrás*	125
	Memory alephs and the unspeakable	125
	Case studies: Guernica, Pontevedra, Badajoz and Belchite	127
	A new map of the memory alephs	141
	Notes	142

Part 3   Sites of Memorialization and Conflict

8	Memory on the walls: Violence, memory and the forgetting of sites of violence during the transition to democracy after Franco's death *Iria Morgade Valcárcel*	147
	Oia and Camposancos, the history of two places	147
	Prisoner drawings as places of memory	152

The evolution of the public policies of memory
during the Spanish Transition 156
Final reflections 160
Notes 162

9 Discourses and public policies on memory: The narrative
construction of the violent past in the Basque Country (1936–2020)
Erik Zubiaga Arana 167
The war of 1936 168
ETA, the 'new gudaris' 171
Contemporary narratives 174
The conflicting management of memory 177
Notes 181

10 From the courts of Buenos Aires to the walls of Guadalajara:
The Argentine Lawsuit against crimes of the Franco regime
as a transnational space of memory *Marina Montoto Ugarte* 187
From the Spain of reconciliation to the 'struggles for historical
memory' 189
The opportunity of the Argentine Lawsuit 192
The Ronda de la Dignidad in Sol as a device at a halfway point 194
Comodoro Py and the Spanish National High Court: The judicial
institution as recognition or grievance 196
The 'victory' of the cemetery of Guadalajara: The two deaths and the
two exhumations of Timoteo Mendieta 201
Notes 204

Select Bibliography 208
Index 210

Illustrations

1.1	Falangists (Spanish Fascists) after the triumph of the Coup in Vigo (Galicia, Spain), *c.* 1936	4
1.2	Tribute at the 'Cross of the Fallen' in Santiago de Compostela (Galicia, Spain), civil war years	6
1.3	Memorial to Johan Carballeira, mayor in 1936 of the small village of Bueu (Galicia, Spain), killed by the coup plotters in 1937	13
1.4	Common grave exhumation made by the Asociación para la Recuperación de la Memoria Histórica (Association for the Recovery of Historical Memory). As Pontes (Galicia, Spain), 2006	15
2.1	Falangists marching in the streets of A Coruña (Galicia, Spain), *c.* 1940	35
3.1	Sentencing Site. Palace of the Provincial Government (Pontevedra, Spain)	55
3.2	Sentencing Site. Assembly Hall at the Palace of the Provincial Government (Pontevedra, Spain)	58
4.1	'Peace and Justice'. Memorial plaque to the victims killed by the coup plotters in 1936, Mondoñedo (Galicia, Spain)	74
4.2	Memorial to the neighbours 'killed by Francoism' in 1938. Mondoñedo (Galicia, Spain), 2019	78
5.1	Diary of Casimiro Jabonero, prisoner in a Francoist concentration camp, Lavacolla (Galicia, Spain), 1939	93
5.2	Lavacolla Concentration Camp Memorial. Santiago de Compostela (Galicia, Spain), 2020	98
6.1	Public rally with coup plotters addressing people in the small village of Cangas (Galicia, Spain), civil war years	110
7.1	Public rally of the 'Sección Femenina' (Women's Branch of Falange) in the small village of Cangas (Galicia, Spain) with children marching as soldiers, civil war years	128
8.1	Exhibition of inscriptions and drawings by prisoners from the concentration camp in the Monastery of Oia (Galicia, Spain), 2019	150
8.2	Detail of inscriptions and drawings by prisoners from the concentration camp in the Monastery of Oia (Galicia, Spain), 2019	162

9.1	Monolith in memory of victims of terrorism and violence (San Sebastián-Donostia, Spain), 2007	170
9.2	Sculpture in memory of Francoist repression victims (San Sebastián-Donostia, Spain), 2014	179
9.3	Plaque in English. Sculpture in memory of Francoist repression victims (San Sebastian-Donostia, Spain), 2014	180
10.1	Resignification of public spaces carried by social movements of memory (A Coruña, Spain), 2007	191
10.2	Plaques in memory of the victims of the 1936 coup and Francoist violence at Boisaca's Cemetery, Santiago de Compostela (Galicia, Spain), 2019	200

Map

4.1 Residents of Ribadeo killed without sentencing in Galicia   77

Table

2.1 The civil governor group of Granada in the summer of 1936   38

Contributors

Antonio Míguez Macho is Associate Professor of Contemporary History. Formerly Ramón y Cajal Fellow at the University of Santiago de Compostela (where he completed his PhD) and visiting researcher at the London School of Economics. He has published *The Genocidal Genealogy of Francoism: Violence, Memory and Impunity* (2016). He was Principal Investigator in four funded research projects over one year from 2012 to 2020. His current work-in-progress are two essays: 'The Destruction of Anti-Spain: Coup d'État and Genocidal Practices (Spain 1936–1945)', in *Cambridge World History of Genocide*, vol. 3, *Genocide in the Contemporary Era, 1914-2020*, ed. Ben Kiernan (forthcoming) and 'The Last Crusade: Holy War and Genocidal Practices in the Case of the Spanish Civil War (1936–1939)', *Routledge Handbook on Religion and Genocide*, ed. Sara E. Brown and Stephen Smith (in progress).

Miguel Ángel del Arco Blanco is Associate Professor and Director of the Department of Contemporary History at the University of Granada. His work centres on the study of fascism, the Spanish Civil War and Francoism. He is the co-editor, with Peter Anderson, of *Mass Killings and Violence in Spain, 1936–1952: Grappling with the Past* (2014). He has recently published two essays: 'Famine in Spain During Franco's Dictatorship (1939–52)', *Journal of Contemporary History* (2021) and, with Santiago Gorostiza, '"Facing the Sun": Nature and Nation in Franco's "New Spain"(1936–51)', *Journal of Historical Geography* (2021).

Conchi López Sánchez is a PhD candidate at the University of Santiago de Compostela and member of the research group Histagra. She was a research support technician in relation to several research projects on Franco's violence in Galicia for the history department at the university. Her lines of research focus on the coup of 1936, the Spanish Civil War and the Franco regime, and she is completing her doctoral dissertation on the military trials in Galicia after the coup of 1936.

Xabier Buxeiro Alonso is a PhD candidate at the University of Santiago de Compostela and member of the research group Histagra. He was visiting researcher at Birkbeck College in London. His doctoral research concentrates on the cycle of mass violence initiated as a result of the 1936 coup in Galicia.

Rafael García Ferreira is a PhD candidate at the University of Santiago de Compostela and member of the research group Histagra. He was previously involved in the research project 'Genocidal practice, memory and transitional justice in comparative perspective'. He is completing his doctoral thesis on how violence transformed the city and the people who lived through it (Santiago de Compostela, 1936–1939).

Claudio Hernández Burgos is Assistant Professor at the University of Granada. He has been a Postdoctoral Fellow at the university and visiting fellow at the Università della Sapienza in Rome, the London School of Economics and the Universidad Autónoma in Madrid. In 2013 he co-edited a book about political attitudes in Franco's regime: *No solo miedo. Opinión popular y actitudes sociales bajo el franquismo* and recently edited *Ruptura The Impact of Nationalism and Extremism on Daily Life in the Spanish Civil War (1936–1939)* (2020).

Aldara Cidrás is a PhD candidate at the University of Santiago de Compostela and member of the research group Histagra. Her doctoral research examines mass violence during the Spanish Civil War focusing on perpetrators and perpetration. He was visiting researcher at Princeton University in 2019.

Iria Morgade Valcárcel is a PhD candidate at the University of Santiago de Compostela and member of the research group Histagra. She holds a degree in Political Science from the Complutense University of Madrid and two Master's degrees, one in International Migrations from the University of A Coruña and the other in Teaching from the University of Santiago de Compostela. She is completing her doctoral thesis on the activity of the Spain's historical memory movement since 1975.

Erik Zubiaga Arana is Lecturer at the Public University of Navarre. He gained his PhD at the University of Basque Country and has published several books and articles on Basque Studies, Spanish Civil War and ETA terrorism. His first book is titled *La huella del terror franquista en Bizkaia. Jurisdicción militar, políticas de captación y actitudes sociales (1937–1945)* (The footprint of Franco's terror in Bizkaia. Military jurisdiction, recruitment policies and social attitudes [1937–1945]) (2017).

Marina Montoto Ugarte gained a PhD from the Department of Social Anthropology at Complutense University of Madrid. Her PhD research was focused on the judicial process initiated in Argentina by the victims of Francoism, the so-called *querella argentina* (Argentinian Complaint). Her primary research interests include the representation of the victims of Francoism in the context of the political as well as biological challenges that mark the present time.

1

'Where forgetting resides ...'. Twentieth-century sites of violence and present-day sites of memory: A global vision from the Spanish case

Antonio Míguez Macho

The era of justification

In the era of memory, as our period has come to be known, it seems paradoxical that the most frequent phenomenon is forgetting: our societies encourage the forgetting of pasts that are traumatic, uncomfortable and not very practical for the purposes of the present. This is why we often feel disorientated when we move across the inhabited/uninhabited spaces of our cities and our countryside. We are continually in need of a guide: Google Maps to determine our location and give directions, a QR code to tell us what we are seeing, Tripadvisor to justify our journey according to the opinions of others. Spaces force us to materialize memory and therefore constitute a fascinating field of study.

It was a French sociologist, Maurice Halbwachs, who was the first to perceive the topophilic potential of memory. He also understood that memory not only refers to individual remembering, but is a construct in which the processes of social construction, shared meanings and policies of commemoration converge as well. Halbwachs's 'discovery' took place in the post-First World War historical context. In fact, his life was marked by the Franco-German rivalry for a territory, a space, in dispute (Alsace and Lorraine) that changed hands twice during his lifetime. It was German when he was born – an occupation that resulted from the Franco-Prussian War – it became French after the Great War but returned to German control at the end of his days in the Second World War. The death of the Frenchman in Buchenwald after being arrested by the Gestapo is the perfect example of those wars. His life is summed up in the question: 'how did war twice encounter Halbwachs, and how did he twice live and understand it?'.[1]

The semantic load of places as memory spaces is a characteristic that arose in the profoundly shaken world of post-war Europe through the public authorities' policies of commemoration. In the First World War, military cemeteries were institutionalized, realizing the idea that those who fought together would lie for eternity together. They constituted the number one space for the modern worship of the 'fallen'.[2] Meanwhile, the need to face the reality of the absence of bodies, frequently buried in distant places, or to make the thousands of disappeared present in some way became clear.[3] In 1920 the Cenotaph was inaugurated in Whitehall, London: the prototype of the empty tomb, the place that commemorates all places.[4] It was a monument that was replicated in every town and square in France, Italy and Portugal, amongst many other countries, accompanied by lists of those who had died for the homeland.[5] These lists were expanded and expanded again with each new conflict.[6] As if that were not enough, the great powers still wanted to highlight the enormity of the sacrifice and its 'just memory' even further. In Duaoumont and Hohenstein, Pétain and Hindenburg inaugurated the great ossuaries in 1927.[7] It is these magnificent monuments to the dead that magnify and justify their sacrifices.

Until the beginning of First World War, the main liberal states had been engaged in a process of nationalization built on the basis of great figures who represented the milestones of the homeland. The statues and monuments erected in the main European capitals between the end of the eighteenth century and throughout the nineteenth century are testimony to this: the equestrian statue of Peter the Great (the Bronze Horseman) in Saint Petersburg, Nelson's Column in Trafalgar Square, the Vendôme Column crowned by Napoleon in Paris, and the equestrian statue of Frederick the Great in Unter der Linden. In revolutionary periods, this monumentalization was briefly dedicated to the people, as an agent of social transformation. Examples of this include Goya's masterpieces on the Spanish uprising against the Napoleonic invasion or the evolution immortalized in the Arc de Triomphe from its conception in the Napoleonic period to its inauguration in 1836. The initial recognition of revolutionary citizens in the Arc de Triomphe's sculptures was finally transformed into the tastes of the post-revolutionary era. Beyond these ephemeral yet transcendental revolutionary moments, up until the First World War, the way to commemorate the myths of nation-building was based on exceptional kings, soldiers or heroes, rather than the faces of anonymous citizens.[8]

The memory regime established in Europe after the end of the First World War, for its part, is defined as a regime of justification. The move to total war and the never-before-seen number of victims caused by the confrontation that broke out in 1914 changed everything. Nation states turned their efforts to providing a sense of justification for the sacrifice of the hundreds of thousands of young men on the fronts of Europe. The protagonists of memory became them, those who had 'died for the homeland', in the cenotaphs, cemeteries, memorials and *Te Deum* that were repeated annually.[9] Dates of national commemoration were also established, for instance Armistice Day on 11 November, with the objective of giving meaning to the magnitude of the massacre: 'Armistice Day was part of a sustained and creative effort to give meaning and purpose to the terrifying and unexpected experience of mass death.'[10]

Although all these experiences were common to the countries that had fought in the conflict, those that did not fight in the Great War were not totally left out of these changes either. Other experiences of mass violence precipitated the emergence of the new regime of justification memory, as in the case of Spain after the civil war (1936–1939). Until then, the memory regime prevailing in Spain did not differ substantially from what had been the norm in European states before 1914. Following in the wake of European countries, at the beginning of the twentieth century there was a true monumentalist outpouring. Monuments and place names were dedicated to what were considered great milestones of Spanish nation-building. The cities and towns of Spain were filled with references that ranged from the resistance of the Celtiberians against the Romans to the war against Napoleon, including figures of the great kings, warriors and heroes of all time.[11]

Thus, when the Second Republic was proclaimed, the prevailing memory regime in Spain was fundamentally one of nationalization with liberal nineteenth-century roots. Within this framework, the nascent Republican state began to exalt its own heroes. This was done with the 'heroes of Jaca', for example, a group of officers who failed in an attempt to proclaim the Republic only a few months before it was established by much more peaceful means. Spanish cities and towns were filled with streets, squares and monuments dedicated to the 'heroes of Jaca', frequently replacing the pantheon of names from the monarchical period. This fact was not only due to the effusiveness of the moment but also to the lack of consistent alternatives. Spain had not gone through the First World War and its only deaths for the homeland were those of the colonial wars, which were not at all an excuse for national consensus and recognition.[12]

Figure 1.1 Falangists (Spanish Fascists) after the triumph of the Coup in Vigo (Galicia, Spain), c. 1936. © Histagra Collection / Histagra Research Group.

With the coup d'état of July 1936 and the ensuing civil war, Spain had its experience of mass violence. The military coup leaders took control of large swathes of Spanish territory: Galicia, in the northwest of the peninsula; Castilla La Vieja, Navarre and Álava in the northern plateau; Extremadura in the east; and western Andalusia in the south down to the Portuguese border; as well as the Spanish protectorate in Morocco, the Canary Islands, and the island of Mallorca in the Mediterranean. In these territories, the newly established military regime abolished all pre-existing constitutional rights and guarantees. Mass incarceration began of all those who were deemed enemies. Within this category, the coup leaders included political militants from leftist organizations, unions and parties, but also those from moderate centrist and conservative organizations. Legitimate authority figures, civil governors, mayors, military members who were not part of the coup and public officials from all branches of the administration were subject to immediate persecution. The coup leaders also persecuted people who fell into the category of 'anti-Spain' because of their ideas, attitudes and public presence in the fields of culture, education and the arts. This group included those considered enemies of tradition, Catholicism and the reactionary values that the coup plotters defended. The arrests were followed by military summary trials with no guarantees of any kind for the defendants that resulted in severe sentences: from life imprisonment to the death penalty. Meanwhile, many of the detainees were removed from prison to be killed on the outskirts of towns and cities, against cemetery walls. In the summer of 1936, the appearance of corpses in roadside ditches was a daily occurrence. Many of the victims were buried in mass graves. The climate of terror that prevailed was intensified by the beatings, humiliations and purges that expelled hundreds of thousands of people from their jobs. Under military authority, and in collaboration with state security forces and squads, the practice of violence was carried out by various militia units, chief amongst them the Falange (the Spanish branch of the Fascist Party).[13]

As this process unfolded in the areas controlled by the coup plotters, a political and social revolution broke out in the territory loyal to the Republic. Various trade unions and militias took control of public order. They retaliated against military members and security forces sympathetic to the coup, as well as against prominent figures associated with the Right: landowners, politicians and militants of conservative parties, along with members of the clergy. This violence was concentrated in the period between July and November 1936, at which point the Republican government gradually brought public order under its control. From then on, although the violence in the Republican rearguard did not completely disappear, it lost much of its intensity.[14]

In the territory under coup control, the violence continued its systematic development during the war, spreading to the areas that were gradually conquered by the coup plotters thanks to their military superiority and the support of their German and Italian allies. Makeshift prisons gave way to an extensive network of 400 concentration camps.[15] The persecution and purging followed systematic rules aimed at eliminating those deemed enemies of the coup in order to build a 'new Spain'. The coup plotters who finally triumphed in 1939 made every effort to commemorate those who had died 'for God and for Spain': the dead soldiers of their own army. Similar to the end of the civil war in Finland in 1918, the victors of the so-called Spanish Civil War created a memory of exclusion.[16] In reality, it seems more accurate to point out that this was a way for the regime to express the justification of its victims, ignoring of course the soldiers of the other side. The war's defeated at that time were confined to concentration camps or had already been tried, sentenced and executed by the regime's firing squads.[17]

Through regulations issued in 1938, as the war was still going on, it was decided that a list of the 'fallen' should be placed in each town and parish of Spain.[18] All of these lists were preceded by the name of José Antonio Primo de Rivera, the founder of the Falange, considered to be the first of the 'martyrs'.[19] In 1940 work also began on the large construction project for the Valley of the Fallen, a building of fascist aesthetics that was erected some forty kilometres from Madrid through the slave labour of Republican prisoners. It was originally designed as an immense ossuary with a connected basilica dedicated to the 'martyrs of the Crusade', which became the tomb of José Antonio himself.[20]

In addition to building this monument, the Franco dictatorship carried out an active policy of resignification of public space in the early 1940s. The names of streets and squares in tribute to the liberal-Republican tradition were replaced by new ones dedicated to exalting the values of the homeland, Christianity and the very figure of Francisco Franco, the dictator. The emblematic premises and buildings of political parties, unions and civil associations linked to that same world of political pluralism and the already long-established Spanish liberal

Figure 1.2 Tribute at the 'Cross of the Fallen' in Santiago de Compostela (Galicia, Spain), civil war years. © Histagra Collection / Histagra Research Group.

tradition were also seized and looted. These buildings frequently ended up in the hands of the Spanish Falange – the sole party – and its related organizations. In other cases, they ended up at bargain prices in the hands of individuals or companies that made their fortune with the new regime.[21]

The predatory desire of the Franco regime towards public space also extended to the figure of the dictator. Amongst many other private assets that made up an immense private fortune during their long years in power, the Franco family acquired valuable properties that they used for their own personal enjoyment. To acquire them as property, Franco used a series of tricks such as the formula of the 'popular donation', or 'voluntary surrender'.[22] The passage of time ran in favour of the usurper of goods, subtly relying on a Visigothic source of law called 'usucaption'. In a recent ruling, this principle was used to justify the looting of a valuable statue by the Franco family in the 1950s and the continued recognition of the heirs as legitimate owners today. This same principle affects the ownership of other assets that were also appropriated, such as the Pazo de Meirás (Galicia), where Franco spent his summers.

In this sense, the Franco regime acted according to logic similar to that of its fellow Nazi-fascist regimes, which were concerned about the destruction of the liberal-democratic world that preceded them and obsessed with a new beginning. However, at the same time, and in contrast to the revolutionary and Bolshevik regimes, the Franco regime took great care to guarantee the continuity of the rights acquired by allied companies and private entrepreneurs. Like Nazism or Italian fascism, the Franco regime never questioned the right to property or inheritance, except in the case of its enemies. Just as Nazism expropriated the property of its racial and ideological enemies with measures such as the Nuremberg Laws, the Franco regime approved a whole set of measures that aimed to guarantee dispossession and to condemn its ideological enemies to ruin. The military trials by which the regime sentenced hundreds of thousands of Spaniards to death or harsh prison terms went hand in hand with financial penalties, fines or the expropriation of their property and professions. As a rule, purging affected all public employees: innocence had to be justified, rather than guilt being proven. The regime passed laws that established retroactive punishments, such as the Political Responsibilities Law of 1939, which imposed huge financial penalties on the families of those previously punished. This was a useful way to plunder those who had been killed without sentencing (the 'paseados'), and who therefore had not been able to receive formal financial penalties at the time. As a result, not only did numerous public spaces change their name to erase the memory of the previous liberal-democratic pluralism, but also numerous private properties, farms, businesses and companies also fell into the hands of new owners who made sure that no one could reclaim them in the future.[23]

The era of denunciation

Memory regimes varied globally with the end of the Second World War. In principle, monumentalization was still associated with the logic of justification, with military cemeteries or the inscription of the names of dead young men on monoliths or tombstones. For example, the French completed their 'morts pour la patrie' with Resistance fighters and the Americans allowed their 'fallen' to remain forever buried in Allied cemeteries in Normandy, not far from German cemeteries. The victors of the war and those who considered themselves as such endeavoured to assert their sacrifices in victory. But in addition, a new issue emerged that had not been present until that moment: the large number of non-combatant victims that the conflict had produced. No memorial device was dedicated to those who died in the war but were not part of the battle. Russian banker Jan Bloch's prophecy of future warfare had come true in a terrible way. Non-combatant victims clearly outnumbered combatants, because total war did not make distinctions between the two. In addition to those who died as victims of bombings, in crossfire or as a result of armed reprisals, there was the enormity of the extermination policy carried out by the Axis powers. Europe was a cemetery, and it was flooded with places destroyed by the violence of war, mass graves and the skeletons of concentration and extermination camps.[24]

The first initiatives in regard to these spaces, particularly the extermination camps, were very different. There are examples of a desire for early conservation and the transformation of a site into a memorial space, as in the emblematic case of Auschwitz.[25] In other cases, such as Treblinka, the destruction carried out by the Nazis themselves in abandoning the camps, combined with a lack of interest in their conservation, physically erased them from the land. And we also have examples of continuity of use, as in the case of Dachau, converted after the end of the war into a 'refugee' camp, which sheltered a small part of the millions of displaced people left by the war in Europe.[26]

However, between 1945 and 1960 there was an important transformation in how to conceive of the past of mass violence and, consequently, how its memorialization should be treated. A variation in the dominant discourses shifted the main focus of attention from the combatant to the victim. In 1945 what was considered worthy of memorialization was the fighting of the soldiers or the resilience of the civilian population. This explains why the Auschwitz memorial museum only recognized the space as a detention centre for the various resistant peoples of Europe, including the Jews. The founding leitmotif of the Yad Vashem memorial complex is to commemorate the 'resistance' of European Jews against

Nazi devastation. At the centre of this account is the Warsaw ghetto uprising.[27] However, as of 1960, there was a shift towards accepting the vindication of victims as victims, without needing to justify their combatant nature.[28]

This revolutionary change to the hegemonic discourses on memory began with efforts to preserve the material legacies of Nazi extermination, now recognized as such. The suffering of the victims is monumentalized and their total innocence is exalted. Such efforts have saved complexes such as Dachau, which, having been abandoned in 1960 after its post-war use, was in danger of being demolished. A commission was created that not only succeeded in stopping these plans of destruction but also that intends to turn Dachau into a symbol of Nazi barbarism and to dedicate the site to the victims. Moreover, through this process Dachau becomes an instrument for combatting denialism, in parallel to the enactment of the first laws in Germany from 1960 aimed at persecuting this phenomenon.[29] In this specific process, three crucial elements of the new memory regime are visualized: the centrality of the victims, the activation of social movements of memory and the discourse of denunciation.

The power gained by this new significance of the past transcended the Jewish extermination itself and was soon incorporated by other victims of different phenomena of mass violence across the globe. These victims felt equally excluded by the hegemonic account of justification, for instance, those who were sentenced by regimes of exclusion, such as the Red Finns, or by regimes of denial, such as the Armenians. Indeed, in 1967 a huge monument dedicated to the victims of the 'Armenian genocide' was erected in Yerevan after a process of struggle with the Soviet authorities.[30] But beyond Europe or Asia Minor, various groups demand the recognition of their suffering, the memorial preservation of their memory and the need to denounce the past of mass violence.

While this was happening in Europe and the rest of the world, the Franco regime faced a very uncertain moment in 1945. The defeat of fascism in Europe – the allies and friends of the Francoist regime since 1936 – forced the regime to reformulate itself as Catholic and traditional rather than fascist. The beginning of the Cold War ultimately allowed the Franco regime to save itself as a reliable Western ally, under the umbrella of the new American policy in the Mediterranean. In parallel to these processes, the vestiges of the violence deployed against the ideological enemies of the 1936 coup and the Franco dictatorship were systematically dismantled. Concentration camps, numbering more than 300 in the early 1940s, were completely closed and dismantled between 1945 and 1947. Their former buildings and spaces were demolished or used for completely different purposes. Mass graves, scattered throughout the entire

Spanish territory, were abandoned to their destiny, which alternated between concealment, forgetting and the small clandestine symbols of denunciation that continued to exist throughout the dictatorship. A similar fate befell the execution sites, where people were killed from 1936 to 1945, which were condemned to forgetting by official ostracism.[31]

The Miranda de Ebro concentration camp (north of Castile and León), known as one of the first to be created and the last to be closed (1937–1947), was briefly used after its closure for military purposes before finally being demolished. An industrial estate was built on its land. This was not a unique case, but part of a systematic logic of concealing those networks built by the Franco regime to punish, persecute and exterminate its enemies.[32]

We can thus establish a correspondence between the fate of sites of violence from 1936 to 1945 and their transformation into places of amnesia. In the Spanish case, the practice of mass violence was produced via itineraries of violence with three major landmarks: sites of confinement, sites of execution and sites of burial. The sites of confinement were assembled through a dense network of prisons and concentration camps, housing an estimated figure of just over one million prisoners in the course of the process. The execution sites included those spaces where the systematic execution of victims who received sentences took place, as well as a whole series of places where the 'executions' were carried out without sentences, or as paseos. The former are obviously easier to systematize, compared to the latter, which are by definition scattered and sometimes circumstantial. To better understand this difference, compare a site of execution such as the southern cemetery of Madrid, where it is estimated that more than 2,600 people were shot, with the place where Federico García Lorca and his two companions were executed, which to this day has not been identified. Despite search efforts, the place where Lorca's remains lie is completely unknown. The case of Lorca is similar to that of two-thirds of the victims of the violence led by coup plotters and Francoists. This is why most of the victims are buried in small or medium-sized mass graves scattered throughout the territory and difficult to locate.[33]

The attitude of the Franco regime towards its own past, however, was also influenced by the paradigm shift in the global context. The regime's discourse regarding the war changed, presenting a supposed dignity of the victims of the defeated side. While the vestiges of mass violence were destroyed and the pain of the victims was silenced, the Franco regime converted its emblematic memorial monument, the Valley of the Fallen, into a memorial for 'all the victims'. For this purpose, around the time of the monument's inauguration in 1959, the remains of thousands of Republican soldiers buried in various cemeteries throughout Spain were seized and taken to the immense ossuary built under the basilica.

In the 1960s, while witnessing the aforementioned transition towards a memory regime that materialized denunciations and placed the victims at the centre, the Franco regime moved from justification to an active policy of denial. This extended to all the monumentality built on the violence of the civil war by the regime, which was carefully moved into the background, leaving the fate of the victims under the protection of projects such as the Valley of the Fallen. In this context, the dictatorship's decision to close the responsibilities for the civil war, adopted in 1969, no less than thirty years after achieving victory, can be understood. Carried out from the new logic of amnesia, this closure of responsibilities kept one eye on the past and another on the increasingly immediate problem of succession after Franco's death.[34]

The era of memory

The Spanish transitional process from dictatorship to democracy occurred in the 1970s, together with what Huntington calls the third wave of democratization in southern Europe (including the cases of Portugal and Greece). In this decade there was a new transformation in the memory regime, which has prevailed since 1945, that turned memory itself into the centre of the memorialization narrative. If denunciation had made the victim the centre of the narrative, and memory a globalized phenomenon, in 1970 it was 'memory' itself that occupied a central place on the stage. Memory, which until then had not been the preferred object of attention among scholars or a fundamental concern of the media, became a new paradigm of modernity.

It is difficult to point out a milestone in this process, but perhaps the international success of the 'Holocaust' series (1978) is a cultural turning point. The success of the series not only makes the Jewish genocide a point of reference in European and world memory, but also establishes memory as an essential device for understanding the past.[35] No one can now conceive of destroying a vestige of the past where acts of mass violence have been committed unless it is done with denialist intentions. Similarly, the value of preserving the material legacies of the past is seen as an end in itself. This is the process by which memory acquires the meaning of heritage.

Concern for preserving the past was also established in academia through such grand projects as Pierre Nora's work on *lieux de mémoire*. In the introduction to his publication in 1984 he writes something transcendental: it is 'the rapid disappearance of our national memory' that makes him think that an 'inventory of the places where it has been electively incarnated' is necessary.[36] In his work, Nora reflects a desire to preserve memory as a good in itself, which accompanies a new transformation of memory into memory-heritage. New material possibilities were considered that until then had only been contemplated as an afterthought. If memory-heritage is ideally exemplified in a material way, it opens up the possibility that the memory of mass violence must also be preserved or recreated in its materiality.

Along with this, a subtle but relevant transition took place from the drive of memory-denouncement to a new way of understanding memory as a cultural product. This can be fully visualized in the Berlin memorial complex *Topographie des Terrors*. The memorial complex stands on the site of the headquarters of the Reichssicherheitshauptamt (Reich Main Security Office). The first exhibition was inaugurated in the space in 1987, and after various vicissitudes that included an initial museum project that was not completed, a brand-new building was finally inaugurated as a museum and documentation centre in 2010. The patrimonial meaning of the space was marked with the installation of the initial exhibition outdoors, through some successful but very simple panels, with the Berlin wall still standing in the background. Content regarding denunciation of the past was consciously present, after years of the place being designated by scholars and guides as a place of amnesia.[37] The transformation from that initial exhibition into the current memorial complex is mediated by the new memorial drive, which the 'era of memory' represents.[38]

It is impossible to account for the profusion of memory sites that have emerged across the globe in the period from 1980 to the present. There is such a variety of sites that trying to cover them in a few lines is impossible. Only in the city of Berlin, for example, have memorials been built that not only remember the Nazi genocide as a whole but also single out the most diverse victimized groups. Huge amounts of money and resources have been invested in memorials, museums and re-enactments of the past, which in turn generate an incessant flow of visitors and tourists.[39] This has resulted in the spread of the phenomenon of 'dark tourism', combining sites of memory, sites of morbid fascination and sites of business.[40]

Memory itineraries constructed in the present time in relation to traumatic pasts feature a series of globalized common characteristics. Strictly speaking, sites of memory are of at least three types: memorials, dedicated sites and sites of denial. Memorials have a direct or indirect spatial relationship with the area

Figure 1.3 Memorial to Johan Carballeira, mayor in 1936 of the small village of Bueu (Galicia, Spain), killed by the coup plotters in 1937. © Histagra Collection / Histagra Research Group.

where the traumatic events being commemorated took place. Various cases have been mentioned throughout this chapter, but their proliferation in the present has been exponential. Not only are they growing in number, but their originality is increasingly important. The Vélodrome d'Hiver in Paris, now defunct, was marked early on with a modest plaque that commemorated the fact that it had served to hold French Jews who were rounded up to be deported to Nazi extermination camps. Once the building was destroyed, the plaque was left as a memorial testimony of the site's significance. However, in the 1990s it was decided that this mention was not enough. The memorialization was strengthened with a new monument, signed by the artist and much more elaborate, to which a new plaque was affixed. Similarly, the previously mentioned case of the *Topographie des Terrors* is an example of the same process: the evolution from the initial guided walks of the late 1970s to the current museum is the expression of the changes that memory regimes have experienced on a global scale.

There are also places dedicated to the memory of the traumatic past that no longer correspond, more than indirectly, with the place of the events.[41] We call these spaces 'dedicated sites'. One of the largest monuments dedicated to the memory of the Holocaust in Europe, the Memorial to the Murdered Jews of Europe, in Berlin, is an example of this. With a remarkable level of abstraction, the monument is a crowd-drawing object of tourist attraction.[42] The United States Holocaust Memorial Museum in Washington, DC, a huge complex of resources for the study of the topic, evidently has no direct relationship with the place of the events. This dedication stands in contrast with the difficulties in the United States to establish a museum dedicated to forms of mass violence that did take place in its territory, regarding phenomena such as slavery or Native Americans.[43]

This last issue leads us directly to the paradoxical multiplication of sites of denial in the present, in sharp contrast to the multiplication of memorials and dedicated sites. Such practices can be extended to entire countries, as in the prominent case of Indonesia regarding the genocide of the 1964 to 1965 coup: a paradigmatic case due to the enormity of the victims and the absolute nullity of memorial recognition. But they also involve numerous cases of human rights violations and mass crimes in places such as China, whose reformulation of space as a result of the exponential growth of the last decades has been accompanied by a policy of denial of crimes committed by the state and its agents.

The Spanish case is once again part of this global panorama of memory itineraries, presenting abundant evidence of the three types of approaches regarding the memory of its own traumatic past. Any interested traveller in Spain can find abundant examples of memorials dedicated to the victims of the Franco regime, dedicated sites and also sites of denial. This complexity of memory sites in Spain corresponds to the course of memory policies undertaken from the Transition to the present. But far from signifying a kind of Spanish uniqueness, the analysis of memory sites in Spain in relation to the experience of its traumatic past reveals its full insertion into the globalized memory of the twenty-first century.[44]

The treatment of memory sites in Spain is related to the way in which the process of transitional justice was carried out after Franco's death.[45] Between 1975 and 1978 a process of institutional transition was completed that turned Spain into a country with a democratic system comparable to that of its Western neighbours. In this context, it was decided that Spanish transitional law could include various measures of reparation, as in fact was the case with the laws of amnesty and the reintegration of rights to certain groups, including financial compensation for the prisoners of the Franco regime. Many reparation measures were also proposed at the symbolic level, which began with the changing of names and the conversion of monuments and removal of Francoist symbols. This process intensified with the approval of the Historical Memory Law in 2006 and reached a milestone with the transfer of Franco's remains from the Valley of the Fallen to a private cemetery in 2019. There are, and have been, multiple initiatives at various levels of the administration, in combination with civil society or not, in relation to the issue of 'historical memory'.[46]

This whole paradigm, which is at a distant extreme from cases of institutional denial such as Indonesia or China, nevertheless, presents an area that has been and is being revealed as very relevant. The Spanish transitional model decided to deny the victims the possibility of criminal justice in the persecution or purging of the perpetrators. This circumstance has meant that the spaces of memory related to criminal acts of the past were never treated as 'the scene of the crime': a place of not only historical but also forensic evidence. In a unique way, this factor has affected the issue of mass graves, making it impossible to implement an institutionalized policy of searching for the remains of buried people or to adopt indirect methods. Therefore, the legislative and judicial systems have conditioned the reading of space in memorial terms in Spain, but only the judicial system has fostered the discourse of denial.[47]

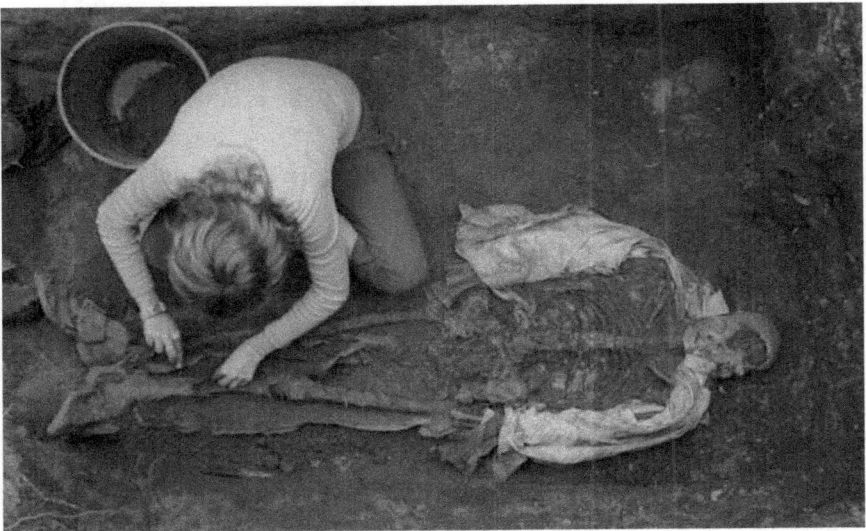

Figure 1.4 Common grave exhumation made by the Asociación para la Recuperación de la Memoria Histórica (Association for the Recovery of Historical Memory). As Pontes (Galicia, Spain), 2006. © Histagra Collection / Histagra Research Group.

How can we otherwise understand that hundreds of exhumations have been carried out in Spain without the presence of a single investigating judge? In the same way, without this active participation of the legal dimension, it is very difficult to understand the absolute impunity of the perpetrators. Given the extraordinary duration of the Franco regime, this impunity has benefited the executioners of 1936 and of 1975.[48] Sites of torture in the last years of the dictatorship, such as the General Directorate of Security in Madrid or Barcelona, continue to be spaces of denial today.

So that forgetting does not triumph: What we have done with this work

The reader who approaches these pages will come across a series of studies that can be read independently but that aim to offer, like a mosaic, an image of where the Spanish case is located on the scale of globalized memory that we have been exploring. These studies are the result of the work coordinated by a research project and by the existence of multiple doctoral studies in progress. They are works of history, but they do not leave out anthropology, sociology and even political science. Above all, they approach the study of history and memory as necessarily intertwined, united by ties that exist in the events studied and that disciplinary traditions should not break.

This idea of intertwining historical facts with memorial phenomena is fundamental to this book and can be found throughout its three parts, which group the chapters based on a combination of thematic and chronological criteria. The first part, 'Sites of Sentencing and Death', focuses on the places that primarily represent the perpetration of physical violence. To approach the study of the traumatic past of the Spanish case from a spatial perspective, the spaces of violence created since 1936, first by the dynamics of coup violence and then by Francoist violence, are analysed. The sites of this violence, which were deployed to create the network of mass violence led by the coup plotters, are identified. The work is based on the study of two fundamental places that served these purposes: military authority headquarters and civil authority headquarters, which were subordinate to those of the military.

In the case of the headquarters of civil authorities, Miguel Ángel del Arco analyses the centrality of civil government buildings in the implementation of immediate violence following the coup of July 1936. His chapter reflects on what occurred in civil government buildings: the true hearts of Francoist rebel violence in the civil war. During the Republic, civil governments were the key institutions in the mediation and regulation of Republican legislation. At the time of the coup, they were also vital: these were the places where the government of Spain's representatives could be found. Ordering the detention of the representative and, in most cases, their execution also meant the death of the Republic in each province. In addition, the seizure of the civil governors' offices gave the starting signal for Francoist rebel violence during the bloody summer of 1936 and later. Civil government buildings were thus essential spaces in the mass violence unleashed in the summer of 1936, which would annihilate Republicans and underpin Franco's future regime: sites that would be forgotten and remain shrouded in silence until today.

The chapter by Conchi López Sánchez underpins the importance of the trials carried out by the military against its enemies not only to punish them but also as a fundamental means of socializing violence. For this reason, the specific places chosen to hold the trials had special meaning; they provided publicity and carried a dimension linked to the eliminationist policy of the new holders of power. Similar to other major processes of mass violence that were nearly simultaneous although very ideologically distant, such as the Stalinist trials with their theatricality, military trials in Spain were not held for the majority of the victims, but they played a key role in making the violence real. Trials were not the fundamental method of elimination for the Stalinist regime either, but their existence somehow made it possible for other forms of violence without sentencing to run systematically in parallel.

The places where these killings without a sentence were carried out are the focus of Xabier Buxeiro's chapter. The author reconstructs with surgical precision the specific spaces where killings took place, creating a new map of terror. These killings represent more than two-thirds of the total fatalities of the violence unleashed by the coup plotters. However, as the author shows, their spatially dispersed nature also makes them part of a diffuse memory. We know of their existence without a doubt, but it is difficult to identify such spaces and their subsequent memorial treatment. In this way, the so-called paseos (or strolls) are part of a certain denialist account of spontaneous and unsystematic violence. They are therefore a substantial component of the account to justify the fact that individuals are not held responsible for what happened.

The second part, 'Sites of Confinement and Denial', addresses the prolongation of physical violence through the punishment of incarceration, but also through daily punishment. Chronologically, the chapters advance into the post-war period, with the Franco dictatorship firmly established. Rafael García Ferreira analyses the history and memory of concentration spaces. Concentration camps in Spain existed at the same time as camps elsewhere in Europe. The origins and purpose of Spanish camps was not to exterminate prisoners, but to exploit them as a workforce and ensure their political re-education (or simply to prevent them from acting politically), necessary for the reconstruction of a country during the war and post-war era. Internally, these camps coincided with other types of illegal detention centres. Prisoners in camps and those of regulated, authorized prisons shared, on many occasions, the same precarious living conditions and their exploitation as manual labour. Such camps thus constituted yet another arm of the apparatus of violence deployed against the defeated since 1936. These characteristics are perfectly visible in the field and city that is the object of this chapter: the Lavacolla concentration camp, located on the outskirts of Santiago de Compostela.

The coup plotters' war victory created a new spatial reality where terror extended beyond the walls of prisons and concentration camps. Claudio Hernández Burgos's chapter examines the spatial dimensions of the violence and social control deployed by the Francoist state during the post-war years. In this way, it aims to contribute to the study of the Francoist violence from a different point of view. On the one hand, it explores the policies of the Franco dictatorship and the role of violence with respect to space. The objective is to demonstrate that this space was a complex reality – inhabited by a heterogeneous variety of actors, where diverse practices occurred – so our view of it must be equally complex. The second part, on the other hand, assesses the dictatorship's ability to control everyday spaces, whether from a political, social or moral perspective. In doing so, it highlights once again the multiplicity of agents that travelled through such spaces and their ability to redefine these spaces on a daily basis, making such places disputed and negotiated realities.

Until this point, the chapters first address the spatiality of violence, followed by the spatiality of memory. The chapter that follows subtly turns this order of analysis around. It poses questions directly related to the spatiality of memory to then return to the sites of violence. In this way, the chapter by Aldara Cidrás analyses how the account of violence of the coup and the Spanish Civil War was constructed in part by concentrating on a relatively small number of events confined to very specific places, even when these episodes may not have been the bloodiest. In other words, it examines how certain events came to represent the totality of the horrors of the conflict, with the peculiarity that, by metonymy, the city in which such events took place came to symbolize all the violence of the coup and the war in the collective imagination. A paradigmatic example is the case of Guernica: the entire city becomes a vast *lieu de mémoire* that both includes and represents the different memories derived from 1936.

The third and final part, 'Sites of Memorialization and Conflict', features a review of how the past leaves its mark in more recent times. These chapters begin in the period of the Transition, when Spain shifted from a dictatorial regime to a democratic one (1975–1978). During this period, various conflicting processes of memory converged in relation to the war, the Franco regime and also the violence of armed groups such as ETA. From this point on, the chapters address the process of memorialization until the present, including the case of the so-called *querella argentina* (Argentine Lawsuit) against the crimes of the Franco regime.

The chapter by Iria Morgade features a first approach to studying two sites of violence located in the northwest of Spain, in Galicia: the Jesuit school of Camposancos (A Guarda) and the monastery of Santa María de Oia (Oia), which were used as concentration camps from 1937. In particular, it analyses the role of the drawings made by inmates on the walls of both camps during their captivity. This chapter argues that the action of drawing and writing on the walls, and the result – drawings that have remained, more or less hidden, with a greater or lesser degree of degradation – constitute actions of memory in themselves. Thus, an examination of the fate of these drawings, their preservation or obscurity, yields more global insights on the treatment of memory in Spain in recent decades.

Within this process of the recent treatment of memory in Spain, there is an intersection with another memory of violence. Erik Zubiaga's study shows how the memory of the violence of 1936 intersects with the memory of the armed Basque group ETA in the same shared space. The treatment of the memory of political violence continues to arouse numerous controversies among different Basque political groups today. This chapter analyses how, in the Basque case, the management of public memory is constantly being built and rebuilt within a conflictive context that changes depending on the political persuasions and interests of the moment. A wide variety of plaques and monuments have been erected in honour of the victims of the various forms of violence that have taken place in the Basque Country in recent decades. The Basque case is analysed here as a paradigm of the challenges represented by managing the memory of an uncomfortable past, the conflicts generated at the social and political level, and the different memories and interpretations made visible by sites of violence and memory.

In closing, the anthropologist Marina Montoto addresses how the judicial process initiated in Argentina by the victims of Francoism, the Argentine

Lawsuit, has become a place of memory. This chapter reviews the lawsuit filed by the collective groups of victims of the Franco regime, as well as the process by which the Argentine Lawsuit has turned into a place of memory. The chapter concludes by examining what the future may hold for the representation of the victims of Francoism in the context of the political as well as biological challenges that mark the present time.

These ten chapters are the result of a research project in which the authors participated, but they have also benefited from the participation of many more people.[49] First of all, I would like to thank Peter Anderson for his valuable comments on the texts, as well as his advice to frame them from a global point of view. Without his help, the work would not have been feasible.

Likewise, I wish to thank Lisandro Cañón, César Manuel Román Sánchez, Lourenzo Fernández Prieto and Daniel Lanero Táboas for their participation in the debates that gave rise to this book. I would also like to express my gratitude to Gustavo Hervella for looking after the management of everything related to the research project and the results obtained.

Of course, I thank the authors for their willingness to generously participate in this study. Finally, I would like to extend my thanks to all the patient families who are often behind these research efforts, who are not always sufficiently recognized.

Notes

1 Annette Becker, *Maurice Halbwachs, un intellectuel en guerres mondiales 1914–1945* (Paris: Agnès Viénot, 2003), 24.
2 George L. Mosse, *Fallen Soldiers: Reshaping the Memory of the World Wars* (Oxford: Oxford University Press, 1990), 70–106.
3 Daniel J. Sherman, *The Construction of Memory in Interwar France* (Chicago: University of Chicago Press, 1999), 100.
4 Thomas W. Laqueur, 'Memory and Naming in the Great War', in *Commemorations: The Politics of National Identity*, ed. John R. Gillis (Princeton, NJ: Princeton University Press, 1994), 156–57.
5 Silvia Correia, 'Forgotten Places of Memory. First World War Memorials in Portugal, 1919–1933', in *Twentieth Century Wars in European Memory*, ed. Józef Niżnik (Frankfurt: P. Lang, 2013), 37–66; Patricia Dogliani, 'Les monuments aux morts de la grande guerre en Italie', *Guerres mondiales et conflits contemporains* 167 (1992): 87–94.

6 Daniel J. Sherman, 'Bodies and Names: The Emergence of Commemoration in Inter-War France', *American Historical Review* 103 (1998): 447.
7 Anna Von Der Goltz and Robert Gildea, 'Flawed Saviours: The Myths of Hindenburg and Pétain', *European History Quarterly* 39, no. 3 (2009): 439–64.
8 M. Christine Boyer, *The City of Collective Memory: Its Historical Imagery and Architectural Entertainments* (Cambridge, MA: MIT Press, 1994), 321; Clifford Geertz, 'Centers, Kings, and Charisma: Reflections on the Symbolics of Power', in *Rites of Power: Symbolism, Ritual and Politics since the Middle Ages*, ed. Sean Wilentz (Philadelphia: University of Pennsylvania Press, 1985), 25.
9 Robert Wohl, *The Generation of 1914* (Cambridge, MA: Harvard University Press, 1979), 231–32.
10 Adrian Gregory, *The Silence of Memory: Armistice Day, 1919–1946* (London: Bloomsbury, 2014), 19.
11 Carlos Reyero, *La escultura conmemorativa en España. La edad de oro del monumento público, 1820–1914* (Madrid: Cátedra, 1999), 77–8; María del Carmen Lacarra Ducay and Cristina Jiménez Navarro, *Historia y política a través de la escultura pública, 1820–1920* (Zaragoza: Institución Fernando el Católico, 2003); Fernando Sánchez-Costa, 'Cultura histórica y nombres de calles. Aproximación al nomenclátor contemporáneo de Barcelona y Madrid', *Memoria y Civilización* 12 (2009): 217–51.
12 Antonio Míguez Macho, 'Apropiación do espazo público e memoricidio: do golpe de 1936 ás políticas públicas da memoria', in *Estudos de Onomástica Galega IV. Os nomes das rúas*, ed. Ana Isabel Boullón and Luz Méndez (A Coruña: Real Academia Galega, 2019), 58–9.
13 For a general overview of this process, see Paul Preston, *The Spanish Holocaust: Inquisition and Extermination in Twentieth-Century Spain* (London: HarperPress, 2012); Antonio Míguez Macho, *The Genocidal Genealogy of Francoism: Violence, memory and Impunity* (Brighton: Sussex Academic Press, 2016).
14 J.L. Ledesma, 'Total War Behind the Frontlines? An Inquiry into the Violence on the Republican Side in the Spanish Civil War', in *If You Tolerate This. The Spanish Civil War in the Age of Total War*, ed. Martin Baumester and Stefanie Schuler-Springorum (Frankfurt: Campus Verlag, 2008), 154–68.
15 Javier Rodrigo, 'Exploitation, Fascist Violence and Social Cleansing: A Study of Franco's Concentration Camps from a Comparative Perspective', *European Review of History* 19, no. 4 (2012): 553–73.
16 Tuomas Tepora, 'Changing Perceptions of 1918: World War II and Post-War Rise of the Left', in *The Finnish Civil War 1918: History, Memory, Legacy*, ed. Tuomas Tepora and Aapo Roselius (Leiden: Brill Academic Publishers, 2014), 364–400.
17 Peter Anderson, *Friend or Foe? Occupation, Collaboration and Selective Violence in the Spanish Civil War* (Brighton: Sussex, 2016), 59–60.

18 Miguel Ángel del Arco, 'Las cruces de los caídos: instrumento nacionalizador en la "cultura de la victoria"', in *No solo miedo. Actitudes populares y dictadura franquista*, ed. Miguel Ángel Del Arco, Carlos Fuertes, Claudio Hernández and Jorge Marco (Granada: Comares, 2013), 65–82.
19 Zira Box, *España, año cero: la construcción simbólica del franquismo* (Madrid: Alianza Editorial, 2010), 119–23.
20 Andrea Hepworth, 'Site of Memory and Dismemory: The Valley of the Fallen in Spain', *Journal of Genocide Research* 16, no. 4 (2014): 463–85.
21 Míguez Macho, *The Genocidal Genealogy*, 56–64.
22 Paul Preston, *A People Betrayed: A History of Corruption, Political Incompetence and Social Division in Modern Spain 1874–2018* (London: William Collins, 2020).
23 Miguel Ángel del Arco Blanco and Peter Anderson, 'Property, the Forging of Francoism and Collective Memory', *International Journal of Iberian Studies* 30, no. 2 (2017): 73–92.
24 Tony Judt, *Postwar: A History of Europe since 1945* (New York: Penguin Press, 2005); Keith Lowe, *Savage Continent: Europe in the Aftermath of World War II* (London: St. Martin's Press, 2012).
25 Amalia Rosenblum, 'Time in the Museum, the Museum in Time: The History of the Auschwitz-Birkenau State Museum', *Anthropology of East Europe Review* 19, no. 1 (2001): 42–55.
26 Aline Sierp, 'Memory, Identity and a Painful Past: Contesting the Former Dachau Concentration Camp', in *Excavating Memory: Sites of Remembering and Forgetting*, ed. Maria Starzmann and John Roby (Gainesville: University Press of Florida, 2016), 316–35.
27 Boaz Cohen, 'Setting the Agenda of Holocaust Research: Discord at Yad Vashem in the 1950s', in *Holocaust Historiography in Context: Emergence, Challenges, Polemics and Achievements*, ed. David Bankier and Dan Michmann (Jerusalem: Yad Vashem, 2008), 255–92.
28 Raul Hilberg, *The Politics of Memory: The Journey of a Holocaust Historian* (Chicago: Ivan R. Dee, 1996).
29 Jenny Wüstenberg, *Civil Society and Memory in Postwar Germany* (New York: Cambridge University Press, 2017); Noah Benezra Strote, *Lions and Lambs: Conflict in Weimar and the Creation of Post-Nazi Germany* (New Haven, CT: Yale University Press, 2017), 231–42; Emanuela Fronza, *Memory and Punishment: Historical Denialism, Free Speech and the Limits of Criminal Law* (The Hague: Asser Press, 2018).
30 Rebecca Jinks, 'Situating Tsitsernakaberd: The Armenian Genocide Museum in a Global Context', *International Journal of Armenian Genocide Studies* 1, no. 1 (2014): 39–52; Serafim Seppälä, 'The "Temple of Non-Being" at Tsitsernakaberd and Remembrance of the Armenian Genocide: An Interpretation', *Art Approaching Science and Religion* 6, no. 2 (2016): 26–39; Armen T. Marsoobian, 'Collective

Memory, Memorialization and Bearing Witness in the Aftermath of the Armenian Genocide', in *Multidisciplinary Perspectives on Genocide and Memory*, ed. Jutta Lindert and Armen T. Marsoobian (Cham: Springer, 2018), 305–20.

31 Antonio Míguez Macho, 'Un pasado negado. Lugares de violencia y lugares de memoria del golpe, la guerra civil y el franquismo', *Confluenze: Rivista di Studi Iberoamericani* 10, no. 2 (2018): 127–51.

32 Alfredo Gonzalez-Ruibal, 'The Archaeology of Internment in Francoist Spain (1936–1952)', in *Archaeologies of Internment*, ed. Adrian Myers and Gabriel Moshenska (New York: Springer, 2011), 53–73; Helen Graham, *The War and Its Shadow: Spain's Civil War in Europe's Long Twentieth Century* (Brighton: Sussex Academic Press, 2012), 104.

33 Francisco Ferrándiz, 'Cries and Whispers: Exhuming and Narrating Defeat in Spain Today', *Journal of Spanish Cultural Studies* 9, no. 2 (2008), 177–92; Robert Barker, *Skeletons in the Closet, Skeletons in the Ground: Repression, Victimization and Humiliation in a Small Andalusian Town; The Human Consequences of the Spanish Civil War* (London: Sussex Academic Press, 2012).

34 Paloma Aguilar, *Memory and Amnesia: The Role of the Spanish Civil War in the Transition to Democracy* (Oxford: Berghahn, 2002), XX, 210 and 213; Carlos Jerez-Farrán and Samuel Amago, 'Introduction', in *Unearthing Franco's Legacy: Mass Graves and the Recovery of Historical Memory in Spain*, ed. Carlos Jerez-Farrán and Samuel Amago (Notre Dame, IN: University of Notre Dame Press, 2010), 2; Carsten Humblebaek, 'The "Pacto del Olvido"', in *Politics and Memory of Democratic Transition: The Spanish Model*, ed. Diego Muro and Gregorio Alonso (London: Routledge, 2011), 183–98.

35 Daniel Levy and Natan Sznaider, 'Memory Unbound: The Holocaust and the Formation of Cosmopolitan Memory', *European Journal of Social Theory* 1, no. 5 (2002): 87–106.

36 Pierre Nora, 'Présentation', in *Les lieux de mémoire. I. La République*, ed. Pierre Nora (Paris: Gallimard, 1984), VII–XII.

37 Svetlana Boym, *The Future of Nostalgia* (New York: Basic Books, 2001).

38 Aleida Assmann, 'The Holocaust – a Global Memory? Extensions and Limits of a New Memory Community', in *Memory in a Global Age*, ed. Aleida Assmann and Sebastian Conrad (London: Palgrave Macmillan, 2010), 97–117.

39 Dominick Lacapra, *History and Memory After Auschwitz* (Ithaca, NY: Cornell University Press, 1998); James E. Young, *The Texture of Memory: Holocaust Memorials and Meaning* (New Haven, CT: Yale, 1993); Alessandro Portelli, 'The Massacre at the Fosse Ardeatine', in *Contested Pasts: The Politics of Memory*, ed. Katharine Hodgkin and Susannah Radstone (New York: Routledge, 2003), 29–41.

40 Philip R. Stone, 'A Dark Tourism Spectrum: Towards a Typology of Death and Macabre Related Tourist Sites, Attractions and Exhibitions', *Tourism: An*

Interdisciplinary International Journal 54 (2006): 145–60; Richard Sharpley and Philip R. Stone (eds), *The Darker Side of Travel: The Theory and Practice of Dark Tourism* (Bristol: Channel View Publications, 2009).

41 Paul Connerton, *How Modernity Forgets* (Cambridge: Cambridge University Press, 1999), 10.
42 Shelley Hornstein, *Losing Site: Architecture, Memory and Place* (Farnham: Ashgate, 2011), 45–54.
43 Andrea A. Burns, *From Storefront to Monument: Tracing the Public History of the Black Museum Movement* (Cambridge: University of Massachusetts Press, 2013), 156–78.
44 Alexandra Barahona and Mario Sznajder, 'The Politics of the Past: The Southern Cone and the Southern Europe in Comparative Perspective', *South European Society and Politics* 15, no. 3 (2010): 487–505.
45 Míguez Macho, *The Genocidal Genealogy*, 89–112.
46 Carolyn P. Boyd, 'The Politics of History and Memory in Democratic Spain', *Annals of the American Academy of Political and Social Science* 617, no. 1 (2008): 133–48; Antonio Cazorla-Sánchez and Adrian Schubert, 'Sites without Memory and Memory Without Sites: On the Failure of the Public History of the Spanish Civil War', in *Public Humanities and the Spanish Civil War: Connected and Contested Histories*, ed. Alison Ribeiro, Antonio Cazorla-Sánchez and Adrian Schubert (London: Palgrave Macmillian, 2018), 19–43.
47 Javier Chinchón, *El tratamiento judicial de los crímenes de la Guerra Civil y el franquismo en España. Una visión de conjunto desde el Derecho internacional* (Bilbao: Deusto, 2012).
48 José Babiano, Gutmaro Gómez, Antonio Míguez and Javier Tébar, *Verdugos impunes. La violación sistémica de los derechos humanos en el franquismo* (Barcelona: Pasado y Presente, 2018).
49 This book stems from research projects RYC-2014-16584, HAR2016-80359-P and 2017-PG128, within the HISTAGRA research group GI-1657 (University of Santiago de Compostela).

Part One

Sites of Sentencing and Death

2

Civil government buildings: Hearts of rebel violence during the Spanish Civil War. The case of Granada

Miguel Ángel Del Arco Blanco

The violence of the Spanish Civil War has long been a popular subject amongst historians. It combines two aspects that have attracted Spanish and international researchers alike: on the one hand, the violence in all its dimensions and complexity, and on the other hand, the civil war itself as a significant aspect in the study of twentieth-century European history.[1] On this tumultuous past, fewer and fewer issues remain to be addressed, despite the interest that current interpretations and debates may continue to arouse. However, this subject can be considered from an innovative perspective if we look at space, at the places where the historical processes of such importance developed.

Cultural geographers have long shown that space is essential to understanding social relations. It is where social processes take place, conditioned by the environment in which they develop.[2] But space is also the result of social actions, practices, relations and experiences, being part of these at the same time. It is not sterile or neutral, but a place that produces social relations and historic processes.[3] All of this applies to the spaces of violence: places where repression was unleashed, producing social results (the annihilation of the enemy), and that simultaneously reflected the power of the authorities and the states which created them. These sites offer another source for confronting the silence that those in power want to impose on the historical record and on history.[4]

Spaces must be included in the study of violence. Death and its mourning strongly mark certain places (battlefields, cemeteries, memorials). But we must expand from those spaces to others where life and death were linked. One of these micro-spaces is that of civil government buildings. By studying them, we not only examine a space of death during the Spanish Civil War, but also recover the memory of this space, generating an awareness of 'place' through past events and experiences that enables the mourning, dignity and memory of the victims.[5]

Little attention has been paid to the role of civil governments in the rebel violence during the war. The studies that exist have focused on analysing the seizure of power in provincial capitals, which led to the triumph of the uprising and the beginning of the persecution and punishment of Republicans.[6] However, taking into account what happened in other places where the coup triumphed and rebel violence was unleashed, I propose taking a closer look at both the space of civil governments as well as the men who commanded them and the actions they took. For this purpose, I examine Granada as a case study, focusing especially on the summer of 1936, when the violence was most intense. The city of the Alhambra can serve as a telling example; it reflects what happened in all the provincial capitals where the coup immediately triumphed and, in spite of this, violence was unleashed to paralyze, eliminate and arrest the supporters of the Republic. Granada also offers a peculiarity: as the place where the poet Federico García Lorca was assassinated, it enables us to access various sources of information and research material in which the civil government and the violence unleashed within appear explicitly or tangentially. Thus, we wade through the rivers of silence that surround the rebel violence and its memory during the Franco dictatorship, as inseparable elements of a single phenomenon that sought to annihilate the Republican enemy.[7]

Through the chosen example, our work aims to show that civil governments were a key piece in the machinery of rebel violence. They were one of the main targets of the coup plotters in 1936; in the early hours of the coup, the plotters seized civil governments while under the command of military forces with the support of civilian volunteers. Located in city centres, civil government buildings were put at the disposal of supporters of the uprising, who gathered there to collaborate or to promote violence against Republicans. Through the events that took place within those walls, we can verify that what happened then marked a rupture with previous uprisings or coups d'état. Denunciations, blacklists, searches, arrests, torture and murders: these were the phases of a deadly and hitherto unprecedented process in which the civil government was an authentic space of death. Military authorities were at the forefront of the civil governments, but they were also accompanied by other entities linked to public order (the Civil Guard, police and Assault Guard) as well as civilian professionals. Prior to the coup, many of them had committed themselves to other uprisings or openly anti-Republican political choices. Civil governments were, in short, essential spaces in the mass violence unleashed in July 1936. Spaces understood in the broadest sense, where social relations took place, where the annihilation of the Republicans was carried out, and which reflected what the Franco regime would become. Spaces that would be forgotten and remain in silence until today.

The coup d'etat and civil governments

In contemporary history, civil governors have been key to the operation of provincial power. Since the time of the Restoration (1875–1930), the role and responsibilities of the civil governor remained fairly constant. The governor's powers were broad but also quite varied: benefits, registration of associations, surveillance of prostitution, performances, statistics of all kinds, child protection, regulation of local life, taxes and contributions, public works and, of course, public order and electoral control. For these reasons, the arrival of the Second Republic and the change in the political profile of appointees would entail a notable shift in the policies to be developed at the provincial level.[8]

This is especially evident after the elections of February 1936 and the victory of the Popular Front. There was a substantial change of civil governors in the country (twenty-three in total), with most of them belonging to the Republican left.[9] Newly arrived in the provinces that spring, they frequently encountered administrative personnel who controlled the information and the means of provincial power, as well as some military garrisons where the coup plot was already being hatched. However, at the time of the coup (between 17 and 19 July) nearly all the governors scrupulously obeyed the orders of Casares Quiroga's Madrid government not to arm the people. When José Giral, the new president, authorized this on 19 July, in many cases it was too late.[10]

Everything seems to indicate that the seizure of power and the unleashing of the brutal violence of the rebels followed similar patterns in most of the provinces. If we look, for example, at Cádiz, Seville, Segovia, Salamanca or A Coruña, we see that the coup started from the barracks, as a consequence of a nationwide plot planned since the end of February 1936.[11] The military took to the streets and occupied city hubs, radio stations, telephone exchanges, town halls and, especially, civil government buildings. It was in this last institution where the incipient 'New State' and its terror policies began to take shape.

In all these provinces, the Republican governors were arrested and usually executed.[12] Their positions were filled by military officials who commanded the repression in capitals and provinces, then appointed mayors and management committees.[13] Throughout the cleansing process, there was active participation from civilians: Falangists, traditionalists, monarchists, Catholics or simply rightwing sympathizers of the coup. Particularly remarkable was the formation of 'civic guards' or armed groups that carried out arrests, killings in the cities or raids on towns throughout the province in search of Republican sympathizers. Such was the case of the 'Tercio Mora-Figueroa' in Cádiz, the group of Ramón de Carranza in Seville, the 'Tercio de Cazadores' of Salamanca or the 'Caballeros de La Coruña' in the Galician capital.[14]

It was different in the provincial capitals conquered over the course of the war, such as Malaga, Bilbao, Santander, Gijón, Barcelona or Madrid.[15] The process did not consist of seizing the Republican institutions and, from there, unleashing terror. When the rebel troops arrived in these cities, the first structures of the rising Franco dictatorship were already in place. 'Hot terror' ensued in the conquest, including indiscriminate killings of civilians trying to escape: such was the fate of entire families who fled on foot from Malaga to Almería in February 1937 and were bombarded by land, sea and air.[16] Later, the institutions of the rising dictatorship were moved to occupied terrain: Republican enemies were classified and ruthless military justice began, this was followed by confiscations and professional purging.[17] After the occupation, civil governments, despite their relevance and position under military control during the war, became yet another institution in the repressive Francoist plot.[18]

Granada belongs to the group of capitals where the coup triumphed. The last Republican civil governor, César Torres Martínez, had been appointed on 24 June 1936. Linked to the Republican left and a lawyer by profession, he had extensive experience as the head of provincial governments during the Republic in provinces such as Lugo, Almería, Ávila and Jaén. However, when he arrived in Granada, the coup plot had already been organized. Torres Martínez had begun his political career in the Autonomous Galician Republican Organization (ORGA), founded by Casares Quiroga, with whom he had a close relationship. Thus, it is not surprising that, at the time of the coup, he scrupulously followed Casares Quiroga's instructions not to arm the people.[19]

The rebellion against the legitimate government of the Second Republic began on 17 July 1936 in the Spanish protectorate in Morocco, and the following day in various parts of the peninsula. However, what the rebels would later call the 'Glorious National Uprising' took place in the city of Granada on 20 July.[20] Until then, the hours that followed the first news of the uprising were spent in the capital of Granada in maximum tension. Trade unions and leftist groups turned to the civil government to defend the Republic. The governor managed to calm the workers, assuring them that the city's military commander, General Miguel Campins Aura, had sworn allegiance to the government. Campins, a monarchist and a friend of Franco, was honest and true to his word. However, the officers under his command were not. On the afternoon of 19 July, the civil governor and Campins authorized the delivery of arms to the population to control the situation and also sent a column of troops to Córdoba, where the coup had triumphed.[21] However, the Granada military opposed the order, and the uprising took hold on 20 July, at 5.30 pm Campins was forced to sign a proclamation of martial law and was later jailed; he would be condemned for 'rebellion' and shot by General Queipo de Llano in Seville on 16 August 1936.[22] That was the charge that all citizens loyal to the Republic would be tried for in Spain after the uprising.[23]

On the afternoon of 20 July, even before the proclamation of martial law was released, the key points of the capital were seized, including the main squares, where artillery was placed. Although the actions were carried out by the military, they had the support of some Falangist volunteers and other right-wing parties.[24] However, the army directed all operations and any civilian elements were subordinate to it.[25]

The first building to be taken was the police station, located on Duquesa Street, next to the civil government office. Even before the uprising took hold in the city, at 4.00 pm the captain and Falangist Nestares Cuéllar carried out the operation to try to stop the shipment of weapons meant to aid the Republicans in Jaén.[26] When the troops took to the streets, the postal service, telegraphs, pro-Republican newspapers and radio came next: EAJ 16 Radio Granada was occupied at 6.30 pm, and broadcasting began of the martial law declaration and coup propaganda.[27] At that same time, the Security and Assault Guards also backed the coup. The uprising then reached the town hall, where the Republican mayor Manuel Fernández Montesinos (brother-in-law of Federico García Lorca) and other authorities were arrested, putting the city council in the hands of the infantry lieutenant Miguel del Campo Robles. The following day (21 July) the provincial government office was taken, and its council members arrested.[28]

Quite the opposite occurred with the civil government office of Granada. The building was seized early, at 5.15 pm on that same afternoon of 20 July.[29] It was the most important location for the coup's success: as mentioned earlier, this was where the representative of symbolic and effective governmental power could be found. The civil governor had numerous powers; perhaps the most important was control over the Assault Guards and the rest of the police force.

At the time of the seizure of the civil government, the civil governor was with some of the main Republican authorities, the most prominent being the governor himself and the president of the Provincial Council. Unlike what happened in other provinces, such as Seville, Cádiz and Córdoba, there was no resistance.

The commander of the Quartermaster Corps, José Valdés Guzmán, arrived at the building raising a flag: he was at the head of a column of officers (including Captain Nestares, who had joined with his men from the neighbouring police station), soldiers and volunteers. Although the Republican authorities ordered the Assault Guards to fire, the guards responded passively and allowed the assailants to enter.[30] Soon, all civil government servants were at the orders of the new civil governor, Commandant Valdés.[31]

Although the operation was ordered, directed and carried out by the military, the presence of civilian elements in the operation should also be noted. Falange volunteers participated, which was partly to be expected since Valdés was also the party's chief of militias in Granada.[32] The following day, the Catholic newspaper *Ideal* made this clear in a published note: while the operation took place 'the public, stationed in front of the Civil Government, did not cease to warmly applaud the soldiers and to utter long live Spain, the Army, the Assault and Security Guards and the Civil Guard'. Throughout the afternoon and evening 'the cheering of the forces and the public in front of the building did not stop'.[33] Evidently, the press was attempting to give proof of popular support for what would later become known as the 'Glorious National Uprising', but at the same time these testimonies revealed the presence of ordinary citizens. Shortly after the institution's seizure, many such citizens came to place themselves under the command of the coup leaders: thus, 'the corridors were filled with civilian elements, who came to place themselves under the new governor, for the various services of surveillance and assistance of the Army and the public force'.[34] The last stronghold of the Republic in the province had been taken. Then the violence and terror began.

In the following hours and days, the rebels took control of the working-class Albaicín neighbourhood, whose inhabitants withstood the bombardments and the advance of military columns until the afternoon of 23 July.[35] Just after the coup, the plotters occupied the towns surrounding the city as well. By 25 July, most of these towns were in their possession. However, the rebel-controlled perimeter was isolated from other areas in revolt, and the Republican lines were only a few kilometres from the city. Subsequently, to underscore the heroism of the 'Uprising' and to justify the repression, the rebels would claim that the city was completely besieged by the Republicans.[36] This was not true, for two reasons. First, because the weapons capacity and the skills of the troops on the rebel side placed them in a very advantageous position compared to the Republicans. And second, because on 18 August General Varela captured the strategic town of Loja, thus entering the valley where Granada is located. He arrived in the capital a few days later, connecting it with the rest of the territory controlled by the rebels.[37]

The rebels continued to kill with equal virulence beyond that date, totalling 5,500 victims throughout the province during the war alone; in the city and province of Granada, the number of victims was higher than average.[38] That perception remained in the memory of some Granadans: on a trip to the city in the late 1940s, the Hispanist Gerald Brenan affirmed that it was widely believed that the killings of Granada per inhabitant were much higher than anywhere else.[39] As with other fascist regimes, violence was a political instrument to eliminate the enemies of the nation, thus regenerating the 'authentic and imperial Spain' with which Francoism would identify.[40] Throughout this entire process, the civil government played a prominent role.

The civil government building and surrounding silence

The civil government building was located at 14 Duquesa Street, a relatively central street in the capital, close to the most important parts of the modern city. The property was located between the main building of the university and Duquesa Street, bordering the sheltered Botica Street (closed in the 1940s) to the west and the Botanical Garden to the east. The building belonged to the University of Granada and was leased to the Republican government. This had been the case since numerous buildings and plots of land in the area had been expropriated from the Jesuits during the Spanish Confiscation. Since then, practically no reforms had been made to the property.[41]

The civil government building consisted of three floors plus a 'covered tower'.[42] This can be seen in the photograph of the property that appears in Molina Fajardo's book *Los últimos días de García Lorca*, which shows three stories, with balconies on the upper two floors, and a small protrusion on the overhang that would be the tower. Both during the Republic and during the war, the ground and first floors were dedicated to administrative offices, while the second floor housed the personal offices of the governor, who lived there with his family.

The building had two courtyards: a larger, stately patio and a smaller one in the northeast part of the building.[43] In an aerial photograph of Granada taken around 1930, the courtyards can be seen by applying an orthophoto technique and noting the shadows cast by the building on the free surfaces. The first square patio on the left is clearly visible, as well as the second one, elongated and bordering the University building. The latter was a more private service patio, designed to provide the building with ventilation and light, and for carrying out domestic tasks.[44]

We know how some of the building's offices were used during the war, which brings us to another side of rebel violence. 'Provisional cells' were set up, where some detainees were temporarily held; these cells may also have been the setting for the brutal interrogations that I will describe later.[45] It seems that they were mainly located on the ground floor, probably close to the service patio so that they would be less visible from the main courtyard. However, there were some detention facilities on the first floor as well: for example, the small office overlooking the Botanical Garden, where the poet Federico García Lorca was held following his arrest on 16 August 1936.[46]

The condition of the property left much to be desired. In fact, as early as December 1932, the Republican civil governor Mariano Joven Hernández, a radical socialist from Aragon, had asked the Ministry of Governance to move the civil government offices to the police premises, also located on Duquesa Street (number 21), 'since the stated premises meet sufficient conditions for this'.[47] Through the measure, the property would be returned to the university, which 'today lacks a place to expand its premises and laboratories'.[48]

This initiative finally came to nothing. Both during the remaining Republican years and during the civil war and the immediate post-war period, the civil government continued to occupy the old building. This situation lasted until 1944, when the property was returned to the University of Granada and the civil government moved to another part of the city. The building was badly deteriorated, being 'in a bad state of solidity and conservation', and not being 'apt for the necessary reform'.[49] A new building was erected with a similar plan to the old one, where new university units would be housed.[50] The inauguration took place on 4 March 1955 in the presence of the Minister of Public Education, Catholic politician Joaquín Ruiz Giménez. Speeches were given that day and other buildings were inaugurated in the city. Even today, in what is currently part of the Faculty of Law, a marble plaque commemorates that event right at the entrance.[51] Silence continues to cover past violence. Today, nothing suggests that this place was the setting for the persecution, punishment and elimination of the Republicans of Granada – and the universal poet Federico García Lorca. I will analyse this next.

The civil government and its men in the summer of 1936

After the coup, the civil government building was turned into a completely militarized space. In addition to being occupied by the military and presided over by an army commander, José Valdés Guzmán, we know that the building had a permanent surveillance squad at its doors and in strategic places such as the patio. Following the capture of the building on 20 July, a 'surveillance service, both outside and inside the building' and at 'the doors of the different offices' was established. In addition, the occupiers placed artillery at certain points, mounting 'machine guns at the doors'.[52]

It appears that different functions were split among the main coup authorities of the province. On the one hand, the military command (the former military government) was primarily concerned with handling military jurisdiction, determining military operations and directing the war effort.[53] The military command building was where the first courts martial against the Republican authorities were held and the first death sentences were issued.[54]

On the other hand, the civil government (now called the 'military government') was responsible for ensuring order in the capital and the province, as well as arresting and executing supporters of the Republic. In the civil government building, courts martial were not held, but killings were carried out that were entirely extrajudicial. Although the civil government was controlled by the military, military and civilian elements mixed, overlapping and feeding the virulence of the repression, especially during the summer of 1936. However, it was the civil governor who had absolute authority in the building and certain autonomy from the military government for the work of repression.[55]

Figure 2.1 Falangists marching in the streets of A Coruña (Galicia, Spain), *c.* 1940.
© Histagra Collection / Histagra Research Group.

All the public participation that made the violence possible revolved around that old building on Duquesa Street. In the first hours after the coup, numerous denunciations began to arrive against left-wing people who should be arrested.[56] As previously mentioned, volunteers also arrived: in lines stood 'hundreds of people to volunteer to maintain order', while 'quota soldiers' (those who normally paid to avoid military service), temporary officers holding university degrees and reservists appeared at their respective barracks or at the military command building. In addition, 'more than fifty owners of cars and trucks offered their vehicles to the authorities for the transfer of forces and *other services*'. It was acknowledged that many of the cars that evening 'provided service' 'with patrols doing *surveillance rounds through the capital*' (my emphasis).[57] This was how suspects were arrested that summer, but also the means by which they were transferred to execution sites. In the case of Granada, that often meant going up to the city cemetery, or moving them to the Víznar ravine, about fifteen kilometres from the capital.

Volunteers went to the civil government building to enlist and then arm themselves. There were 'three enlistment departments', where volunteers were given the necessary weapons for the tasks they were going to carry out.[58] Prior to receiving the weapons, they needed to register and obtain a licence.[59] The number of licences granted is proof of the mobilization and public participation at that time: just four days after the coup, nearly 1,000 firearms permits had been granted in the city.[60]

Military and civilian elements coexisted in the building. The Infantry and Artillery Forces, Security Corps, Assault Guard, Civil Guard and volunteers took turns in the 'service of surveillance and crowd containment'.[61] Falange militiamen were among the volunteers, but (as in other Spanish provinces where the rebellion triumphed) they also organized 'patriotic militias' such as the 'Spanish Patriots' or the 'Armed Defence of Granada'.[62] Thus, the military and civilians intermingled, forming 'mixed guards'.[63] The presence of ordinary citizens was not unusual, and many of them spent a lot of time in the building, even staying overnight: the 'youth volunteer groups', while taking turns doing night surveillance shifts, 'slept on the cool slabs of the patio floor and the main stairwell of the building'.[64] There were even mishaps confirming the presence of civilian volunteers, such as when one was wounded 'when a weapon was accidentally fired at one of those providing surveillance services'.[65]

This mix between the military and civilians was also reproduced among the main commands of the civil government. It is true that its leadership was in the hands of the military: Commander Valdés was the governor, and his private secretary and right-hand man (who would represent him on many occasions) was Lieutenant Colonel of the Civil Guard Nicolás Velasco Simarro. Valdés was an Africanist military man who had participated in numerous operations in the Moroccan protectorate, as well as in the events of October 1934 in the city of Granada; a long-time Falangist, he was the chief of militias at the time of the uprising, to which he contributed with previous conspiracy plots and meetings in his own home.[66] For his part, Velasco Simarro, also a resident and with notable personal ties to the city, had been involved in the failed 1932 coup (the 'Sanjurjada') and had participated in the persecution and arrest of Republicans on the occasion of the October 1934 revolution in Granada.[67] Both had extensive conspiracy experience against the Republic, and had noted the failures of the previous uprisings (1932) and the limits of the legal system to punish those whom they considered the enemies of Spain.

The governor and his secretary were surrounded by an entourage of collaborators. Among them the mixture of military and civil elements was once again clear, as well as their anti-Republican experiences: military members, Civil Guards, Assault Guards, police, politicians, landowners and lawyers would take charge of the Granadan repression unleashed from the civil government.[68] Not to mention the 'Black Squad': a group of men in the service of Valdés with plenty of freedom of movement who went in and out of the civil government building, then headed towards the houses of Republicans where at night they carried out the removal of prisoners and executions 'on the fly', leaving the corpses abandoned. Many of these men belonged to wealthy families, but others belonged to the middle or lower-middle class.[69]

We have managed to reconstruct part of the group of men who led the anti-Republican violence in the city (see Table 2.1). They became known in popular memory as the 'civil government clique' or the 'Valdés clique'. The results are illuminating. The first detail that stands out is the military hierarchy, leading the entire machinery of violence (starting with the civil governor and private secretary). Next come other collaborators linked to the police, the Assault Guards or the army. These elements were intertwined with those representing professions far from the militia or the control of public order (lawyers, a typographer, a teacher). Nonetheless, they were all united by a shared sense of political commitment preceding 1936: Africanists, participants in the 1934 coup d'état or in the repression of the 1934 strike in Granada, active right-wing politicians (CEDA and Falange), etc. Finally, they shared another common denominator: they all had roots of some kind in the city, where most had been born and lived for a long time.

Table 2.1 The civil governor group of Granada in the summer of 1936

Name and surnames	Position	Profession in July 1936	Organization	Political party before coup	Background	Familiar with the city
José Valdés Guzmán	Civil Governor	Commandant	Army	Falange	Africanist, October 1934, chief of Falange militias	Yes
Nicolás Velasco Simarro	Personal secretary	Lieutenant Colonel	Civil Guard		Sanjurjada, October 1934	Yes
Julio Romero Funes	Public order delegate	Police inspector	Surveillance Corps		CEDA sympathizer	Yes
José Nestares Cuéllar	Chief of Surveillance Corps	Captain	Army	Falange		Yes
José Mingorance Jaraba	Collaborator		Surveillance Corps		Political-Social Brigade	Yes
Rafael Martínez Fajardo	Collaborator	Captain	Assault Guard	Falange	Africanist, dismantling anarchist cells 1934	Yes
Ramón Ruiz Alonso	Collaborator	Typographer		CEDA		Yes
Federico Martín Lagos	Collaborator	Teacher			Member of Falange after the coup	Yes
Manuel Jiménez de Parga	Collaborator	Lawyer		Falange		Yes
José Jiménez de Parga	Collaborator	Judicial secretary		Falange		Yes
Antonio Jiménez de Parga	Collaborator	Lawyer		Falange		Yes
Francisco Angulo Montes	Collaborator and military judge	Lawyer				Yes

Sources: Ian Gibson, *Granada en 1936 y el asesinato de Federico García Lorca* (Barcelona: Crítica, 1979); Agustín Penón, *Miedo, olvido y fantasía. Crónica de la investigación de Agustín Penón sobre Federico García Lorca. Granada-Madrid (1955–1956)*, ed. Marta Osorio (Granada: Comares, 2009); and Miguel Caballero, *Las trece últimas horas en la vida de García Lorca* (Madrid: La Esfera de los Libros, 2011).

After the seizure of power, columns of troops were sent out to control the rest of the province. Arrests, searches and persecutions began in the city. The activity of the coup plotters was frenzied, often turning into multiple and overlapping functions: acts of war, arrests, searches, executions, social control, censorship, etc.[70] In fact, various testimonies describe the corridors and offices of the civil government full of guards and volunteers, in a bustle of coming and going of coup supporters and detainees. They slept little and many even rested in the building: the governor 'Valdés spent fifteen days without trying a bed. He kept himself going on coffee and cognac. The security squad, with straps loosened and rifle between their arms, slept on the floor', in the room next to his office.[71] Those men spent several intense days together, sharing experiences that were extreme and highly compromising for their future. They also shared leisure: they visited bars and restaurants, having dinners and drinks together. An example of this appears in the striking photograph of Valdés and many of his collaborators at the 'Bar Jandilla', where some of the conspirators had been meeting since before the uprising.[72]

One of the first steps in unleashing the repression was to prepare lists of Republicans. For this, the participation of people who knew the city well, who had certain roots there, was crucial. As pointed out earlier, the 'clique' of the civil government highlights the importance of such insider knowledge. In Granada, it seems that this responsibility fell to several professionals linked to the world of law: the Jiménez de Parga brothers (Manuel, José and Antonio), law graduates of the University of Granada and Falangists, actively collaborated in the preparation of these death lists.[73] Their power was remarkable: on certain occasions, they removed certain names without the civil governor's knowledge. The lists would then reach the desk of Valdés, who decided on the fate of the lives of those included. Valdés's personal doctor would later remember seeing in the governor's office a 'list with forty names of people who would be shot'.[74]

It is very likely that many of the lists were created based on denunciations from individuals or even drawn up by staff working in the civil government. The role of the jurists in serving the repression thus gave an appearance of 'lawfulness' to the arrests and killings. Lists were also drawn up elsewhere in Granada, such as the military government office. According to some testimonies, certain people with close ties to the civil government also wrote lists in cafes in the city and would later take them to the Duquesa Street building.[75]

Military and militia groups would leave the civil government building to carry out searches and arrests in different parts of the city. This happened as soon as any denunciation or information reached the civil government offices, and was subsequently authorized by the signature of the governor.[76] After the coup and the crushing of the resistance in the Albaicín, the newspaper acknowledged that 'house searches were still being carried out with intensity to find weapons and dangerous elements'. Only on 23 July, 'some thirty people were arrested for possession of firearms, extremist propaganda, being undocumented and suspicious'. From there they were taken to the civil government building, where they were identified, interrogated and detained.[77] We even have graphic testimony of one of these events. An image shows how, from their car, a soldier and a Civil Guard (accompanied by a standing civilian driver) delivered some confiscated weapons to the door of the civil government.

There is plenty of evidence to demonstrate that the civil government was a place of repression. Agustín Penón revealed this long ago in his research, which compiled the first testimonies detailing the brutality of Governor Valdés and his men, as well as the terror that prevailed in the city at the time.[78] The detainees would go through the civil government building before finally being taken to execution sites (especially the Víznar ravine), where they arrived with an order that they had to deliver to the garrison chief Nestáres Cuellar, a captain and also a Falangist.[79] The property was definitely not a place where legal proceedings of any kind were held; instead, procedures were limited to identifying the detainees. Neither were the detainees led afterwards to any of the jails set up in the city. On the contrary, the testimonies reveal guards and militia volunteers tightly controlling the entrances, crowded into certain rooms and moving from one place to another, bringing in and taking out detainees.[80]

Torture was the common currency, applied in particular to those who were thought to have more links with leftist parties or union organizations to force them to denounce their comrades. Various testimonies cite the brutality of a character known as 'Italobalbo', as well as the existence of instruments of torture. The building doormen Gibson spoke to for his research 'constantly heard the screams of the victims'.[81] On several occasions, prisoners threw themselves out of the windows to escape the horror, but they also threw themselves into the small interior courtyard or the neighbouring Botanical Garden.[82]

Given the brutality of the violence, one might wonder if, as elsewhere in Spain, there were people who tried to intercede on behalf of the detained Republicans, in an attempt to save their lives.[83] Faced with the disappearances of relatives and acquaintances, and also the news of the executions, some approached the civil government with the intention of mediating on behalf of the detainees. Proof of this is that, on 15 August, a note from the civil governor was posted at the door of the building and published in the press that prohibited recommendations 'about detained persons', under penalty of a fine of 150 pesetas.[84] Despite this, these intervention attempts continued. One example is the sad case of García Lorca. After his arrest, the Rosales brothers visited the civil government to obtain his release; Lorca was close to the Rosales family, in whose house he had been hiding until the moment of his arrest, and they were among the most prominent Falangists in Granada. Another attempt was made by the composer Manuel de Falla, who tried to intervene for his friend when, in fact, Lorca had already been assassinated.[85]

Knowing the truth about the killing of the poet Federico García Lorca has led various researchers to concern themselves with his terrible last hours. Some of them he spent in the Granada civil government building, the heart of rebel violence in the city and the province. More lives were cut short before and after that of the poet. In the post-war period, the civil government was transferred to another building, which was demolished. The new construction, extravagantly inaugurated by a Francoist minister and other Granadan authorities who may have known the poet, still commemorates that festive day with a plaque. Silence has covered everything ever since. Paradoxically, investigations into the brutal killing of Lorca have allowed us to explain, reconstruct, revive and remember that space of mass violence.

Notes

1 Javier Rodrigo, *Hasta la raíz. Violencia durante la Guerra Civil y la dictadura franquista* (Madrid: Alianza, 2008).
2 Derek Gregory and John Urry (eds), *Social Relations and Spatial Structures* (Basingstoke: Macmillan, 1985).
3 Henri Lefebvre, *The Production of Space* (Cambridge: Blackwell, 1991), 73 and 84–5.
4 Michel-Rolph Trouillot, *Silenciando el Pasado. El poder y la producción de la historia* (Granada: Comares, 2017), 44–54.
5 Avril Maddrell and James D. Sidaway, 'Introduction: Bringing a Spatial Lens to Death, Dying, Mourning and Remembrance', in *Deathscapes Spaces for Death, Dying, Mourning and Remembrance*, ed. Avril Maddrell and James D. Sidaway (Farnham: Ashgate, 2010), 2–3.
6 For a study covering all of Spain, see Paul Preston, *The Spanish Holocaust: Inquisition and Extermination in Twentieth-Century Spain* (London: Harper Press, 2012).
7 Antonio Míguez Macho, *Genocidal Genealogy of Francoism: Violence, Memory & Impunity* (Brighton: Sussex Academic Press, 2016).

8   Joan Serrallonga Urquidi, 'El aparato provincial durante la Segunda República. Los gobernadores civiles, 19312011939', *Hispania Nova* 7 (2007): 4–6.
9   Ibid., 24.
10 Paul Preston, *The Spanish Civil War: Reaction, Revolution and Revenge* (London: Harper, 2006), 98.
11 On the coup and repression in these cities, see Francisco Espinosa Maestre, *La justicia de Queipo: violencia selectiva y terror fascista en la ll División en 1936: Sevilla, Huelva, Cádiz, Córdoba, Málaga y Badajoz* (Barcelona: Crítica, 2005); Juan Ortiz Villalba, *Del golpe militar a la guerra civil: Sevilla 1936* (Sevilla: RD, 2006); Santiago Vega Sombría, *De la esperanza a la persecución: la represión franquista en la provincia de Segovia* (Barcelona: Crítica, 2005); Ricardo Robledo (ed.), *Esta salvaje pesadilla: Salamanca en la Guerra Civil española* (Barcelona: Crítica, 2007); Jesús De Juana and Julio Prada, *Lo que han hecho en Galicia. Violencia política, represión y exilio (1936–1939)* (Barcelona: Crítica, 2006). On the plot and the involvement of civilian elements, see Ángel Viñas, *¿Quién quiso la guerra civil?: historia de una conspiración* (Barcelona: Crítica, 2019).
12 The exception was Varela Rendueles of Seville. Espinosa Maestre, *La justicia de Queipo*, 76–7.
13 However, in Seville General Queipo de Llano appointed a civilian as mayor of the capital (Ramón de Carranza Gómez). Ortiz Villalba, *Del golpe militar*, 92.
14 Ibid., 116–17; Santiago López García and Severiano Delgado Cruz, 'Que no se olvide el castigo: la represión en Salamanca durante la guerra civil', in *Esta salvaje pesadilla. Salamanca en la Guerra Civil española*, ed. Ricardo Robledo (Barcelona: Crítica, 2007), 106–07; Emilio Grandío Seoane, 'Golpe de Estado y represión franquista en la provincia de A Coruña: ¿Qué pasa con Coruña?', in *Lo que han hecho en Galicia. Violencia política, represión y exilio (1936–1939)*, ed. Jesús De Juana and Julio Prada (Barcelona: Crítica, 2006), 36–41.
15 See Preston, *The Spanish Holocaust*, 207–9, 474–5, 476–7, 482–3, 506–8.
16 Lucía Prieto and Encarnación Barranquero, *Población y Guerra Civil en Málaga caída, éxodo y refugio* (Málaga: Diputación de Málaga, 2007), 180–209.
17 Peter Anderson, *Friend or Foe? Occupation, Collaboration and Selective Violence in the Spanish Civil War* (Brighton: Sussex Academic Press, 2017).
18 Gutmaro Gómez Bravo, *Geografía humana de la represión franquista: del golpe a la guerra de ocupación (1936–1941)* (Madrid: Cátedra, 2017).
19 Ian Gibson, *Granada en 1936 y el asesinato de Federico García Lorca* (Barcelona: Crítica, 1979), 59–60.
20 Various books give a detailed account of the coup in the capital, see Gibson, *Granada*, 70–90; Rafael Gil Bracero and María Isabel Brenes, *Jaque a la República (Granada, 1936–1939)* (Granada: Osuna, 2009), 151–208. For an update on the military coup in Granada, see Joaquín Gil Honduvilla, *Y cayó Granada. La sublevación de julio de 1936 en la capital y la provincia* (Comares: Granada, 2019).

21 Gil Honduvilla, *Y cayó Granada*, 129–34.
22 Preston, *The Spanish Holocaust*, 172.
23 José Babiano, Gutmaro Gómez Bravo, Antonio Míguez and Javier Tébar, *Verdugos impunes. El franquismo y la violación sistémica de los derechos humanos* (Barcelona: Pasado & Presente, 2018), 63.
24 Rafael Gil Bracero, 'Granada en manos de las autoridades militares', in *La guerra civil en Andalucía oriental, 1936-1939* (Granada: Ideal, 1987), 91; Gil Bracero and Brenes, *Jaque a la República*, 185–95. See testimony of Patricio González of Canales in Eduardo Molina Fajardo, *Los últimos días de García Lorca* (Barcelona: Plaza & Janés, 1983), 114–15.
25 Gil Honduvilla, *Y cayó Granada*, 163.
26 Joaquín Arrarás, *Historia de la Cruzada española*, vol. 3 (Madrid: Ediciones Españolas, 1956), 285.
27 'Notas leídas por Radio', *Ideal*, 21 July 1936: 4. The Republican newspaper *El Defensor de Granada* was closed the same day, 20 July. Francisco Vigueras, *Granada, 1936: muerte de un periodista* (Granada: Comares, 2015), 226.
28 Rafael Gil Bracero, *Revolucionarios sin revolución: marxistas y anarcosindicalistas en guerra. Granada-Baza, 1936-1939* (Granada: Universidad de Granada, 1998), 95.
29 This information comes from later courts martial. The newspaper *Ideal* would set the time of the seizure at 6.00 pm. See 'El comandante comisario de Guerra de la plaza, don José Valdés Guzmán, se posesiona del Gobierno Civil', *Ideal*, 21 July 1936: 3.
30 Gil Honduvilla, *Y cayó Granada*, 167–69; Gibson, *Granada*, 86–8; Gil Bracero and Brenes, *Jaque a la República*, 189–90.
31 'El comandante comisario', *Ideal*, 21 July 1936: 3.
32 Agustín Penón, *Miedo, olvido y fantasía. Crónica de la investigación de Agustín Penón sobre Federico García Lorca. Granada-Madrid (1955-1956)*, ed. Marta Osorio (Granada: Comares, 2009), 45 and 49.
33 These attitudes lasted for quite a long time: 'El entusiasmo por el movimiento militar es grande en toda la provincia de Granada', *Ideal*, 22 July 1936: 3.
34 'El comandante comisario', *Ideal*, 21 July 1936: 3.
35 Gibson, *Granada*, 93–5.
36 For example, Ángel Gollonet Mejías and José Morales López, *Rojo y azul en Granada. Más datos para la historia de la guerra civil española* (Granada: Librería Prieto, 1937); Cándido G. Ortiz De Villajos, *Crónica de Granada en 1938. II–III Año Triunfal* (Granada: Urania, 1939), 145–46.
37 José Enrique Varela Iglesias, *Diario de operaciones 1936-1939* (Madrid: Almena, 2004).
38 Preston, *The Spanish Holocaust*, 777.
39 Gerald Brenan, *The Face of Spain* (London: Serif, [1950] 2010), 109.

40 Claudio Hernández Burgos, 'Making the "New Spain": Violence, Nationalism and Religion in the Rebel Zone, 1936–1939', in *Ruptura: The Impact of Nationalism and Extremism on Daily Life in the Spanish Civil War (1936–1939)*, ed. Claudio Hernández Burgos (Brighton: Sussex Academic Press, 2020), 125–64.

41 Juan Manuel Barrios Rozúa, *Guía de la Granada desaparecida* (Granada: Comares, 2006), 366. See also Mercedes Fernández Carrión, 'Del edificio central de la Universidad a Facultad de Derecho', in *Universidad y ciudad. La Universidad en la Historia y la cultura de Granada*, ed. Ignacio Henares Cuéllar and Rafael López Guzmán (Granada: Universidad de Granada, 1997), 171–77.

42 As it was pointed out in the 'Acta de Entrega del edificio a la Universidad': *Archivo de la Universidad de Granada* (AUG), box 01842/001, 'Acta de entrega', 13 March 1944.

43 Some have pointed out that there was only one *patio*: Fernández Carrión, 'Del edificio central', 180.

44 In fact, one of the investigations on Lorca would collect a testimony mentioning a 'small cobbled service patio, where the caretaker's family hung clothes'. Testimony of Carlos Jiménez Vílchez in Molina Fajardo, *Los últimos días*, 233.

45 Gibson, *Granada*, 101.

46 Miguel Ángel del Arco Blanco, 'Un espacio para rescatar del olvido: la Facultad de Derecho y el asesinato de Federico García Lorca', *Revista del Centro de Estudios Históricos de Granada y su Reino* 31 (2019): 177–200.

47 On Joven Hernández, see José Luis López Casamayor, *Mariano Joven Hernández: la ética de un demócrata* (Almonacid de la Sierra: Ayuntamiento, 2006).

48 AUG, box 01803/10, 26 December 1932.

49 Archivo General de la Administración (AGA), *Memoria del Proyecto de ampliación y cierre del recinto universitario – Granada*, box 17331. The building would be demolished according to the tender of 14 March 1944. See AUG, box 03080/001, Act of 14 March 1944 del Rector Magnífico de la Universidad de Granada. The demolition was granted to Ángel Quesada Martínez.

50 The new civil government 'had been installed' in the sumptuous Müller Palace 'acquired by the state, located at number 50, Gran Vía de Colón' in the capital. AUG, box 01842/001, Acta de entrega, 13 March 1944.

51 *Boletín de la Universidad de Granada* 14, no. 169 (1955). The news was also picked up by national papers. See 'El ministro de educación inaugura la nueva facultad de ciencias de Granada', *ABC*, 5 May 1955: 34.

52 'El comandante comisario', *Ideal*, 21 July 1936: 3.

53 After the coup, the command was led by Colonel Basilio León Maestre, but from 29 July it would be led by General Antonio González Espinosa, sent by Queipo de Llano from Seville. At the command post 'as many people wishing to collaborate with the cause of maintaining order for the good of Spain and the Republic' should show up, also making available to the authority 'means of locomotion (cars,

trucks, etc.)'. See 'Notas leídas por Radio', *Ideal*, 21 July 1936: 4. On the extension or suspension of military jurisdiction in the province, see 'Alzamiento de la suspensión de términos y actuaciones judiciales (Bando del Excmo. Sr. Gobernador Militar de la plaza)', *Ideal*, 11 September 1936: 5.

54 Gibson, *Granada*, 98–100. Testimony of Fernando López Nebrera, in Molina Fajardo, *Los últimos días*, 122.
55 Acknowledged by the Falangist José Rosales. Penón, *Miedo, olvido y fantasía*, 702. Another testimony, see p. 53.
56 Ibid., 166.
57 'Notas leídas por Radio', *Ideal*, 21 July 1936: 4.
58 'El entusiasmo por el movimiento militar', *Ideal*, 22 July 1936: 3.
59 'Se ha infringido un duro castigo a los aviones enemigos', *Ideal*, 30 July 1936: 5.
60 Joaquín López-Mateos Matres had license number 949, signed on 24 July 1936. For his testimony, see Molina Fajardo, *Los últimos días*, 246.
61 'El entusiasmo por el movimiento militar', *Ideal*, 22 July 1936: 3.
62 Something recognized in Bonifacio Soria Marco, *Cruzada nacionalista. Memorias de guerra de un vanguardista de 'Españoles Patriotas' en el frente de Granada* (Granada: Urania, 1937). See also Rafael Casas De Vega, *Las milicias nacionales* (Madrid: Editora Nacional, 1977).
63 For the testimony of Julián Fernández Amigo, see Molina Fajardo, *Los últimos días*, 237.
64 'El entusiasmo por el movimiento militar', *Ideal*, 22 July 1936: 3.
65 'Continúan realizándose registros en busca de armas. Herido por disparo casual en el Gobierno civil', *Ideal*, 24 July 1936: 4.
66 Personal file of José Valdés Guzmán, Archivo General Militar de Segovia, 1ª/B-201, Exp. 0.
67 Miguel Caballero, *Las trece últimas horas en la vida de García Lorca* (Madrid: La Esfera de los Libros, 2011), 39–62.
68 Gibson, *Granada*, 100–1; Caballero, *Las trece últimas horas*, 123.
69 Penón, *Miedo, olvido y fantasía*, 63; Gibson, *Granada*, 107–9.
70 Gibson, *Granada*, 98. For the testimony of Vicente Lara Jiménez, see Molina Fajardo, *Los últimos días*, 232–4; Caballero, *Las trece últimas horas*, 144–6.
71 For the testimony of Carlos Jiménez Vílchez, see Molina Fajardo, *Los últimos días*, 232.
72 For the testimony of Antonio Pérez Funes, see Molina Fajardo, *Los últimos días*, 252.
73 Caballero, *Las trece últimas horas*, 123, 136–9.
74 For the testimony of Luis Morell Cuéllar, see Molina Fajardo, *Los últimos días*, 138.
75 See the testimony of Luis García-Alix Fernández in Molina Fajardo, *Los últimos días*, 198.
76 Several Falangists acknowledged this to Agustín Penón. Penón, *Miedo, olvido y fantasía*, 53.

77 'Continúan realizándose registros', *Ideal*, 24 July 1936: 4.
78 Penón, *Miedo, olvido y fantasía*, 159, 162–3.
79 Marta Osorio, *El enigma de una muerte (Crónica comentada de la correspondencia entre Agustín Penón y Emilia Llanos)* (Granada: Comares, 2015), 271.
80 Gibson, *Granada*, 98. For the testimony of Vicente Lara Jiménez, see Molina Fajardo, *Los últimos días*, 232–4; Caballero, *Las trece últimas horas*, 144–6.
81 Gibson, *Granada*, 110–11.
82 For the testimony of Carlos Jiménez Vílchez, see Molina Fajardo, *Los últimos días*, 232–4.
83 Carlos Gil Andrés, 'También hombres del pueblo. Colaboración ciudadana en la gran represión', in *No solo miedo. Actitudes políticas y opinión popular bajo la dictadura franquista (1936–1977)*, ed. Miguel Ángel del Arco, Carlos Fuertes, Claudio Hernández and Jorge Marco (Granada: Comares, 2013).
84 'Prohibición de recomendaciones', *Ideal*, 15 August 1936: 8.
85 Ian Gibson, *El asesinato de García Lorca* (Barcelona: Ediciones B), 230. For the testimony of Julián Fernández Amigo, see Molina Fajardo, *Los últimos días*, 237. The Rosales's intervention before Valdés is discussed in the testimony of the poet Luis Rosales, see *A fondo. Luis Rosales* (1977) [TV Programme], Televisión Española, 23 October, from minute 1:04:00. Available online: http://www.rtve.es/alacarta/videos/a-fondo/fondo-luis-rosales/2795955/ (accessed, 7 April 2020). Also: Penón, *Miedo, olvido y fantasía*, 165–66.

3

The staging of 'formal' violence: Sentencing sites

Conchi López Sánchez

The Francoist regime used triumph at war as a source of legitimacy and the beginning of a propaganda discourse that would be key to perpetuating the dictatorship for more than thirty years. The use of violence since 18 July 1936 was essential for 1939 to become the 'Year of Victory' and for the coup plotters to achieve their most desired goal: power. To identify the mechanisms and the key reasoning behind the operation of this violence, it is worth analysing the relationship between society and the military coup's leadership. Shortly after the coup, in the rearguard territories dominated by the insurgents, the command forces began to search for the individuals who had hindered their access to power. Consequently, they prepared reports on certain people regarding their 'political antecedents' or their behaviour during the coup, which led to military court investigations. To make this great legal machinery work, they combined the Code of Military Justice (CMJ) from the Second Republic with new elements that changed and perverted the previous legal framework. Military lawsuits were thus developed as part of the construction of legal *inventio*, in response to the need to justify coup violence and involve society. In this regard, the selection of venues is a particular aspect that enables us to observe the military leadership's desire to turn trials into events that could attract and promote social participation.

This chapter explains how the coup plotters used military justice in a way that was targeted, carefully shaped and opportunistic. First, I will try to point out the main parts of the coup strategy. On the one hand, the military organization of the territory according to organic divisions and the main hubs of power was key to designing the process of occupying the different garrison towns. On the other hand, the perverse twisting of Republican legal legitimacy, which constituted the *inventio*, enabled the justification of the coup and was carried out in several ways: the publication of proclamations of martial law was one of the most important. Second, I will delve into the structure of military trials, since their very nature allows us to explain the opportunistic use that coup plotters made of the process to achieve collective participation. Subsequently, I will analyse in depth the sites and spaces that were chosen to hold such trials and issue sentences.

The distorted use of military justice: The *inventio* – legal legitimacy of the coup

Emilio Mola Vidal, an Africanist of dubious loyalty to the constituted government, was the main military organizer of the 1936 coup d'état. Through his *Instrucciones reservadas* – instructions sent secretly from April 1936 to military coup plotters – he elaborated a plan of action in which military organization of the territory and the use of violence were key.[1] Indeed, once Spain was divided into two zones, the side that fell under control of the coup plotters was reorganized according to these guidelines, which involved the coordination of civil organization (related to provinces) and military organization (based on organic divisions).[2]

The ordinance in force in 1936 divided the Spanish Army into eight Organic Divisions (together with the Moroccan Army), territories among which the different infantry, cavalry, troops and garrison forces were divided.[3] Using this map, Mola designed a coup plot that prioritized attacking the centre of military power followed by civilian command centres, depending on the administrative category of the territory.[4] Beneath this plan was a violent line of reasoning that was designed and executed vertically, in which the conquest of military capitals – which were usually provincial capitals as well – was essential to seizing control of the areas under their influence. The most important hubs of power in the capitals were military headquarters, civil government offices, provincial government offices and town halls. Once the capitals were under control, military troops were sent to occupy the remaining space – smaller population centres – through the use of violence.

In the case of the Navy, territorial planning divided the Spanish coastline into three maritime departments whose capitals were Ferrol, Cádiz and Cartagena. These areas were then subdivided according to a descending scale into thirds, provinces and maritime districts where different naval bases and forces were distributed. From 18 July, Cartagena remained faithful to the Republic until the end of the war; meanwhile, Ferrol and Cádiz fell into the hands of the coup leaders, who immediately took control of the warships from these arsenals. Consequently, key authority figures who did not join the uprising were punished, for example, Rear Admiral Antonio Azarola, head of the Ferrol Arsenal and former Minister of the Navy.[5]

The control of space was key to the coup strategy. This task was carried out through various means, one of which was the subjugation of garrison towns through 'proclamations of martial law'. These territorial organizational units were also used to plan and execute military justice. The concept of the garrison town (*plaza militar*) has been abstract and vague throughout history, but since the CMJ of 1890 we can define it as the smallest structure of space subject to military jurisdiction. Wherever the coup triumphed, the organization of physical space was particularly military in nature, and administrative and political divisions became secondary. Consequently, this imposed territorial organization would condition the selection of venues for trials beyond the spaces of the barracks.

The military legal structure used by the coup plotters from 18 July to dismantle the democratic state of the Republic and seize power began with a series of decrees, codes and laws promulgated at the end of the nineteenth century and in force until 1945.[6] In other words, during the war, the coup plotters did not create a new code, but started from the previous legal framework. Through a perverse strategy, they distorted it and prepared themselves to build a discourse on the legitimacy of the coup that, initially, was linked to the issuing of proclamations of martial law.

The proclamations were documents outlining the seizure of key garrisons and were published by the main coup leaders in each area. These documents were relevant because they were the starting point for the establishment of military coup power: they eliminated the individual guarantees enshrined in the 1931 Constitution, and placed the armed forces, common justice, public order and civil power under military jurisdiction.[7]

The first proclamations followed a pattern of stating the consequences of the declaration of martial law as indicated in the CMJ: the militarization of the armed forces under the control of the army. However, despite sharing points in common, and even repeated paragraphs, most constituted different texts with certain nuances. All of them defined crimes subject to the jurisdiction of war, but the specification and definition of such crimes would change as the days passed. At first, the war Proclamation of Santa Cruz de Tenerife – published on 18 July 1936 and signed by Francisco Franco – indicates in Article 8 crimes that violate public order, as stated in the Ordinary Penal Codes of Military Justice in the CMJ and the Law of July 1933.[8] The Proclamation of A Coruña – published two days later – continued the previous line with a succinct description, referring to 'all criminal acts of political-social origin'. Subsequently, other documents such as those published in Ourense (Articles 5 and 7) and in Lugo (Article 5) specified what these crimes were and what they consisted of. Broadly speaking, in the first proclamations, those who disobeyed or attacked military forces and disturbed public order would be considered guilty of rebellion.[9]

The proclamation of martial law was more than a document; its publication and reading turned into public and social events that filled the main squares of the rearguard. These events were like a starting gun for the coup plotters to impose physical and specific domination over the territory. After the proclamation of the state of war, the coup military commanders began to issue orders that reorganized the power and space under their control. They dismissed local councils, ordered the purging of public servants, appointed delegates of their authority, ordered the creation of an armed militia under the responsibility of a Subdelegate for Public Order, and distributed the responsibilities of military and civil powers to delegates of the Army and the Civil Guard, representatives of the armed forces.[10]

While these actions took place at the local level, on 25 July 1936, the Junta de Defensa Nacional (Council of National Defence) was established and assumed all powers of the state. At the end of July, the president of the Junta, Miguel Cabanellas, published a proclamation of martial law that united different elements that were already visible in the previously published declarations.[11] It proclaimed the legal foundations that would be applied with regard to the classification of crimes and the powers of the military jurisdiction. These foundations constituted the initial guidelines that would be completed with successive decrees and laws, such as the creation of the High Court of Justice on 24 October 1936 or the Supreme Council of Military Justice on 5 September 1939.[12]

One of the keys to the proclamation of 25 July was Article 6, which clarified and redefined the concept of 'rebel' with respect to Article 237 of the CMJ: 'They are guilty of the crime of military rebellion those who rise up in arms against the State constitution, against the King, the Legislative Bodies or the legitimate Government.'[13] In the proclamation, 'rebellious' behaviour was categorized as follows:

> spreading false or biased news in order to undermine the prestige of the military [...], those in possession of weapons or flammable or explosive substances [...], those who hold any meeting, conference or public demonstration without prior notice [...], those who tend to impede or hinder the supply of basic necessities [...] or those who restrict the hiring of workers.[14]

This was one of the first steps in the process of inverting justice, which years later Franco's brother-in-law and right-hand man Serrano Suñer would call 'reverse justice'. In other words, the coup-plotting rebels were moved to the realm of 'legality' and vice versa: 'rebel illegality' now applied to the defenders of the established order.[15] This incongruity was of vital importance because it articulated a good part of the coup strategy; however, to validate it, the plotters needed public approval and society participation in the violence they were perpetrating. Such publicity – given to the trials after repurposing the crime of rebellion – had a double function, since it was also a way to denigrate those who were previously 'authorities' and were now 'criminals'.

Later, we will see how the decision to hold trials outside of military spaces fulfilled these functions and turned trials into public spectacles with large audiences. While the passing of sentences was one of the main executive branches of coup violence, the places where key political leaders were sentenced were one of the mechanisms used to generate publicity and involve the participation of society.

The violence of the coup was mainly carried out in two ways: either hand in hand with legal *inventio* through trials or via the more immediate channel of 'paseos' (or 'strolls'). Both methods existed in parallel, at least until the end of the war, although they resulted in disparate numbers of victims. According to data from early rearguard areas such as Galicia or Cádiz, the victims of paseos were far greater in number, making up two-thirds of the total. Military courts became particularly active from the moment the rebels took power in each garrison town, and this lasted for the next twelve or eighteen months, at which point the activity declined and acquired new characteristics. Collective summary proceedings became less frequent – in favour of individual cases – and, in general, military courts became more complex and acted less harshly.[16]

The CMJ established various types of procedures; however, the one used by the coup plotters to carry out unprecedented violence was of a summary inquisitorial nature. In these lawsuits, the accusation weighed on the defence and was always initiated by means of *notitia criminis*: a denunciation, a statement, a purging investigation or an investigation originating in the detention camps. Subsequently, the corresponding judicial authority (normally, the garrison commander) was contacted to appoint an investigating judge to whom the 'evidence' would be sent, launching the military case. This figure was usually one of the military's fiscal commanders, or a captain or junior officer who would be directly involved with the military judicial authority coordinating the entire process. An example of this dynamic is 'the standard form' that was usually used by the military commanders – on whom the other garrison towns under their jurisdiction depended – to appoint investigating judges:

> for the purposes of building the corresponding case, I refer Your Honour to the statements heard by the Civil Guard of this town, against the individuals who are implicated on the back, indicating that Your Honour is empowered to act as a military judge in the proceedings to be held on the occasion of events that occurred in the territory of that Court.[17]

From there, the procedure consisted of two phases. The first was the pretrial proceedings: the judge appointed a secretary to assist him in the corresponding tasks, statements were taken, denunciations or statements were confirmed, and conduct reports were requested from 'persons of order' who could give accounts of the social, political and moral background of those concerned. At this stage, social participation in the lawsuit was essential; the military authorities required key local authorities and witnesses who could corroborate the facts to support the accusation. However, these statements lacked supporting evidence, and only those voices that reinforced the guilt of the defendant were considered and used to build and strengthen the initial accusation. Witnesses who testified in favour of the victim and rebutted or contradicted the original statement that prompted the trial were dropped from the lawsuit and later ignored by the prosecutor in the conviction request. An example of this can be found in the case against the Popular Front council deputy mayor and Republican left president of Monforte de Lemos (Lugo), Víctor Martínez. He was prosecuted for the alleged crime of military rebellion, and the prosecutor asked for the maximum sentence based on the reports and declarations of the Civil Guard and some neighbours regarding four actions: organization of armed people to defend the legitimate government in the provincial capital; coercion and threats to right-wing people before the coup; unwarranted possession of weapons during a state of war; and being a supposed Marxist propagandist.[18] However, both the prosecutor and the court that handed down the sentence ignored the testimonies that contradicted such conduct and defended the accused, including those from 'persons of order'. The priest declared that '[the defendant] did not mistreat any right-wing person, nor did he demonstrate against religion'; the notary 'had shared conversations with the defendant from which he deduced with certainty that he was anti-Marxist'; the vice-consul of Germany in the city 'knew nothing of his acting as a leader in Monforte on the occasion of the charges'; and in short, the veterinarian, the doctor and important local businessmen and industrialists agreed that 'the political conduct of Víctor Martínez was always orderly'.[19] Even by accepting the logic of the coup plotters, there was not enough evidence to resolve the apparent contradiction between the arguments in favour and against the accused; therefore, the logical structure of the reasoning based on the evidence was weak. Despite this, he was sentenced to life in prison; after the intervention of three private votes, he was finally sentenced to death.[20]

The prosecution's accusations were a key part of the process to determine the impact and use of legal *inventio* by the coup plotters. In making these accusations, they used the twisting of previous laws enabled by the war proclamations, a perverse means that turned citizens defending Republican legitimacy into rebels. Subsequently, the Chief of Staff of the Division would announce the courts martial to be held throughout the day, along with their time, place and composition. Once the court martial had been set up, it was held, a sentence was pronounced, it was recorded in legal proceedings and, with the auditor of the Division's approval, the sentence was carried out. In short, it was an operating scheme that in practice provided no guarantees to the accused. Of all its complexity, the places where courts martial were held represent a fundamental aspect that allows us to understand the logic of the whole.

Spaces of legal domination: Maritime jurisdiction and land jurisdiction

The administration of military justice was organized by territory according to the responsibilities of land and maritime jurisdictions. Although the number of trials heard differs in each case (there were many more under land jurisdiction), broadly speaking they shared the same procedural logic.

Maritime jurisdiction applied to crimes committed by people in the coastal territories under this authority. The degree of harshness with which the Navy used violence, by holding military trials, was adapted to the conditions of each territory as the war progressed. In early rearguard territories, such as the north-western peninsular area captained by Ferrol (Galicia), the maritime jurisdiction authorities ordered trials against a third of the total victims indicted, and (as on land) accusations were frequently based on the crimes of desertion or rebellion.[21] The actions that gave rise to this type of accusation were mainly two: on the one hand, individuals who did not show up when called to join replacement ranks and, on the other, coup and counter-coup actions that were carried out on the ships themselves.[22]

In the case of Ferrol, capital of the Northern Maritime Department, those trials that thrived and consisted of courts martial deliberating sentences were held primarily in three spaces: prison warships and two areas within the General Command of the Maritime Department – the courtroom and the naval engineering academy (Academia de Maquinistas). An example of the first group of places was the 'Contramaestre Casado', a ship that had been part of the transport fleet under the orders of the General Staff of the Navy since 1927. On 20 July 1936, when the coup d'état began in the capital, the crew detained the seditious officers and led the resistance. The following day, the loyal sailors surrendered to the coup forces. They were detained and a case was opened; they were sentenced to death and executed. Later, the uses and functions of the ship were reconverted by the coup authorities. From then on, the ship became a place of confinement where military trials were carried out. One of the most extensive and relevant examples was the case brought against the crew of the 'Mar Cantábrico' steamboat,[23] seized by the national fleet while carrying a shipment of war material for the Republic. The ship, which had been a symbol of resistance to the coup, was now one of the scenes of coup justice.[24]

Other sites used to hold most of the trials in Ferrol were the different rooms of the General Command of the Maritime Department. One of these was the courtroom, located in the heart of the city.[25] At first it was the headquarters of the General Services of the Navy, where legal services were located; later, it housed the Naval Archive, and currently it houses a military residence inaugurated in 2013. In the last refurbishment of the building, a Francoist-era coat of arms presiding over the façade was replaced, and the archive was moved to the military district headquarters. Another place where war trials were held was the naval engineering academy. For a time, this place was used as a courtroom for the department, and it also served as the headquarters of the Public Order delegation, the Falange and the Civil Guard. It is located within the naval base itself and currently forms part of the publicly accessible area of the arsenal.[26]

What happened in Ferrol was not an isolated reality. The rebels' capture of the main Galician naval base along with those of the department of Cádiz overthrew two-thirds of the legitimate command of the maritime capitals of the Spanish state. These circumstances allowed for the trial of hundreds of naval officers, the occupation of their spaces of power and the reassignment of new functions to ships, all as part of the violent spiral used to achieve the goals of the coup plotters. However, in the only naval area that resisted until the end of the war – the Mediterranean coast commanded by the Cartagena maritime department – the violence exerted through the military courts in the post-war period acquired certain nuances. The strategic importance of the only naval base that the Republic held until its fall in March 1939 conditioned the relevance acquired by the cases heard under the marine jurisdiction of this area. Half of the military courts that operated in the Murcia region after 1939 did so under the jurisdiction of the Cartagena maritime department.[27] In this way, and following the pattern of what happened in Ferrol and Cádiz during the war, public trials in Cartagena were brought against the enemies of the coup plotters, who were now victorious.

The majority of the trials fell under land jurisdiction, which mainly handled cases related to the resignified crime of rebellion. In addition to their numerical significance, the trials of this jurisdiction played a fundamental role in executing the most violent sentences while attracting and involving the general population through their testimonies, and establishing the coup leaders' authority through the occupation of the most important physical centres of political power.

Military courts were initially formed in the headquarters of the most important regiments. This had been the case since before 18 July 1936 and subsequently there was some continuity in the different 'national rearguards' during the civil war. The San Hermenegildo barracks in Seville, the San Francisco barracks in Las Palmas, the Don Julián Sánchez 'El Charro' barracks in Salamanca, the

Figure 3.1 Sentencing Site. Palace of the Provincial Government (Pontevedra, Spain). © Histagra Collection / Histagra Research Group.

number 22 infantry regiment barracks of Burgos and the Atocha barracks in A Coruña were places used for this purpose.[28] Nonetheless, military trials took place beyond military spaces in the rearguard and occupied other civilian buildings, depending on the needs and circumstances.

The city of A Coruña was the capital of the province and also of the VIII Organic Division, which was located in the Palace of the General Military Headquarters in the Plaza de la Constitución. In addition, it was where one of the main regiments of the division was based, as well as the highest body of civil judicial power in Galicia, the Palace of Justice, located in the centre of the expansion district of the city. Thus, the city housed the headquarters of the most important civil, judicial and military powers. Like other cities in the rearguard, the main military barracks was where A Coruña's military court of justice carried out its work on a regular basis.

The barracks mentioned here is located in the city centre and its history is closely linked to that of the number 29 infantry regiment of Zamora, as it was the regiment's residence from 1903 to 1943. At the height of 18 July 1936, this garrison was part of the 15th Infantry Brigade under Salcedo Molinuevo, as part of the permanent forces and detachments of the VIII Organic Army Division.[29] It was Colonel Martín Alonso's company that revolted in the city on 20 July and took to the streets to read aloud the proclamations of martial law. The company later participated in numerous acts of war on the front of Alto de León, Oviedo and in the campaigns of Teruel, Aragón, Ebro and Catalonia.[30] The departures of the troops were seen by the new powers as patriotic events, in which military might was showcased through the marching troops accompanied by the music band.[31]

In the rearguard during the civil war, the military barracks was a space with its own entity that fulfilled an essential function for the coup plotters: the organization and execution of violence. In addition to serving as the headquarters of the armed forces of the army, it was a place of confinement, where the civil governor Francisco Pérez Carballo and the commander José Auz Auz were detained, amongst other authorities.[32] It also served as a meeting point for exalting and commemorating the new power through celebrations for the different bodies of the Eighth Military Region, as well as a hub for the organization of rearguard contingents. At the end of August 1936, in the same room where the trials were held – the weapons room or the justice room – a fraternization event was organized by the accidental commander-in-chief for his soldiers and other officers of the detachment.[33]

But it is also true that the coup strategy's capacity for adaptation and rearrangement – which inverted the previous legal legitimacy – allowed the new authorities to strategically choose the places where they would impart their justice. Based on the needs as well as the propagandic and strategic uses of the trials as public events, they changed facilities:

> Perhaps out of a noble and wise desire to give as much publicity as possible to a matter of such magnitude [...] it had the aim, fully achieved, to show how the anguished mission of judging can be accomplished before the greatest possible number of people, within the possibilities of the premises; that was the reason that the Military Court abandoned its offices in the Atocha barracks for just a few hours, and moved to the large building in the Plaza de Galicia occupied by the Palace of Justice. [...] In the morning and in the afternoon, a large audience, with all social classes represented, filled the corridors and the Section Hall as soon as it was ready for viewing. [...] Relatives of the victims, wives, sisters, daughters, occupied benches meant for them [...]. Not to mention their presence, the sadness reflected in their faces, the tears that sometimes flooded the room and spread everywhere, penetrating even the hardest of hearts. Terrible predicaments, frightful tragedies that life holds for us, and which justice, firm, serene, implacable but just, has to face![34]

The event described in the news report is the trial brought against the mayor and prominent political and union leaders of the city at the main headquarters of the civil justice system.[35] The Palace of Justice, therefore, was one of the symbolic places displaying the coup plotters' usurped power that suffered a reconversion of its uses and functions. In addition to serving as the venue for the military trials, it was one of the public spaces conquered by campaigns and national events.[36]

The use of new spaces to provide the military trials with new character was not exclusive to this city. The military officials that dominated other rearguard garrison towns also 'removed' sentencing from the barracks to achieve greater dissemination and social participation. The Cajasol building, headquarters of the Seville Provincial Court; the Palace of Justice in Vigo; the assembly hall of the Tenerife Provincial Court; and the courthouses of the Provincial Councils of Palencia, Lugo and Pontevedra were spaces used for this end.[37] Gradually, a completely refined mechanism was developed to turn the act of justice into a public spectacle. Frequently, military cases against prominent figures in the community – such as mayors, councillors, deputies and civil governors – became events that the coup plotters promoted. The press helped to spread the social response to the call for public attendance and to transform it into a sign of support for the coup authorities. At the trial against the civil governor of Palencia, 'many onlookers attended who not only completely filled the public

Figure 3.2 Sentencing Site. Assembly Hall at the Palace of the Provincial Government (Pontevedra, Spain). © Histagra Collection / Histagra Research Group.

gallery and part of the room in which the proceedings took place, but also formed large groups on the stairs, hallways and around the main door of the Provincial Courtroom'; the same phenomenon occurred in the auditorium of the institute used to judge the civil governor of Ourense.[38]

The choice of one space or another was also related to the venue's capacity, the physical and material state of the property and the geographical location of the place. They were often large, solemn civil buildings located in the town centre and headquarters of important civil institutions. In the city of A Coruña, the headquarters of the provincial government and the civil government were not used because they were located in a building that suffered significant damage during the armed confrontation of 20 July 1936.[39] In other cities, where the headquarters of civil authority remained intact and provided the ideal conditions for publicizing coup justice, they were the places of choice, as in the case of Lugo or Pontevedra.

The provincial manor and the San Marcos courtroom – the headquarters of the provincial governments of Lugo and Pontevedra, respectively – were built in the nineteenth century, and their existence has always been closely linked to that of the provincial government itself.[40] As of 24 July 1936, in Lugo and Pontevedra, the Managing Committee of the Provincial Council was suspended and the president delegate took over. The assault on the physical headquarters of power began, along with the usurpation of administrative positions to 'control it, take care of administrative matters and especially attend to essential collections and payments, adopting the necessary solutions for the proper operation of the functions of charity, administration and social assistance'.[41]

The coup plotters' control was latent in all means of power, since it extended from the military hubs to civilians through the use of force and violence. The physical headquarters of the civil government were not only occupied to issue sentences, but were also established as places to commemorate the new authorities, through acts such as raising the two-colour flag on the balcony or holding campaign events.[42] They were also key spaces for displaying the power of the Falange forces and celebrating the coup army's victories on different fronts.[43] These spaces simultaneously hosted official receptions of prominent military authorities or national events such as the Fiesta del Caudillo.[44] Such propaganda activities were combined with other administrative and bureaucratic functions throughout the dictatorship, mainly in the areas of charity, health, education and communication.[45] The political activities that this institution had developed in the Republican period – notably, that related to the approval of the Statute of Autonomy of Galicia – were suppressed in favour of efforts to assist the consolidation of the coup powers.[46]

The rooms where the trials were held – in the cases that I have been able to analyse – continue to maintain a very similar appearance today. Broadly speaking, they are wide spaces with high ceilings that present careful use of lighting, eye-catching decorations and noble materials. The coup authorities chose rooms that were conceived and designed as places to be seen and enjoyed, inspiring a feeling of luxury and grandeur. Undoubtedly, the characteristics of the space reflected the coup plotters' elaborate and intentional use of legal processes to carry out their violent project. They were considered ideal places for public celebrations such as the trials because they flaunted the power that resided in them and could accommodate many attendees to support this propagandic project. Despite the important role such civic spaces played in our history, currently only a few exceptions have a symbolic reminder that indicates how the plotters used these spaces. For example, in the Pontevedra provincial government building, since 2016, the plenary hall – where the military trials took place during the war – is used annually to host a public event in favour of the recovery of our memory. This recent tradition began with an act of redress and reparation on the 80th anniversary of the shooting of a member of the Managing Committee and two of the institution's presidents in 1936. Portraits from the Republican period were added to the collection of portraits of provincial government presidents, and a plaque was placed in the garden with the inscription: 'In memory of the people who were imprisoned, tortured and tried in these two buildings for defending democratic legitimacy against the fascist uprising of 1936.'

Military trials sites and the legal spectacle

Violence was intrinsic to the 1936 coup d'état and took on different forms and intensities according to the coup plotters' needs to achieve power. The conquest of territory and the persecution of society suffered the effects of the violent dynamics of the coup; consequently, the administrative and legal order imposed on society acquired a fundamentally military tone. The state of war proclamations brought dominated spaces and justice administration together under the garrison towns. As a result, military courts formed in the main provincial garrison towns prosecuted, convicted and executed a third of the victims of the coup rearguard. The coup plotters decided to make society actively participate in this process through different mechanisms, such as issuing mass calls to the civilian population to testify or holding trials in public places and the headquarters of key institutions of civil authority. Military trials were moved from the barracks to provincial government headquarters, civil government buildings and territorial courts. This change in setting mainly applied to trials against significant individuals in the Republican public sphere such as politicians, mayors, governors, councillors and deputies, amongst others. The main aim was to transfer the perversity of the *inventio* to public sites and to turn the military trials into mass social events. For this purpose, the plotters chose spacious rooms with a large capacity, ornate or even luxurious decoration, good lighting and a careful arrangement of space that would serve as a reminder of the magnitude of the power of the institution at hand – in this case, the military coup leaders. In short, the coup plotters removed the civil and judicial authorities of the Second Republic from their natural settings and then occupied these spaces to carry out the legal spectacle that would condemn their leaders and part of society.

The current treatment of our past through public memory policies rarely recognizes the use that the coup plotters and Francoist authorities made of public places and civil government facilities to persecute and kill part of society during the war and the dictatorship. Even less recognition is given to the case of spaces that are still used by the military today, such as certain barracks and general military buildings. Sometimes, the guidelines established in the

Historical Memory Law of 2007 result in small changes, such as the modification of street names or the removal of certain anti-democratic symbols from the façades of buildings. However, most of these changes are driven by local groups and associations of citizens with little collaboration or support from political authorities. Many modifications to public spaces have involved a rearrangement of Francoist symbols to fit the democratic reality, and those problematic references to the uncomfortable past have been eliminated. These interventions thus open the door to a debate on the real resignification of symbols and places; in spite of these small changes, the existence of a shared effort to create a conscious democratic memory remains in doubt.

Notes

1   'Carpetas 26 y 27, caja 2550, fondo Guerra Civil', Archivo General Militar de Ávila (AGMA).
2   Gabriel Cardona, *El poder militar en el franquismo* (Barcelona: Flor del Viento, 2008), 29–32.
3   Ramón Salas Larrazabal, *Historia del Ejército Popular de la República*, vol. 1, *De los comienzos de la guerra al fracaso del ataque sobre Madrid (noviembre de 1936)* (Madrid: La esfera de los libros, 2006), 821.
4   Ramón Salas Larrazabal, 'Aspectos militares de la guerra civil española', *Anales de Historia Contemporánea* 7 (1989): 93–110.
5   Lourenzo Fernández Prieto and Antonio Míguez Macho, 'Os verdugos no golpe de Estado de 1936. Quen matou a Antonio Azarola?', in *Golpistas e verdugos de 1936. Historia dun pasado incómodo*, ed. Lourenzo Fernández Prieto and Antonio Míguez Macho (Vigo: Editorial Galaxia, 2018), 13–87.
6   On the one hand, the regulations for the Army and Navy start from the CMJ published by Royal Decree on 27 September 1890, the Penitentiary Code of 24 August 1888 and the Laws of Organization and Powers of the Courts of the Navy and Military Marine Prosecution of 10 November 1894 – all three were in force until they were grouped under the law of 17 July 1945. For more information, see Fernando de Querol Durán, *Principios de Derecho Militar Español* (Madrid: Editorial Naval, 1946).
7   Raúl C. Cancio Fernández, *Guerra civil y tribunales: de los jurados populares a la justicia franquista (1936–1939)* (Cáceres: Universidad de Extremadura, 2007), 125–29.
8   *La Gaceta de Tenerife*, Santa Cruz de Tenerife, 19 July 1936: 1.
9   Ibid.
10 *Boletín Oficial de la Provincia de A Coruña*, A Coruña, 28 July 1936, no. 170.

11 'Bando', *Boletín Oficial de La Junta de Defensa Nacional de España* (BOJDNE), Burgos, 30 July 1936, no. 3.
12 'Decreto núm. 42 de creación de un Alto Tribunal de Justicia Militar de 24 de octubre de 1936', *Boletín Oficial del Estado*, 1 November 1936: 18. 'Ley de 5 de septiembre de 1939 de creación del Consejo Supremo de Justicia Militar', *Diario Oficial del Ministerio de Marina*, 10 November 1939 (annex 1).
13 'Código de Justicia Militar', *Gaceta de Madrid*, 4 October 1890: 277.
14 'Bando', BOJDNE, 30 July 1936: 3.
15 Ramón Serrano Suñer, *Entre el silencio y la propaganda, la Historia como fue. Memorias* (Barcelona: Planeta, 1977), 245.
16 Francisco Espinosa Maestre and Fernando Romero Romero, 'Justicia Militar y represión fascista en Cádiz', *Historia* 16, no. 297 (2001): 74–91. Lourenzo Fernández Prieto and Antonio Míguez Macho, 'Nomes e Voces: balance. Preguntas e interpretaciones. Las huellas del golpe de Estado en Galicia', in *Otras miradas sobre golpe, guerra y ditadura*, ed. Aurora Artiaga Rego and Lourenzo Fernández Prieto (Madrid: Catarata, 2014), 80–110.
17 'Causa 601/36', 1, AIMNOR.
18 'Causa 601/36', 3, 8, 18, 22, 54, 86, 92, 94, 95, 135 and 154, AIMNOR.
19 'Causa 601/36', 64, 151–4, AIMNOR.
20 'Causa 601/36', 155–74, AIMNOR.
21 In the case of Galicia, 11,558 people were indicted and 30.6 per cent were prosecuted under authority of the Navy and jurisdiction of the Ferrol maritime department. 'Nomes e Voces' database, nomesevoces.net.
22 Some of the analysed cases on this topic are 2529/38 of the maritime district of Bueu, held on the fishing steamboat 'Nuevo Celta' of the port of Vigo the night of 1 October 1938; or the case 2103/38 of the Marine command of A Coruña, held against the crew of the fishing boat 'Rafael de Palacio' on 26 September 1938; maritime department of Ferrol, Archivo Naval de Ferrol (ANFER).
23 'Causa 29/36', ANFER.
24 'Causa 50/37', 79 and 174, ANFER.
25 'Causa 65/36', 206; 'Causa 199/36', 39; 'Causa 1204/38', 46; and 'Causa 1657/38', 80, ANFER.
26 Juan Antonio Rodríguez Villasante Prieto, *El arsenal de Ferrol. Guía para una visita* (Ferrol: Armada-Concello de Ferrol-Fundación Caixa Galicia, 2000), 10. 'Causa 2154/38', 57, ANFER.
27 Antonio Martínez Ovejero, 'La represión franquista en la Región de Murcia (1936–1948)', *I Congreso víctimas franquismo, Madrid, 20–22 de abril de 2012*, 2, 4.
28 Examples that account for the case of Seville: *Guión*, 2 September 1936: 2; the case of Las Palmas: *La Prensa*, 4 August 1936: 2; the case of Salamanca: *El Adelanto*, 6 September 1936: 1; the case of Burgos: *El Diario de Burgos*, 30 July 1936: 2; and the case of A Coruña: *La Voz de Galicia*, 27 August 1936: 1.

29 José Manuel Martínez Bande, *Los años críticos. República, conspiración, revolución y alzamiento* (Madrid: Encuentro, 2007).
30 José Ricardo Pardo Gato, *Del cuartel del Príncipe al acuartelamiento de Atocha. Vida militar coruñesa* (A Coruña: Publicaciones Arenas, 2015).
31 *La Voz de Galicia*, A Coruña, 18 July 1936: 3.
32 Emilio Grandío Seoane (ed.), *Anos de odio. Golpe, represión e Guerra Civil na provincia da Coruña (1936–1939)* (A Coruña: Deputación Provincial, 2007).
33 *El Pueblo Gallego*, Vigo, 29 September 1936: 9.
34 *La Voz de Galicia*, A Coruña, 27 August 1936: 1.
35 Alfredo Suárez Ferrín, mayor of the city during the Republic, along with the secretary of the city council Joaquín Martín Martínez, the secretary of the civil government Leovigildo Taboada, the deputy Manuel Guzmán García, the socialist leaders Ramón Maseda and Francisco Mazariegos, and four other individuals accused of military rebellion. Most of them were sentenced to death and executed: 'Causa 207/36', A Coruña, AIMNOR.
36 *Vida Gallega*, 15 September 1936.
37 Examples that give an account of the case of Seville: Concha Morón Hernández, 'Audiencia Provincial', in *Lugares de la memoria. Golpe militar, represión y resistencia en Sevilla. Itinerarios*, ed. Rafael Gómez Fernández (Sevilla: Aconcagua, 2014), 115–20; the case of Vigo: *El Progreso*, 23 August 1936: 4; the case of Tenerife: *La Gaceta de Tenerife*, 29 September 1936: 5; the case of Palencia: *El Diario Palentino*, 11 September 1936: 2; the case of Lugo: 'causa 175/36', 30; 'causa 510/37', 70; and 'causa 314/36', 171; Lugo, AIMNOR or the case of Pontevedra: 'causa 728/37', 32 and 34; 'causa 1308/36', 73; and 'causa 1363/36', 130 and 154; Pontevedra, AIMNOR.
38 *El Diario Palentino*, Palencia, 11 September 1936: 2. *La prensa*, 26 September 1936: 2.
39 F 8-5-273, *Arquivo da Deputación de A Coruña* (ADAC). *La Voz de Galicia*, A Coruña, 24 July 1936: 1; 25 July 1936: 1 and 6.
40 Plácido Ballesteros San José and José Ramón Rodríguez Clavel, *Los archivos de las diputaciones. Qué son y cómo se tratan* (Asturias: Trea, 2010).
41 *Arquivo da Deputación de Pontevedra* (ADPO), 'Libro de actas da comisión xestora', 1931–1938, 36038 050-1, 24 July 1936.
42 *El Pueblo Gallego*, 30 August 1936: 7 and 11; 1 September 1936: 14.
43 *El Pueblo Gallego*, 28 September 1936: 2.
44 *El Diario de Pontevedra*, 28 October 1936: 2. *Ciudad*, October 1945: 3.
45 *Ciudad*, 29 October 1945: 3. *El Diario de Pontevedra*, 20 August 1936: 1.
46 Xosé Fariña Jamardo and Miguel Pereira Figueroa, *A Deputación de Pontevedra. 1836–1986* (Pontevedra: Deputación Provincial, 1986).

4

Memory and forgetting of the 'paseos': Places and accounts

Xabier Buxeiro Alonso

In the context of the cycle of mass violence triggered by the 1936 coup d'état in Spain, the term 'paseo' (or 'stroll') refers to the execution of people who had not been formally sentenced to death. It also refers to the killing of those individuals who, despite being sentenced to capital punishment, were not executed via the mechanisms that the coup authorities claimed were legal.

To establish this difference between the normative and the non-normative is not to recognize the existence of illegal violence as opposed to violence under the penal code. Starting from that dichotomy would require accepting the validity of sentences issued by coup-established courts against individuals for treason and rebellion, when what those individuals had done was, precisely, defend the law. In other words, it would mean validating the propaganda aimed at justifying the uprising of 18 July 1936 on the basis of Republican law.[1]

Arguments of this nature, despite having been consistently discredited and refuted by historiography, continue to appear in public debate. In this way, they continue to condition, in our opinion, explanations of the violence stemming from the 1936 military uprising, thus influencing public policies of memory in Spain.

The objective of this chapter is to analyse how current interpretations influence the way that Spanish society remembers the paseos, both at the public and private level. Thus, we will study the connection between public policies of memory and the memories of victims' families, as well as reflect on the reciprocal influences between history and memory in regard to this form of violence.

Paseos in history: Definition and typology

Paseo is among the terms most widely used within public debates on historical memory in Spain. The identification of victims of this type has been one of the fundamental concerns of historical memory initiatives since the beginning of the twenty-first century.

Despite this, the enormous interest that this form of violence has generated (and continues to generate) has not translated into privileged knowledge on the subject. In fact, the opposite is true; in our opinion, the paseos continue to be one of the most overlooked aspects in studies of so-called Francoist repression. This is logical. It cannot be ignored that this type of killing was designed, more than any other, to hide the responsibilities of its perpetrators, as this chapter will attempt to argue.

In popular culture, there are constant reminders that the 'paseados', or victims of paseos, were killed in roadside ditches, open fields or forests. In short, these were scattered places that were much more difficult to identify than those where people condemned by military trials were systematically and officially executed.[2] Moreover, paseos were usually carried out at night (or in the early morning), and the victims were killed, on many occasions, in places that were quite far from where they lived.

All of this helps to explain why many studies on these killings continue to show recurring problems, ignoring or minimizing the extent of the coup authorities' control over this practice.[3] According to traditional theory, paseos were a form of violence that took place in the initial moments after the coup, and were later replaced by the regulated violence of executions. However, regional studies, such as those carried out in Galicia, have revealed the limitations of the previous argument by demonstrating that paseos and executions occurred simultaneously over time.[4]

Nonetheless, the fact that the term paseo is still in common use today shows the persistence of the account created by the executioners themselves. Thus, it is necessary to be clear that the word paseo is a term that has its origin in the perpetrators, namely, a euphemism used to avoid talking about deaths or, directly, 'killings'.

This idea can be exemplified through the words of Pilar Carballo, daughter of Florencio Carballo, killed on 12 September 1936. According to her testimony, the jailer of the prison where her father was being held (and from which he was taken on the eve of his murder) had told her sister that she did not need to leave her father food (as she usually did) since he 'was out for a *paseo*'.[5]

Among the coup executioners there is a duality. On the one hand, it is possible to distinguish perpetrators who were proud of their actions, making public statements or comments that revealed themselves as responsible for some violent act (of a more or less serious nature). And, on the other hand, there are executioners who, despite being evidently involved in the spread of violence, tried (and in many cases managed) to hide their participation in the events, which does not mean that their crimes cannot be proven through paperwork.

Antonio Moreda Rodríguez, the first coup mayor of a small Galician town called Ribadeo, was, as we have verified, among those who were most active in incriminating their neighbours.[6] However, his name is not even mentioned in the various interviews that have been conducted with relatives of victims from the same town.

Conversely, there is the more openly acknowledged case of the first person to hold the position of Military Commander of Ribadeo: Juan Aranguren Ponte. To illustrate his behaviour, we have the account of Elisa Fariñas, daughter of the paseo victim Santiago Fariñas Reinante. In her testimony, Elisa Fariñas considers Aranguren to be the person most responsible for the killings carried out in Ribadeo. In addition, she says that when some of her mother's friends went to intervene on behalf of her father, Aranguren, far from trying to hide his decision-making capacity and (therefore) his responsibility, said that they should not ask for the detainee's clemency unless they wanted to suffer the same fate.[7]

Cases like this have been etched into the local memory of many towns. However, they represent a clear minority. This is not especially surprising nor is it a reality that should be understood, exclusively, in moral terms. The explanation of why most executioners tended to hide their condition as such is more complex and has to do with the historical reality at the time of the coup and the civil war, as well as with the political climate (both national and international) surrounding the Franco regime throughout its existence. After the Second World War, the disappearance of the regime's natural allies as well as the trial of the main Nazi leaders in Nuremberg marked a before and after for the coup perpetrators, convincing them of the convenience of keeping silent about their crimes.[8] Even so, the executioners, or at least some of them, understood from the first moment the dangers that their actions entailed.

The uprising, despite what its propaganda machinery repeated time and again, was not triggered in response to the murder of Calvo Sotelo. Nor was it the consequence of a situation of pre-revolutionary violence in a country that prevented democratic coexistence.[9] The reality is that a few soldiers, who on many occasions rebelled against their commands (making them traitors), carried out an illegitimate and illegal military insurrection: a very risky bet that turned out well for them, but which could have had the opposite result, with tragic consequences for those involved.

All this helps us to understand why, from the first moment of the coup, there was always a certain resistance to collaboration, as detailed in some of the reports written by direct witnesses to the events described here. On this note, it is worth citing the work of Antonio Ruíz Vilaplana, who recounted, from his exile in Paris in 1937, his experience as secretary of the Burgos investigative court following the military uprising:

> There were real battles not to be part of these Courts, which the professionals called 'the White Chekas'; some of us could avoid them under the excuse of excessive court work, but almost everyone had to accept, since those who did not do so enthusiastically were regarded as factious, or at least 'lukewarm' and apart from the profession. On the other hand, it was easy to fill these positions with young lawyers.[10]

This reality highlights the complexity of studying social attitudes after the coup, as well as the need to overcome a simplistic differentiation between victims and perpetrators. Identifying the executioners is as necessary as it is problematic, as this role required the ability to mutate and adapt to different contexts. This is why, putting moral discussions aside, it is almost impossible to classify a person as a perpetrator in absolute terms. However, it is indeed possible to do so within a specific context, such as the paseos.

To describe more simply and precisely what these paseos were, perhaps it is preferable to start by describing what they were not. The difference between the victims of paseos and the victims of 'executions' is quite clear and does not require an extensive explanation. Essentially, the term 'execution' refers to the killing of people who were arrested, prosecuted, interrogated, tried and convicted. They were victims against whom testimonies were collected to decide (at least theoretically) their fate and who – despite the absence of real guarantees (present in democratic judicial systems) – had access to a lawyer, as well as to the hypothetical possibility of defending themselves by presenting testimonies in their favour. Moreover, executed individuals were killed according to fixed procedures and in specific places, with their deaths officially recorded and documented, and their bodies buried according to the regulations in force.[11]

These characteristics distinguish 'executions' from other categories that can be used to classify the victims of coup violence. In addition, they enable us to make an initial estimate (without taking more detailed studies into account) of the minimum number of individuals involved in the violence as perpetrators, as well as to identify the places where victims were executed.

Another category of victims of the 1936 coup d'état is the 'disappeared': people whose final whereabouts are unknown. Some were listed as arrested and even as prosecuted, but there is no record of their final destination.[12] The individuals included in this group were, with almost total certainty, killed. Nevertheless, the lack of documentary evidence requires us to be cautious. I believe, however, that as research continues, we will be able to classify a large part of these victims within the category of 'paseados'.

Finally, we can identify a heterogeneous group of victims whose deaths were barely or not at all premeditated. Here we can distinguish two profiles: on the one hand, there are people who decided to commit suicide to avoid suffering other forms of violence or being killed. One example of this can be found in the Galician city of Vigo. On 23 April 1937, nine people trying to flee the coup-controlled area by boat (in the trawler EVA) decided to commit suicide together to avoid falling into the hands of Falangists who had assaulted the boat.[13] On the other hand, there are those who were killed in the context of armed confrontations or chases. In this last group, we find individuals who suffered a fate very similar to that of many 'paseados'.

Within what is commonly understood by the term 'paseados', we find two significantly different profiles. On the one hand, there are individuals who were 'removed' from a (more or less improvised) prison and later killed without a prior conviction that could justify their fate. On the other hand, a number of deaths that can be characterized as unplanned have also been included in the paseo category. Establishing this difference is quite complicated and, obviously, is not intended to excuse the action of the executioners. On the contrary, since in dissecting the paseo category, the aim is to determine (as clearly as possible) the circumstances in which different deaths took place, helping to identify those responsible.

To explain this difference, it is useful to start from two examples, two cases of paseos whose reconstruction exemplifies the differences between the two types of killing that have been alluded to previously. The first is the aforementioned case of a paseado from Ribadeo: Santiago Fariñas Reinante. The second is that of the paseado Antonio Díaz y Díaz Villamil, resident of the nearby town A Pontenova.

The reconstruction of the Santiago Fariñas case perfectly illustrates what a 'saca' (removal) is. The details of his killing instantly conjure up the iconic image of a paseo. Thus, the fate of Santiago Fariñas (with the exception that his family was able to recover his body) was very similar (based on existing data) to that suffered by the Granadan poet Federico García Lorca, one of the most well-known and honoured victims of the coup and the Spanish Civil War.

The evidence indicates that Santiago Fariñas Reinante was killed on 4 September 1936. The day before, he had been 'removed' from the Ribadeo municipal prison, where he had been held since 3 August.[14] According to the records of the judicial proceedings, on 3 September Santiago Fariñas Reinante was transferred (by order of the Military Commander Juan Aranguren Ponte) to the municipal prison of Navia, a town about thirty kilometres away in the neighbouring province of Asturias. During the trip, according to the statement by the Carabineros Sergeant Ignacio García de Frutos, the detainee managed to escape (after faking an anxiety attack) from the forces guarding him.[15] This account is evidently false and intended to exonerate the killers of Santiago Fariñas, being a resource commonly used by coup executioners to justify this type of killing. We know that the victim was taken in the opposite direction to that of the Navia municipal warehouse and killed in the municipality of O Vicedo, seventy-five kilometres from Ribadeo.[16]

The second type of paseo is exemplified in the case of Antonio Díaz y Díaz Villamil. Perhaps the most significant difference between his case and that of Santiago Fariñas is the place of death. While Santiago Fariñas was killed in an indeterminate place in O Vicedo (his body was thrown into the sea), Antonio Díaz y Díaz Villamil died in the hospital in Lugo, the provincial capital. This fact allows for the hypothesis that his killers did not want to kill him, at least not at that time, as they tried to argue during the judicial proceedings in which the details of his death are described.[17]

Now that both types of paseos have been described, it is time to answer the question posed earlier: what was the fate of most paseo victims? In other words, were they murdered after being 'removed' from prison? Or, conversely, were they killed during a capture?

Our reasoning revolves around two axes. The first is memory. It makes sense to postulate that sacas were more frequent than unplanned killings because they appear more often in the accounts of these events given by the victims' families. The second is the unexpected nature of the coup and the violence, which meant that most individuals did not resist arrest, even going so far as to voluntarily present themselves when requested by the authorities.[18]

The veracity of this last idea can be verified, quantitatively, by analysing the relationship between the number of arrests and the number of killings during capture. To illustrate this argument, we can once again examine the case of

Ribadeo. In that town, the only death of an individual whom the authorities were trying to capture was Juan Antonio Ardao Seijido, who died in the local hospital on 9 August 1936.[19] However, in July and August alone of that same year, 128 people (at least) were arrested, their names listed in the record book of the town's prison.[20]

With these two categories, I think that it is possible to explain the deaths of the vast majority of individuals killed as a result of the coup in Spain as a whole. Large massacres, such as the Badajoz massacre in the town's bull ring, were exceptional from a quantitative point of view, but not from a qualitative perspective, and should be studied within the logic of the so-called sacas. The coup plotters in Badajoz decided to carry out the mass killing of prisoners who were in their custody, something they had already been doing in many of the towns (in Andalusia and Extremadura) they had occupied in their advance towards northern Spain.[21] These practices differ from those in the previously mentioned case of Galicia in the total number of killings committed. However, in essence, they are the same.

Paseos in memory: Absences and tributes

The coup d'état of 18 July 1936 in Spain opened the gates to rivers of blood, but also of ink. From the first moment, the military rebels understood the need to justify their actions in the face of public, national and international opinion. To this end, they tried to blame their enemies for all kinds of atrocities, publishing manipulated (or directly fabricated) reports blaming the Madrid government for horrendous crimes.[22] On the other hand, they made an effort to justify their own actions, mainly through two mechanisms. The first consisted of holding some of the victims responsible for their own fate. The second was based on direct denial of some of the killings.

Within this double strategy, the paseados were a central element, as can be seen in the previously mentioned two cases. Antonio Díaz y Díaz Villamil was killed (theoretically) for not surrendering to the 'authorities' who were trying to arrest him. Meanwhile, the case of Santiago Fariñas reveals an even more perverse reality: the denial of killing. Crucially, the official account (which was established in the case brought against him) states that the accused had successfully fled from the forces guarding him.

This account had a clear aim: to turn the victim into a disappeared person. Thus, as his daughter described in the aforementioned interview, the appearance and registration of the body of Santiago Fariñas was unforeseen by the coup authorities. His body was rescued from the sea by some fishermen and officially registered by the municipal judge of Viveiro, who was able (and wanted) to recognize him, as he had previously known the murdered man.

However, beyond what might happen in practice, the concealment of violence was a constant part of coup strategy. The official discourse of the dictatorship could be challenged thanks to the work of foreign authors, who were able to publish works on the Spanish Civil War on account of living in democratic countries.[23] In the interior of Spain, the memory of the violence was able to survive in secret thanks to the families of the victims. These families had the courage and will to rescue and honour the memory of their relatives through symbolic acts, such as leaving flowers on roads, in ditches and at cemeteries: the places where their relatives had been killed and/or buried.[24] With these acts, they laid the foundations for the creation of numerous associations for the recovery of historical memory, which would come to light with the consolidation of democracy and continue to exist today.

With the arrival of the twenty-first century, interest in learning about 'Francoist repression' has increased greatly. In fact, the change has been qualitative, not just quantitative. In 2000, the first exhumation using scientific methodology of a mass grave from the Spanish Civil War was carried out.[25] This action led to the establishment of the Association for the Recovery of Historical Memory (ARMH), whose main objective has been to exhume the remains of the victims of coup violence dumped outside burial grounds as well as in mass graves within cemeteries.[26]

However, the memory movement has not been limited to unearthing the dead. An exhumation is not an end in itself. It is linked to acts of reparation and public recognition of the victims.[27] These actions have given way to practical translations beyond changes at the educational level or certain institutional declarations. In this way, they have enabled the resignification of numerous spaces in many towns and cities throughout the Spanish territory.

Within the process of recovering memory, physical elements enable the past to be permanently attached to the territory, contributing (in this case) to democratic learning.[28] This idea leads us to the concept, popularized by the French historian Pierre Nora, of *lieux de mémoire*, sites created to preserve the memory of disappearing human communities (such as the victims of coup violence), where collective memory and history interact to create a discourse considered necessary to transmit to future generations.[29]

In the construction of these memorial spaces (as well as in most tributes to the victims of coup violence), the paseados have had, in our opinion, a prominent position. This statement should not be surprising. Paseos were the mechanism used to kill two-thirds of all victims of coup violence in the whole of Spain.[30] In addition, the extreme violence of this type of crime, as well as the trauma caused by practices such as the concealment of bodies, has left an indelible mark on the relatives of the victims and on Spanish society as a whole. However, the focused interest taken by historical memory groups in these killings has not translated into privileged knowledge about this form of violence. This has had evident repercussions on public policies concerning the past, turning certain places of memory into places of forgetting or places of denial.[31]

At this point, it is worth noting that despite the large amount of published work and the efforts of associations for the recovery of historical memory, there are still no systematic investigations that study places of violence and their hypothetical transformation into places of memory.[32] Consequently, we lack an updated census listing and classifying these spaces, which forces us to point out (and comment on) only some of these *lieux*. To this end, I will combine the macro perspective, when speaking of large regional areas or the whole of Spain, with the micro perspective, focused on specific locations. In doing so, I aim to raise questions of a general scope without forgetting the advantages of focusing on a specific space of analysis that allows for more systematic assessments.

If we examine the whole of Spain, we can divide the sites of memory related to paseos into two large groups, depending on their spatial relationship with the violence. The first group is made up of spaces where a violent event that took place there is remembered. Two examples of this are the Campo da Rata in the city of A Coruña and the San Esteban de las Cruces cemetery in Oviedo.[33] The second group of sites of memory consists of places where a tribute to a victim is made in a location that had nothing to do with their victimization. This is the case of the Ánxel Casal library (dedicated to the paseado mayor of the city of Santiago de Compostela) or that of the statue, placed on Granada's Constitution boulevard, in memory of the poet Federico García Lorca.

In this chapter, the *lieux* that we are interested in analysing are, fundamentally, those belonging to the first group. This is because our objective is to study how certain places of violence have not become places of memory: a circumstance that, as I will explain, has a lot to do with the approach to the past adopted in Spain in recent decades.

Based on this idea, I have approached the *lieux* of the autonomous communities of Galicia, Asturias, Cantabria, the Basque Country, Catalonia and Andalusia through the existing literature. I have reached the conclusion that the sites of memory that share a spatial relationship with the paseos correspond to execution and burial points or, in other words, the spaces in which victims were killed and/or buried.[34]

This kind of intervention has been carried out in locations of all kinds, both in the north and south of Spain. In the northern part of the country, we can highlight the memorial monuments built in the Ciriego cemetery, about five kilometres from the centre of the city of Santander, as well as those located in the cities of A Coruña and Oviedo (mentioned above). Within this same geographical area, there are also numerous commemorative plaques in many forests and mountainous areas of the Cantabrian Mountains. The distribution of sites of memory throughout the territory is a reality that is also present in the south of the country. In Andalusia there are more than 600 mass graves in 359 towns, which are the preferred locations among memory groups for constructing *lieux*.

Figure 4.1 'Peace and Justice'. Memorial plaque to the victims killed by the coup plotters in 1936, Mondoñedo (Galicia, Spain). © Histagra Collection / Histagra Research Group.

We have found this general reality while carrying out a more systematic study focused on a total of nine municipalities located in the north of the Province of Lugo, within the former legal districts of Ribadeo, Mondoñedo and Viveiro, in which paseos against certain residents have been recorded.[35] In this analysis, I have classified each of these spaces into four groups based on how the victims were treated:

1. municipalities with no sites of memory: A Pastoriza, A Pontenova, Cospeito, Muras y Viveiro;
2. municipalities with sites of memory in which no specific mention is made of paseo victims: Ribadeo;
3. municipalities with sites of memory dedicated to paseo victims in locations unrelated to the violent act: Mondoñedo; and
4. municipalities with sites of memory dedicated to paseo victims in locations related to the violent act: O Vicedo, Mondoñedo.

Ribadeo's *lieu de mémoire* consists of a plaque in honour of the town's Republican democrats. In O Vicedo there are two commemorative plaques at the O Barqueiro bridge, a place that marks the border between the provinces of Lugo and A Coruña, and where numerous killings were perpetrated. Finally, in Mondoñedo, we have three sites of memory related to paseos. The first is located in the town's old cemetery; it honours six residents of Ribadeo and one of Viveiro who were killed in other parts of the Mondoñedo municipality. The second, a monolith in the vicinity of the same cemetery, is dedicated to Mondoñedo residents Siervo González, Graciano Paz and Manuel Rodríguez, who were killed without sentencing in that same space. The third consists of a plaque in memory of José Antonio Díaz Álvarez, a paseo victim from Ribadeo, and is located at the site of his killing.

The selection of these types of memory sites excludes one of the fundamental spaces of violence that must be considered when analysing paseos: places of confinement. Such spaces have become places of amnesia or, at best, places of partial forgetting. In other words, they are spaces where only certain types of violence are remembered. What is mainly transmitted is the memory of the overcrowded and unsanitary conditions that led to the death of many inmates, as well as the executions of those sentenced to death, which were carried out in (some of) these spaces. This can be seen (to take an example from the same region as the cases presented above) in the memorial exhibition currently on display in the provincial prison of Lugo at the time of this chapter's writing.

However, many other (or most) confinement spaces have been completely excluded from memory policies. This is the case of the municipal warehouses of Ribadeo and Mondoñedo. In Mondoñedo, according to records (in oral memory), the three residents of the town who were killed in paseos on 11 January 1938 were previously 'removed' from prison.[36] This idea has also come to light in acts for the recovery of historical memory held in the town, in which relatives of the killed Mondoñedo residents have participated.[37]

In Ribadeo, as I have pointed out, there are no specific references in public places to the residents of the town who were victims of paseos. The only sites of memory where their names are given are located in the municipality of Mondoñedo, the place where they were killed. In this way, a spot that is perfectly easy to locate (in the town centre) has been excluded from the policies of memory: the municipal prison, a space from which ten of the eleven paseo residents of Ribadeo were 'removed' to be killed, as shown in Map 4.1.

The ten people referred to in Map 4.1 were killed in four different municipalities in the north of the province of Lugo: O Vicedo, Ribadeo, Mondoñedo and A Pontenova. Another victim, César Margolles de la Vega, was taken for a paseo in the neighbouring province of Asturias. In addition, within the aforementioned municipalities (in which more than one resident of Ribadeo was killed) there are several different sites of death, some of them unknown. This is the case of O Vicedo, where Marcelino Álvarez López and Santiago Fariñas Reinante were killed. Regarding the municipality of Mondoñedo, there are three sites of death: the parish of Argomoso (where the body of José Antonio Díaz Álvarez was found), the parish of San Vicente (where Jesús Longarela Maciñeira was killed) and El Prado de Los Remedios (site of the paseos of Florencio Carballo Novigil, Bruno Martínez Fernández, Antonio María Martínez López and Enrique Navarret García).

This omission of the Ribadeo municipal prison from public policies of memory cannot be considered accidental; it follows a trend present in both the municipalities mentioned above and other parts of Spain, which I have examined (although less systematically) through the literature. Nor can the transformation of Ribadeo's municipal warehouse into a place of forgetting be explained as the result of the forgetfulness of the victims' relatives. The sacas carried out there are acts that are strongly remembered in interviews given by family members of the paseo victims of Ribadeo.

Finally, it is important to note that this memory of the sacas is not exclusive to one or two specific municipalities. References to this type of act have appeared since the emergence in 2000 of the movement for the recovery of historical memory, as Emilio Silva, one of its promoters, has written.[38]

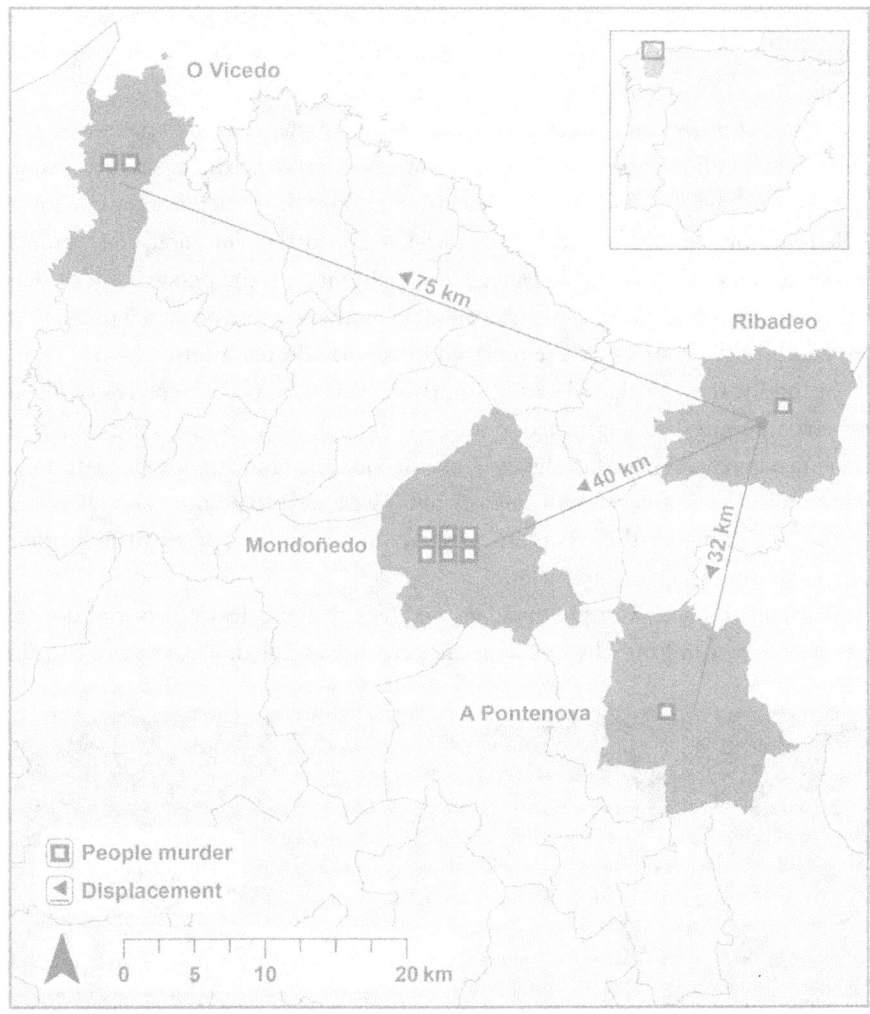

Map 4.1 Residents of Ribadeo killed without sentencing in Galicia.
Source: compiled based on data from nomesevoces.net.

Paseos and memory policies

For all these reasons, I believe that the omission of the sites of sacas from public policies of memory is a reality whose explanation must take into account the relationship between memory and history, and depends fundamentally on three ideas.

In the first place, it is a consequence of the lack of systematic studies on this form of violence, a reality mentioned above. In this way, as I have argued, knowledge of paseos continues to be quite limited, which has resulted in the persistence of certain clichés that originated at the moment of the coup and sought to hide the responsibility of the individuals involved.

Thus, I consider that public policies on memory sites related to paseos do not contribute at all to understanding the modus operandi of the agents who were in charge of carrying them out. The decision to limit the remembrance of people killed without sentencing to spaces unrelated to the violent act, or to points where they were killed and/or buried, is consistent with the persisting idea that paseos were a (more or less) uncontrolled phenomenon that occurred in the first moments of the coup and were replaced by regulated executions.

Secondly, the fact that places of imprisonment have become places of (total or partial) amnesia is connected to the fact that investigations into the coup and its violence have focused exclusively on the victims, ignoring the perpetrators. This reality becomes even more significant if we take into account an idea noted at the beginning of this chapter: most of the victimizers tried to hide their participation in said crimes.

Tributes to paseo victims made at the place of their death or burial do not need to go beyond the obvious fact: the person was killed. Thus, it can be said

Figure 4.2 Memorial to the neighbours 'killed by Francoism' in 1938. Mondoñedo (Galicia, Spain), 2019. © Histagra Collection / Histagra Research Group.

that memory policies on these violent acts have, curiously, focused on locations designed to hide the identity of the executioners. As I have pointed out, paseos used to take place at night, in scattered places, having as sole witnesses the victims (who could not, apart from very few exceptions, relate what happened) and the perpetrators (who have resisted giving their testimony).

However, it is indeed possible to know the names and surnames of the people who were guarding the victims in the different prisons from which they were 'removed'. In this way, by recovering the memory of the sacas, we can study the paseos in a different light, understanding them as an organized violent practice in which the coup authorities were involved, just as they were in the executions of individuals sentenced to death.

Thirdly, the policy of choosing sites of memory related to paseos has its origin in tradition, that is, in continuity with the private tributes carried out by the relatives of those killed on roads, in ditches and in cemeteries. The selection of these types of locations by the victims' families can be easily explained. On the one hand, these sites constituted the spaces in which their loved ones had been killed and/or buried. On the other hand, their location allowed family members to maintain a certain degree of anonymity in their actions, which were moreover a simple act of homage, something difficult for a proudly Catholic regime to prohibit. It would have been completely different to protest in front of a prison, pointing fingers at the coup authorities, just as the Mothers of the Plaza de Mayo in Argentina would do decades later.

Be that as it may, this chapter proposes that memory policies in Spain should go beyond paying the necessary tributes. Such policies should contribute to the transmission of a more complete and rigorous account of the 1936 coup and the violence that accompanied it. In this way, the inclusion of confinement spaces as new sites of memory could help clarify the view that citizens have of what is, without a doubt, one of the most iconic forms of violence associated with the 1936 coup. Furthermore, this shift in the focus of public policies on the past could shed light on a human group that has traditionally been left out of research and accounts of the subject at hand: that of the victimizers.

Notes

1   Fernando Puell de la Villa, 'La trama militar de la conspiración', in *Los mitos del 18 de julio*, ed. Francisco Sánchez Pérez (Barcelona: Crítica, 2013), 72.

2 Antonio Míguez Macho, 'Un pasado negado. Lugares de violencia y lugares de memoria del golpe, la guerra civil y el franquismo', *Confluenze. Rivista di studi americani* 2 (2018): 132.
3 Affirmations of this type appear (though in a nuanced manner) in a significant number of works, such as Paul Preston, *The Spanish Holocaust: Inquisition and Extermination in Twentieth-Century Spain* (London: Harper Press, 2012).
4 Lourenzo Fernández Prieto and Antonio Míguez Macho, 'Nomes e Voces: balance, preguntas e interpretaciones. La huellas del golpe de Estado en Galicia', in *Otras miradas sobre Golpe, Guerra y Dictadura. Historia para un pasado incómodo*, ed. Lourenzo Fernández Prieto and Aurora Artiaga Rego (Madrid: Catarata, 2014), 94–5.
5 Interview of Pilar Carballo Rodríguez, conducted by Eva Vieites Salmonte (Ribadeo, Lugo, Spain, June 2006), 2009. *Fondo Nomes e Voces*, https://www.terraememoria.usc.gal/entrevista/2009 (accessed 30 September 2020).
6 Xabier Buxeiro Alonso, 'Os verdugos e a sociedade. A violencia sublevada en Ribadeo (1936–1941)', in *Golpistas e verdugos de 1936. Historia dun pasado incómodo*, ed. Lourenzo Fernández Prieto and Antonio Míguez Macho (Vigo: Galaxia, 2018).
7 Interview of Elisa Secundina Fariña López, conducted by Eva Vieites Salmonte; Gustavo Hervella García (Ribadeo, Lugo, Spain, 31 May 2006), 2006. *Fondo Nomes e Voces*, https://www.terraememoria.usc.gal/entrevista/2006 (accessed 30 September 2020).
8 Antonio Míguez Macho, *The Genocidal Genealogy of Francoism: Violence, Memory and Impunity* (Brighton: Sussex Academic Press, 2016), 161–2.
9 Julio Aróstegui, 'Una izquierda en busca de la revolución [El fracaso de la segunda revolución]', in *Los mitos del 18 de julio*, ed. Francisco Sánchez Pérez (Barcelona: Crítica, 2013), 186–87.
10 Antonio Ruíz Vilaplana, *Doy fe … Un año de actuación de la España nacionalista* (París: Coopérative Étoile, 1937), 160–1.
11 For more on coup court proceedings, see Peter Anderson, *The Francoist Military Trials: Terror and Complicity, 1939–1945* (New York: Routledge, 2010).
12 For more on the concept of disappearances, see Míguez Macho, *The Genocidal Genealogy*.
13 Interview of Manuel Martínez Montenegro, conducted by Andrés Domínguez Almansa (Bouzas, Vigo, Pontevedra, Spain, 9 October 2007), 2286. *Fondo Nomes e Voces*, https://www.terraememoria.usc.gal/entrevista/2286 (accessed 30 September 2020).
14 *Archivo Municipal de Ribadeo* (AMR). 'Goberno/Pleno. Xunta de Partido Xudicial. Caja 1132. Libro de reclusos que perciben socorro 1931–1962' (1132/3).
15 *Archivo Intermedio Militar Noroeste* (AIMNOR), 'Fondo Lugo, caja 48, causa 309/36', 112 and 112 bis.

16 Interview of Elisa Secundina Fariña López, conducted by Eva Vieites Salmonte; Hervella García, Gustavo (Ribadeo, Lugo, Spain, 31 May 2006), 2006. *Fondo Nomes e Voces*, https://www.terraememoria.usc.gal/entrevista/2006 (accessed 30 September 2020).
17 AIMNOR, 'Fondo Lugo, caja 57, causa 744/36'.
18 Interview of Dolores Torviso Barata, conducted by Lourenzo Fernández Prieto, 2217. *Fondo Nomes e Voces*, https://www.terraememoria.usc.gal/entrevista/2217 (accessed 30 September 2020).
19 *Nomes e Voces*, http://vitimas.nomesevoces.net/gl/buscar/?vecinanza=395 (accessed 26 December 2019).
20 Arquivo Municipal de Ribadeo (AMR). 'Goberno/Pleno. Xunta de Partido Xudicial. Caja 1132. Libro de reclusos que perciben socorro 1931–1962' (1132/3).
21 Francisco Espinosa, *La columna de la muerte. El avance del ejército franquista de Sevilla a Badajoz* (Barcelona: Crítica, 2003).
22 For an example of this type of publication, see Authority of the Committee of Investigation Appointed by the National Government At Burgos, *A Preliminary Official Report on the Atrocities Committed in Southern Spain in July and August, 1936, by the Communist Forces of the Madrid Government* (London: Eyre and Spottiswoode, 1936).
23 For example, see Hugh Thomas, *The Spanish Civil War* (London: Penguin Books, 1961).
24 Iria Morgade Valcarcel, 'Rosa Branca. Accións colectivas da memoria na Transición: vítimas sen verdugos', in *Golpistas e verdugos de 1936. Historia dun pasado incómodo*, ed. Lourenzo Fernández Prieto and Antonio Míguez Macho (Vigo: Galaxia, 2018).
25 Francisco Etxeberria Gabilondo, 'Las políticas de memoria', in *Diccionario de memoria histórica. Conceptos contra el olvido*, ed. Rafael Escudero Alday (Madrid: Catarata, 2011), 77.
26 Mirta Núñez, 'Representaciones de memoria', in *Diccionario de memoria histórica. Conceptos contra el olvido*, ed. Rafael Escudero Alday (Madrid: Catarata, 2011), 34.
27 Etxeberria Gabilondo, 'Las políticas de memoria', 78.
28 Coxita Mir, 'Acción pública y regulación memorial del territorio', in *El Estado y la memoria. Gobiernos y ciudadanos frente a los traumas de la historia*, ed. Ricard Vinyes (Barcelona: Memorial Democràtic, 2009), 523.
29 Pierre Nora, 'Between Memory and History: Les Lieux de Mémoire', *Representations*, no. 26 (1989): 7–24.
30 Jose Babiano, Gutmaro Gómez, Antonio Míguez and Javier Tébar, *Verdugos Impunes. El Franquismo y la violación sistemática de los derechos humanos* (Barcelona: Pasado y presente, 2018), 95.
31 Antonio Míguez Macho, 'Un pasado negado. Lugares de violencia y lugares de memoria del golpe, la guerra civil y el franquismo', *Confluenze: Rivista di Studi Iberoamericani* 10, no. 2 (2018): 127–51.

32 Ibid., 129.
33 Amaya Caunedo Domínguez, 'Espacios y monumentos para el recuerdo de las víctimas en el norte', in *Duelo y memoria. Espacios para el recuerdo de las víctimas de la represión franquista en perspectiva comparada*, ed. Coxita Mir Curcó and Josep Gelonch Solé (Lleida: Universitat de Lleida, 2013), 82, 85.
34 Coxita Mir Curcó, 'Rememorar a las víctimas: un recorrido por los espacios de duelo de las violencias de guerra y posguerra en Cataluña', in *Duelo y memoria. Espacios para el recuerdo de las víctimas de la represión franquista en perspectiva comparada*, ed. Coxita Mir Curcó and Josep Gelonch Solé (Lleida: Universitat de Lleida, 2013); Javier Giráldez Díaz, 'El recuerdo de las fosas comunes de la guerra civil y el franquismo en los cementerios de la Andalucía democrática', in *Duelo y memoria. Espacios para el recuerdo de las víctimas de la represión franquista en perspectiva comparada*, ed. Coxita Mir Curcó and Josep Gelonch Solé (Lleida: Universitat de Lleida, 2013); Caunedo Domínguez, 'Espacios y monumentos'.
35 Information taken from, Nomes e Voces, http://www.nomesevoces.net/ (accessed 30 December 2019).
36 The Mondoñedo residents killed by the coup plotters were, as I have mentioned, Siervo González Rivas, Graciano Paz Amieiro and Manuel Rodríguez Núñez. Information taken from the website of the inter-university project Nomes e Voces: http://vitimas.nomesevoces.net/gl/buscar/?nome=&apelidos=&sexo=0&natural=&vecinanza=283&filiacion=&suceso=4&profesion=&morte= (accessed 30 December 2019). For more information on the sacas in Mondoñedo, see Interview of Orlando Leivas Freire, conducted by Andrés Domínguez Almansa; Somoza Cayado, Antonio (Mondoñedo, Lugo, Spain, 14 May 2008), 2318. *Fondo Nomes e Voces*, https://www.terraememoria.usc.gal/entrevista/2318 (accessed 30 September 2020).
37 For more information, see 'Homenaxe popular: 80 aniversario dos asasinatos de Siervo González, Graciano Paz e Manuel Rodríguez', 15 January 2018. Available online: http://cadernodeantonioreigosa.eu/2018/01/homenaxe-popular-80-aniversario-dos-asasinatos-de-siervo-gonzalez-graciano-paz-e-manuel-rodriguez/ (accessed 30 December 2019).
38 Emilio Silva Barrera, 'Los trece de Priaranza: Mi Abuelo También Fue un Desaparecido', *La Crónica de León*, 8 October 2000. Available online: https://memoriahistorica.org.es/los-trece-de-priaranza/ (accessed 30 December 2019).

Part Two

Sites of Confinement and Denial

5

Francoist concentration camps: Spaces of imprisonment and forced labour

Rafael García Ferreira

In the future, I believe, when the term concentration camp is used, we will think of Hitler's Germany and only Hitler's Germany.

—Victor Klemperer

An overview on the concentration camps systems

Often when speaking of 'concentration camps' one thinks of the system organized and carried out by the Nazi regime during the Second World War. Because of this, the collective conscience tends to associate the term 'genocide' with 'the Holocaust' and, in turn, that of 'concentration camps' with the 'extermination camps' of eastern Europe. However, concentration camps were not only a feature of the 1930s and 1940s, nor were they used exclusively in this context. They were not born in Nazi Germany, and their origins are not from the interwar period or even the European context. Concentration camps also simultaneously existed in other countries, such as the case discussed in this chapter: Franco's Spain. Chronologically, their origin dates back decades before the interwar period to the context of colonial war experiences, when Spain established camps in Cuba; the United States in the Philippines; and the United Kingdom in South Africa, all with the aim of fighting guerrilla armies formed in the colonies. In Cuba, for example, camps were used to imprison the civilian population so that it could not provide aid to guerrilla fighters.[1] Hitler himself claimed that the Nazis had copied the English camp system implemented during the Boer War, while Himmler cynically explained that the German concentration camps were more moderate than foreign camps.[2] Similarly, the history of concentration camps did not end with the conclusion of the Second World War, as they continued to appear in contexts as diverse as the Greek Civil War, the Mao regime, and the Balkan secession wars of the late twentieth century.

Of course, not all camps were the same or served the same purpose; they also did not hold the same type of prisoner, nor did they have the same goals regarding the treatment of prisoners. Likewise, they did not all emerge from the same particular context. The first Nazi camps were established on German soil, shortly after Hitler's appointment as chancellor: the first was Dachau, opened in the vicinity of Munich in March 1933. Initially, the purpose of the camp was not to eliminate the Jewish population; in fact, the first people transferred to the camp were political prisoners of communist ideology. In the USSR, the Gulag, with precedents already in tsarist Russia and origins in the civil war, would be consolidated along with the communist regime during the 1930s. In France, camps existed before the German occupation, appearing as early as the Third Republic to admit huge numbers of exiled Republicans after the Spanish Civil War (1936–1939) ended.[3]

Thus, it is important to highlight the differences between camps, their time periods, their objectives and the types of prisoners they held. That the system was common to many territories in Europe in the 1930s and 1940s does not mean that these camps had the same characteristics, that they were used for the same purpose or that they contained the same type of prisoner. Concentration camps in Spain arose in the midst of the civil war, in a context in which it was necessary to make room for the huge number of Republican fighters who became prisoners as the coup army advanced towards victory. The Republican defeats in the north of the peninsula led to a large number of prisoners of war (POWs) being classified into one of three fundamental outcomes: to be sent back to the front as combatants in the coup army, to be sent to labour battalions or to proceed with their purging. In the summer of 1937, the insurgent authorities created the Inspection of Concentration Camps for Prisoners (ICCP) with the aim of standardizing the situation of POWs. The creation of camps and the treatment of prisoners would be contextualized within a broader prison system that encompassed other types of detention centres. The camps' differences with regard to these other centres would be, at this point, the type of prisoner and their treatment: in addition to ideological enemies, the camp prisoners also included enemies of war, differentiating them from those prisoners detained in the rearguard during the war or, once the war had ended, from the dissidents against the new Regime. On the other hand, the ICCP would advance the system of reducing penalties through labour, created under a 'Redemption of Sentences through Work' scheme operational from October 1938, in relation to the management of prisoners as manual labour.[4]

The context in which the camps emerged is similar to that of the civil wars of Russia (1917–1923), Finland (1918) and Greece (1946–1950), as it was a wartime measure, at the service of the war effort and its objective was to confine internal enemies (fellow citizens) of war as well as political enemies, as has been pointed out.[5] Moreover, they were not extermination camps per se, despite the fact that the prisoners' living conditions led to a significant number dying during their internment. Instead, and in spite of their particular features, they were part of a much broader penitentiary system, which encompassed both established prisons and detention centres that were exceptionally created due to the extraordinary situation of the increased number of inmates since July 1936.[6]

This, then, was the situation in which the Spanish concentration camps began to proliferate. They would coincide in time with camps elsewhere in Europe, but their genesis and purpose, as indicated above, was not the prisoners' extermination, but their exploitation as labour and their political re-education (or inhibition), necessary for the reconstruction of a country in the midst of war and the post-war period. Internally they coexisted, as we have just seen, with other types of atypical detention centres. Inmates of camps, normal prisons and makeshift detention centres shared, on many occasions, the experience of precarious living conditions and labour exploitation. Such spaces were, in short, one more branch of the repertoire of violence deployed against the defeated since 1936.

Spanish concentration camps

The coup plotters and, later, the Franco regime used concentration camps to confine a large number of prisoners. However, the camps were not the only spaces used for this purpose. In the areas controlled by the coup plotters from the beginning (Galicia, Castile and Leon, Navarre, Western Andalusia, Extremadura, Mallorca, the Protectorate of Morocco, etc.), a huge number of prisoners were confined, forcing the authorities to find space to house these inmates. The regular prisons that already existed proved to be insufficient from the start, so it was necessary to set up other places to accommodate the prisoners. In this way, other kinds of places, which were not designed for these purposes and did not meet the necessary conditions to function as prisons, were incorporated into the penitentiary system. They were places set up under exceptional circumstances, prepared to serve the needs of the moment. Many of them, however, remained open for several years, with thousands of prisoners entering reconverted spaces, such as castles, barracks, convents, monasteries, factories, bullrings, and so on. The fact that these spaces were not intended for use as prisons, in addition to their poor condition and the enormous number of people they housed, made the living conditions of the prisoners very precarious. Overcrowding, poor housing and hygiene conditions, and diseases were common. Adding to this, in many cases, was the prisoners' suffering of abuse by the authorities and the harsh conditions under which they were forced to work.[7]

The life of these detention centres would not have the same evolution. As mentioned above, many of them were already set up in the summer of 1936; others would be opened later, according to the needs of the moment. The number of prisoners they housed was also variable, as it depended on the capacity of each space, although overcrowding was the norm. Similarly, the types of prisoners could be very different: from local prisoners, arrested for opposing the coup, to prisoners transferred from other places due to the overcrowding of regular prisons and the need for redistribution. There were also prisoners of war: combatants at the front who, once defeated, were held in different centres throughout the country for their transfer to another prison or for their final confinement.

The Francoist penitentiary system was, therefore, diverse and ever-changing. The centres used as prisons were chosen according to the needs of the moment, which would also mark their evolution over time. The same thing would happen with the network of concentration camps: just as differences existed between different types of concentration camps in a global or European context, differences were also found in post-war Spain. The most recent investigation into the Francoist concentration camp system has revealed the existence of about 300 camps.[8] Some camps would serve as inmate rehousing centres; others were confinement spaces where many prisoners of war were held; and others not only served to confine enemies of the regime but simultaneously functioned as forced work camps, in which prison labour was used to construct infrastructure or other types of buildings. Of these constructions, the best known is probably the Valley of the Fallen, a complex built largely with prison labour starting in 1940, and where the remains of the dictator, Francisco Franco, were buried until October 2019. The architect of the Valley, Diego Méndez, described the prisoners in the following words:

These men, mostly convicted of shocking crimes, by their very nature lacked fear, they cared nothing about facing the greatest dangers. They bore through granite, they went up on unbelievable scaffolds, they handled dynamite [...]. They have played, day by day, with death, [...] without them, the work would have lasted many more years, with the use of machines in greater numbers, and with increased waste.[9]

Even while largely dehumanizing the prisoner, an enemy, their work was recognized as crucial to the success of the construction.[10] The context of the Valley's construction is the end of the Spanish Civil War, in April 1939. During the war, concentration camps were opened throughout the country, as the victories of the uprising army brought with it an increase in the number of POWs. Many of them were assigned to these camps, already created in the midst of the conflict. However, with the final victory the number of prisoners would become even greater: in mid-1939 there would be 500,000 prisoners in concentration camps, 100,000 in labour battalions and some 47,000 in disciplinary battalions.[11] Many camps were opened with the aim of redistributing these prisoners, as permanent places to house them or as work camps. This last aspect is of great interest, since much of this labour, imprisoned and forced, carried out the construction of vital infrastructure for the development of the country, and not only the reconstruction of territories damaged by war. Large public infrastructures and various industries benefited from the slave labour of prisoners. For example, the Lower Guadalquivir Canal, which runs for more than 150 kilometres in Andalusia, was also built with forced prison labour, leading it to be known as the 'Prisoners' Canal'. It was the largest hydraulic work to be carried out.[12]

In 1937, the first prisoners assigned to forced labour were divided into three battalions of workers of about 600 prisoners each. In 1938, the number grew to 40,577 workers, and in 1939, to 90,000, of whom less than 13,000 worked in exchange for a sentence reduction.[13] The growing number of prisoners was in line with the increasing number of POWs that resulted as Franco's army advanced and the Republican army retreated. The number of prisoners who worked for the dictatorship would fall during the 1940s, although on the other hand, common prisoners, and not only POWs, would be incorporated into the system. Despite this, forced labour would continue until 1970, when the last group of 140 prisoners would be dissolved. This was due to the fact that, despite the closing of the various concentration camps, prison labour continued to be used in public works for decades. Other state organizations managed the distribution of such labour to different public works that needed to be completed.[14] Due to their working conditions, many prisoners died, both from accidents and from diseases such as silicosis, a condition that affects the lungs.[15]

From the regime's perspective, the prison population worked to redeem itself for the damage it had caused, under the oversight of the Directorate General of Devastated Regions, which organized the reconstruction of cities and roads as well as other works. On a visit to Spain, Himmler himself said that he found it absurd to accumulate thousands of prisoners without further ado and noted how convenient it would be to take advantage of this workforce. Franco, for his part, stated that he would not consider granting amnesty to the prisoners and that their labour would be used to repair the country, as payment for the 'damage' they had caused:

> It is necessary to liquidate the hatreds and passions of our past war, but not in the liberal style, with its monstrous and suicidal amnesties, which contain more fraud than forgiveness, but through the redemption of punishment through work, with repentance and with penance; whoever thinks otherwise sins of inconsistency or of treason. So much is the damage done to the country, so serious the havoc caused in families and morals, so many the victims who demand justice, that no honest Spaniard, no conscious being can stay away from these painful duties.[16]

Although the conditions of the workers have already alluded to, it is worth mentioning again the causes of these conditions. The movement of workers between the places where they were confined responded to two objectives: the first, to move them away from their place of origin or residence and to break the ties that they might have to these places; and the second, to prevent any friendly relations among the prisoners themselves. It was a way to punish the prisoner, not only physically but also psychologically, by depriving him of any previous relationship he might have or any other that he could develop during his stay in a camp. They were isolated and their lives came to be completely at the mercy of their captors.[17] Their work, on the other hand, was formally considered compensation for the damages they had caused and for their maintenance as prisoners.

The lifespan of the camps fluctuated, and there are examples of spaces that were used for a few months as well as others that operated for several years. They were scattered throughout the country, but there were great geographical differences. The areas with the most camps were Andalusia, with fifty-one, the Valencian Community, with forty-one, and Castile-La Mancha, with thirty-eight. The places where the camps were located were very diverse, just like the exceptionally prepared makeshift prisons: for example, in Madrid, the two largest local football fields were used. But the places where concentration camps were established were among the most diverse, ranging from adapted military facilities and prisons to bullrings, factories, monasteries and convents, or simply adapted land surrounded by barbed wire; in Asturias, a large part of the locality of Grado was fenced in for use as a camp.[18]

As we have already seen, forced labour served to rebuild the country. On some occasions prison labour was used for the reconstruction of towns ravaged by the war, and on others for the construction of infrastructure that was necessary for the new regime. In these cases, collaboration with local authorities was frequent, as they benefited from a workforce that was not under their responsibility and which they did not have to properly compensate; the same was true for those companies that were granted contracts for such projects. Although the camps had their own management, it was not uncommon for third parties to use forced labour for their own benefit, or even arrange its use for their own purposes. In other words, forced prison labour was not only put at the service of the new Francoist state, but also that of many businessmen, who grew visibly wealthy through the use of slave labour.[19] The salary the prisoners received was much less than that of a regular worker, but their availability to carry out the work was greater due to their captive situation. This was how numerous railway tracks were built, for example, in the 1940s and 1950s, which benefited the construction companies that ran these projects.[20] Other organizations benefited in a similar way, such as mining companies, the Madrid Metro and construction companies. Slave labour was also used for the construction of hydraulic works, for the reconstruction of towns and cities, and to carry out other civil and military works as well as projects benefiting the Church.[21]

As indicated above, prison labour was very useful to the regime for the reconstruction of the country. However, the exploitation of the prisoners was not the only reason why they were used as labour. There was a moral burden, at least from a formal point of view, that led the dictatorship to employ its prisoners in this way. Their labour was a form of reparation for the damage to the country that they had supposedly caused, an idea that came from the dictator himself. In the same way, we cannot forget the notable influence of the Church and Christianity on the dictatorship; many prisoners were subjected to processes of re-education and re-Christianization. In other words, they were forced to pay moral reparations, a process considered necessary due to their presumed ideology for having fought on the side of the Republic.[22]

We have not yet mentioned the situation of women, who were also involved as victims in the Franco prison system. Their situation and the hardships they suffered, however, differed from those experienced by men. They suffered abuse and rape, and many of them had their children taken from them at the age of three years old or were abused when they were pregnant.[23] Some of them were also exploited for work in prisons for women, always inside, and as long as they were not considered amongst the worst prisoners by the authorities. They could not choose to lessen their punishment through work, but still, at times, they did textile work to earn an income that helped support their families outside.[24]

A Francoist concentration camp: The case of Lavacolla

The extent and ubiquity of the incarceration system of the coup plotters and the early Franco regime can be observed in different specific cases. In the city of Santiago de Compostela, the capital of Galicia, three different confinement spaces were used in this context alone.[25] The first was the municipal prison, which from the coup of July 1936 went from housing a small number of prisoners to accumulating a much larger number, due to the arrests that followed the coup's triumph in the city. The second space of the city is related to the dynamics of opening new detention centres due to the enormous number of existing prisoners. The Santa Isabel barracks, an old military barracks on the outskirts of the city, was chosen and adapted to be used as a prison. It was a facility in which troops had never felt comfortable due to the poor conditions of the place, as well as the humidity of the environment; for that reason, it had never been occupied long term. From 1940 onwards it served as one of the so-called central prisons, and it came to have some of the highest levels of occupation in the northwest of the peninsula, accommodating up to 1,600 prisoners between 1942 and 1943. The central prisons were exceptionally established detention centres created to support the regular prisons, which were not able to absorb the enormous number of prisoners that existed from the first moment. The last detention centre that was set up in the city was a concentration camp, the Lavacolla camp.[26]

The Lavacolla camp operated under two official names: first, as a concentration camp, and later, as a labour battalion. This change of name occurred in many other concentration camps, but in practice it did not bring about a substantial transformation for the prisoners, their work or the place where they were being held. The inmates of the camp continued to work in the same way before and

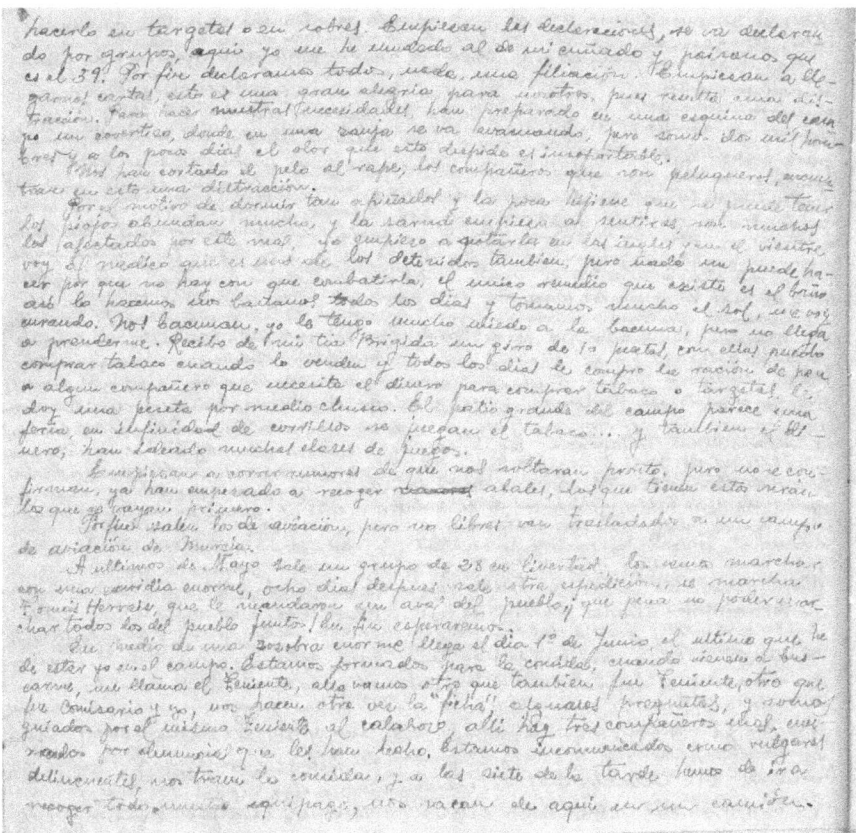

Figure 5.1 Diary of Casimiro Jabonero, prisoner in a Francoist concentration camp, Lavacolla (Galicia, Spain), 1939. © Histagra Collection / Histagra Research Group.

after they were considered one way or another: 'on 15 November of that year (1939) the inmates went to bed as prisoners of that camp and got up on the 16th as members of Workers' Battalion number 90'.[27]

The camp was created in 1939, at the end of the war, and initially served to redistribute prisoners to other detention centres. We have information of its first months of operation through the testimony contained in the diary of one of the prisoners. Casimiro Jabonero was a combatant in the Republican army. At the end of the war, he was sent to Santiago de Compostela and kept in Lavacolla before being sent to other centres, as was the case with many other fellow inmates. In the few days he was in the concentration camp, he saw first hand the conditions in which the prisoners lived and would live:

> We walk to a town called Lavacolla, the Concentration Camp is here. We go in one by one, they search us and collect all sharp and pointed objects, they give us half a bread roll and a tin of sardines. After they put us in some warehouses, we are crowded; we have to sleep on top of each other [...]. Here you have to observe iron discipline, you cannot cross the line at all, otherwise the 'whip' will come to resolve things. In the morning we raise the National Flag and the Falange anthem is sung and in the afternoon we have to lower it, like that every day; meals are somewhat scarce, we have them on time so in that we are doing well [...]. To relieve ourselves, they have prepared a shed in a corner of the field, which empties into a pit, but we are two thousand men and after a few days the smell that this gives off is unbearable.
>
> They have shaved our heads, this gives our fellow inmates who are barbers something to do.
>
> From sleeping so crowded together and the little hygiene that can be maintained, lice are very abundant, and we begin to have scabies. Many are affected by this disease, I begin to notice it on my groin and belly. I go to the doctor, who is also one of the detainees, but he can do nothing for me because there is nothing to fight it with, the only remedy that exists is bathing. That's what we do, we bathe every day and sunbathe a lot. I am healing. They vaccinate us, I am very afraid of the vaccine, but it does not make me sick.[28]

A later report, referring to the inspection of the work battalions, revealed that conditions had not improved much by 1942. This report highlighted that the capacity of the halls in which the prisoners were housed was insufficient, even with the progressive decrease in the number of prisoners, as it was noted that some 2,400 men came to live together in those warehouses. According to the inspection, the hygienic conditions of the premises were very poor, something that even affected the rooms of the workers' guards:

> In general, the characteristics of almost all of them are: insufficient cubic capacity for the number of individuals who sleep in each space; this detail is accentuated by the scarce ventilation, although it is true that the absence of a ceiling allows for complementary air ventilation of some importance through the roof slots. Now, as can be understood, this help is detrimental to the comfort of the room, especially in winter. The lighting is of course minimal and sunshine can be said to barely exist. The floor of the rooms, except for those corresponding to the floors above, is almost always flattened earth, and the wooden floors are quite deteriorated.[29]

Mentioned in the same conditions of misery were other aspects such as hygiene, clothing or food. For the disposal of human waste, a pit was still used. It was close to the river, causing the contamination of both the soil and the river itself despite periodic disinfection using chemical procedures: clearly an insufficient routine. In this sense, little had changed in the situation with respect to what Casimiro Jabonero had described as early as 1939. Clothing also stood out as insufficient and worn out, especially in the case of footwear, which was noted for its *pitiful* state – even that of the guards. The food, in quantity and quality, was manifestly insufficient. But between the description of Jabonero in 1939 and the report in 1942, changes had occurred in the concentration camp. The most important one was that the camp had transformed from a mere prison into a labour camp, where prisoners would work on the construction of the city's airport. In this way, the regime would try to overcome the two obstacles to building the airport: a lack of financing and a lack of manpower.[30]

The manpower issue was resolved in a practical way, as the new regime had large numbers of prisoners who could be forced to work in the service of the new state. In August 1939, the mayor of the city, Juan Gil Armada, carried out the necessary steps to ensure the labour of the prisoners, meeting in Madrid with various ministries and obtaining approval for the project. In April, Casimiro Jabonero had estimated that some 2,000 companions were in the camp; during the summer the figure would reach 2,400 due to the transfer of prisoners from other camps in the area. It is not easy to determine the exact number of prisoners in the compound at all times due to the lack of continuous sources and the frequent movement between centres. But it seems clear, according to official documentation, that at the end of 1939 there were 400 prisoners working on the airport construction.[31] In 1940 a second battalion of workers would be sent from Madrid as reinforcement for the project.[32]

The prisoners were housed in a former tanning factory a few kilometres from their workplace. The working conditions were extremely harsh. The testimony of another prisoner reveals that the prisoners faced an excessive workload and a very precarious food situation, while they also suffered the contempt of the guards:

> To do this, the morning Battalion had to be ready at five. They gave us a pot of coffee and took us in five by five, holding hands [...]. We had to walk three kilometres before reaching the work site. The other Battalion entered from 1 p.m. until 9 p.m. When they gave us dinner, cooked cabbages, it was already eleven at night. The work was exhausting. We had to dig and load eight or ten 1.5-metre wagons of dirt, and we had to take them along a track, to flatten some hills. They gave us very little clothes, and no money, despite the fact that the construction was being carried out by a contractor. [...] A fellow companion from my hometown of Villaralto, Alfonso Luna, was beaten with a stick that had

a tack and they stabbed it into his arm. When they took him to the hospital in Santiago, he died the next day, a victim of gangrene. We were very hungry. The poor man whose family did not send him anything was condemned to death. They sheltered us in an old leather tanning factory; through the roof, at night, we saw the stars, stiff with cold. The commander laughed when he saw us and called us the 'children of La Pasionaria'.[33] Many fellow prisoners were no longer able to work because they no longer had the strength to walk and they fainted.[34]

This dynamic would continue until 1945, the year in which the concentration camp was definitively closed. With the airport construction completed, it was no longer associated with military activity, and sports aviation resumed on the airfield runways. It left behind the living and working conditions to which the prisoners were subjected, by far the harshest of the penitentiary spectrum of the early Franco regime. In another of the city's prisons, the aforementioned Santa Isabel barracks, some inmates also carried out work, but to support the daily needs of the compound (as cleaners, library assistants, cooks and clerks).[35] Meanwhile, in the rest of Spain, concentration camps continued to be opened and maintained. In many of them, forced labour continued to be exploited to carry out construction and infrastructure projects, as in the case of Santiago de Compostela and its airport, but also for other types of construction, such as dams or railroad tracks.

Memory and forgetting of the Francoist concentration system

Although the last of the concentration camps was closed in 1947, the forced labour system lasted until practically the final days of the dictatorship. In more than thirty years, prisons had been set up and a system of forced labour had been consolidated. Sometimes this system shared similarities with its European counterparts, but it certainly had a much longer lifespan than those that were used during the 1930s and 1940s in the rest of the continent. This was partly because the Franco regime had survived the defeat of fascism, enabling it to follow its own dynamics; even so, as we can see, it maintained part of its framework while it tried to show the international community that it had broken its ideological ties with the defeated in the Second World War.

In Spain, initiatives have been carried out to highlight the memory of the civil war and the dictatorship, as well as its victims. For example, there have been projects to recover the names of victims, such as the 'Proxecto Nomes e Voces', dedicated to identifying victims of Galicia, or the 'Todos los nombres' initiative, which identifies victims from Andalusia, Extremadura and North Africa.[36] Debates surrounding the naming of places and streets in honour of the dictatorship's milestones or prominent military officials and leaders continue to raise questions today. Similarly, memorialization projects have been carried out to preserve the memory of victims and to combat the forgetting to which they were subjected by the dictatorship, which exclusively honoured the 'fallen' of its own side during the war of 1936–1939. One of the goals of these projects has been to identify execution sites and the locations of mass graves. In the case of Catalonia, for example, an initiative of memorial significance was launched with the approval of a project to underline the importance of these types of spaces, the 'Memorial Democrático'.[37]

Regarding concentration camps, however, other conditions have meant that their memory is not sufficiently cared for or disseminated today. One reason for this is that as the dictatorship closed its camps, it also ensured that many of them were dismantled, promoting a 'forgetfulness' about these spaces that makes them difficult to locate or search through. Something similar has occurred with those places where the use of space did not disappear, but changed over time, either in the same premises where a camp had been or in a new building built where prisoners had previously been housed. To all this we must add that the policies regarding camps have not been similar to those elsewhere in Europe. Although the camps of central and eastern Europe have undergone a process of museumization that has helped to preserve the memory of what happened there, this process has generally not taken place in Spain. The meagre left-wing initiatives and strong right-wing opposition to addressing the memory of the Franco regime with the aim of making amends to the victims have led this task to fall into other hands, such as associations for the recovery of memory, or initiatives supported by specific instances of funding, and not through a solid, constant and fluid strategy by institutions to contribute resources to research. In this way, in many places there is no memory of the concentration camps that operated nearby; in others, despite the recognition of commemorations carried out over the years, popular memory still does not reflect the reality of the existence of concentration and labour camps close to the places where people currently reside. The symbols that represented some of the enclosures that housed inmates and still stand are in danger of being erased as well, such as the case of the Badajoz bullring, demolished in 2000. The very building that housed the workers of the previously mentioned Lavacolla camp is today a restaurant; of the other eleven Galician camps, only three more have some kind of sign that honours the memory of the victims. The Valley of the Fallen itself is today known as a monument that exalts the memory of the dictatorship, but not many are aware that it also functioned as a camp and that prison labour was used for its construction.

Figure 5.2 Lavacolla Concentration Camp Memorial. Santiago de Compostela (Galicia, Spain), 2020. © Histagra Collection / Histagra Research Group.

There is, moreover, another issue in this regard, and that is the preponderance of the memory of the dictatorship; in many cases, of the 'forgetfulness' to which I have alluded.[38] The Franco regime made an effort to erase from its memory any episodes that could put it in a compromising situation before the international community or before history. Due to this, incidents such as the fact that the largest airport in the northwest of the peninsula was initially built by slave labour have hardly transpired. It was a construction project in which the mayor himself mediated, ensuring that this workforce be used. Subsequently, the contract for the construction was awarded to a local company, which benefited from the labour provided by the prisoners – a fact that has also been buried in memory. This is one of the great differences that exists with, for example, German historiography, which has dealt with identifying the main leaders and collaborators of the Third Reich, as well as the guilt of society. One of the differences between the Hitler and Franco regimes is this: the former lost its war and had to face the Allies' demands of responsibilities; the latter was founded on the basis of victory in a civil war and lasted for almost forty years, enabling it to shape its memory. A memory that, on many occasions, is still imposed today.

To end this section, it seems reasonable to mention the memory of the camp I have studied in Santiago de Compostela and the prisoners who spent time there. In this regard, I must highlight the commemorative monolith that was erected in 2006, a few metres from where the prisoners were housed, through the initiative of an entity dedicated to actions recovering historical memory (Fundación 10 de Marzo) and the city council. However, in this case hardly any names of the camp's guards or leaders have been confirmed. Added to this is the difficulty in many cases of tracing them and learning more about them as well as their previous and subsequent activity. Until a few years ago, Spanish historiography on the civil war and Francoism has mainly focused on the question of the victims. That means that today studies are still emerging on their counterpart: the perpetrators, those who exercised violence. In part, this is also because the sources do not often provide information on the latter.

The punishment of the defeated

The framework of the Francoist penitentiary system was complex. As we have seen, there were detention centres with very different characteristics depending on when they were established, the space they occupied and the prisoners they housed, to which we must add the context in which they were employed. If the prisons were of different types, the same was true of the way the prisoners were treated. The city I have studied provides a very clear example, where there were two exceptional post-war detention centres. In many camps prisoners were used to carry out hard labour, which resulted in significant physical fatigue, and the camps were often associated with very precarious living conditions; these camps coexisted with other types of prisons, where sometimes even more prisoners were housed, but where those who carried out labour on the premises did so, at least, in physical conditions that were much less demanding. Of course, this was also related to space, since some camps were used for the construction of an infrastructure that the territory lacked, and others were simply detention centres, where the prisoners' labour was used to support the administration of the prison.

The question of space is also interesting, as it poses problems for its definition. In Lavacolla, a concentration camp was created, but months later it was called a work battalion. The official documentation refers to the camp in its first months of life; as of November 1939, it refers to the battalion. However, in practice, the changes were minimal. Is there a difference between the camp and the group that made up the battalion? In theory, no. We could argue that the 'camp' was just the physical place where the prisoners were held, while the 'battalion' referred to the group of people who were forced to work. But in practice, the name assigned to them did not change their situation, their conditions or the work they were forced to do. That the camp was closed in November 1939 did not mean anything, since there was no closure; it only changed the way it referred to itself and its prisoners.

The prisoners, for their part, found themselves in degrading and inhuman conditions. For the regime, they were half POWs and half ideological prisoners or enemies. The Franco regime took charge of building a narrative in which its enemy was foreign and dehumanized, so it would not be morally reproached for the conditions in which it held its prisoners. In fact, as we have seen, when forced labour was still being used, sports aviation returned to the same spaces in which the prisoners worked. The violence exercised against them seems obvious, although, again, it presents difficulties in its definition. We cannot consider physical aggression as the only form of violence: so too were the living conditions in which the prisoners were kept and the working conditions to which they were subjected. Was the violence more severe in the camp or in the work site? Neither more nor less, but it did continue, as the prisoner was degraded in both places.

It also seems clear that the prisoners were outsiders. Those people from towns and their surroundings who had considered themselves enemies of the coup plotters and the new regime had already been prosecuted in previous years. The inmates of these centres tended to be transferred from other places, since they were enemies of war and ideological enemies who had been exiled from their hometown to break any links or networks that they may have been part of. This was also a way to try to break the will of the prisoner, who did not know what his next destination would be and who lived with the uncertainty of not knowing when he would be able to return home and see his relatives. These orders were common in camps, but also in other detention centres in which the flow of prisoners was constant while they operated.

Some of the prisoners who worked did so in exchange for a reduced sentence, but not all of them. Sentence reductions stipulated that an amount of the sentence could be commuted for the work done. The system operated across the Franco regime's different spaces of confinement; it also applied to the camp system, but those prisoners who were considered worst by the regime were not allowed to benefit. On the other hand, the workers received a salary that was not proportional to the labour performed, a result of the idea that their work was compensation for all the harm they had previously caused. It was an attitude towards the defeated that the dictatorship would maintain throughout its entire existence.

Notes

1 Ian R. Smith and Andreas Stucki, 'The Colonial Development of Concentration Camps (1896–1902)', *Journal of Imperial and Commonwealth History* 39 (2011): 417–37.
2 Nikolaus Wachsmann, *KL: A History of the Nazi Concentration Camps* (New York: Farrar, Strauss and Giroux, 2015), 15.
3 Robert Gellatelly, *Backing Hitler: Consent and Coercion in Nazi Germany* (Oxford: Oxford University Press, 2001), 77, 80; Álvaro Lozano, *Stalin, el tirano rojo* (Madrid: Ediciones Nowtilus, 2012), 182; Marie-Claude Rafaneau-Boj, *Los campos de concentración de los refugiados españoles en Francia (1939–1945)* (Barcelona: Ediciones Omega, 2018), 6.
4 Gonzalo Acosta Bono, José Luis Gutiérrez Molina, Lola Martínez Macías and Ángel del Río Sánchez, *El canal de los presos (1940–1962). Trabajos forzados: de la represión política a la explotación económica* (Barcelona: Crítica, 2004), 17–20.
5 Javier Rodrigo, *Los campos de concentración franquistas. Entre la historia y la memoria* (Madrid: Siete Mares, 2003), 28–32.

6 Antonio Míguez Macho, 'Un pasado negado. Lugares de violencia y lugares de memoria del golpe, la guerra civil y el franquismo', *Confluenze, Revista di Studi Iberoamericani* 2 (2018): 127–51.
7 Gutmaro Gómez Bravo, *El exilio interior. Cárcel y represión en la España franquista, 1939–1950* (Madrid: Taurus, 2008), 20–1.
8 Carlos Hernández de Miguel, *Los campos de concentración de Franco. Sometimiento, tortura y muerte tras las alambradas* (Barcelona: Penguin Random House Grupo Editorial, 2019), 72.
9 Paloma Aguilar Fernández, *Políticas de la memoria y memorias de la política. El caso español en perspectiva comparada* (Madrid: Alianza Editorial, 2008), 146–58 (p. 147).
10 Sam Jones, '"Spain is Fulfilling Its Duty to Itself": Franco's Remains Exhumed', *The Guardian*, 24 October 2019.
11 Gutmaro Gómez Bravo, *Geografía humana de la represión franquista. Del Golpe a la Guerra de ocupación (1936–1941)* (Madrid: Cátedra, 2017), 229.
12 Isaías Lafuente, *Esclavos por la patria. La explotación de los presos bajo el franquismo* (Madrid: Temas de hoy, 2002), 74–6.
13 Hernández de Miguel, *Los campos de concentración de Franco*, 94–5.
14 Lafuente, *Esclavos por la patria*, 59–63.
15 Aguilar Fernández, *Políticas de la memoria y memorias de la política*, 148–9.
16 Paul Preston, *The Spanish Holocaust: Inquisition and Extermination in Twentieth-Century Spain* (London: HarperCollins, 2013), 616, 643.
17 Antonio Míguez Macho, *The Genocidal Genealogy of Francoism: Violence, Memory and Impunity* (Brighton: Sussex Academy Press, 2015), 37.
18 de Miguel, *Los campos de concentración de Franco*, 17.
19 Preston, *The Spanish Holocaust*, 658–9.
20 Juanjo Olaizola Elordi, 'Destacamientos penales y construcción de infraestructuras ferroviarias', in *Los trabajos forzados en la dictadura franquista*, ed. José Miguel Gastón and Fernando Mendiola (Pamplona: Instituto Gerónimo de Uztáriz, 2015), 116–31.
21 Lafuente, *Esclavos por la patria*, 327–33.
22 Gutmaro Gómez Bravo, *La redención de penas. La formación del sistema penitenciario franquista, 1936–1950* (Madrid: Catarata, 2007).
23 Preston, *The Spanish Holocaust*, 661–3.
24 Fernando Hernández Holgado, 'Esclavas del franquismo: el trabajo de las mujeres presas', in *Los trabajos forzados en la dictadura franquista*, ed. José Miguel Gastón and Fernando Mendiola (Pamplona: Instituto Gerónimo de Uztáriz, 2015), 104–15.
25 To give an idea of the size of the city in relation to the number of detention centres in operation, Santiago had a population of about 43,000 inhabitants in 1930, and about 55,000 in 1940.

26 Rafael García Ferreira, 'Violencia golpista en Santiago de Compostela: verdugos, lóxicas e espazos (1936–1946)', in *Golpistas e verdugos de 1936. Historia dun pasado incómodo*, ed. Lourenzo Fernández Prieto and Antonio Míguez Macho (Vigo: Galaxia, 2018), 137–80.
27 Hernández de Miguel, *Los campos de concentración de Franco*, 98.
28 Víctor Manuel Santidrián Arias, *Diario del soldado republicano Casimiro Jabonero. Campo de prisioneros de Lavacolla, prisión de Santiago de Compostela, 1939–1940* (Santiago de Compostela: Fundación 10 de Marzo, 2004), 99–100.
29 Archivo General Militar de Ávila (AGMA), 'Caja 20904, Carpeta 10'.
30 Xerardo Rodríguez Arias, *100 anos de aviación en Compostela* (Santiago de Compostela: Consorcio de Santiago, 2017), 74–89.
31 Archivo Intermedio Militar Noroeste, 'Caja 104'.
32 AGMA, 'Caja 20974, Carpeta 4'.
33 Dolores Ibárruri, nicknamed 'La Pasionaria', was a communist leader known for her political work and defense of women's rights during the Second Spanish Republic. After the end of the civil war, she was forced into exile in the USSR, returning to Spain in 1977 after the end of the dictatorship.
34 Francisco Moreno Gómez, *Córdoba en la posguerra. La represión y la guerrilla. 1939–1950* (Córdoba: Fernando Baena Editor, 1987).
35 Archivo General de la Administración, 'Fondo de Justicia, Caja 41/11945'.
36 The databases can be accessed at http://nomesevoces.net and http://todoslosnombres.org (accessed 30 June 2020).
37 Jordi Guixé, 'Espacios, memoria y territorio, un memorial en red en Cataluña', in *El Estado y la memoria. Gobiernos y ciudadanos frente a los traumas de la historia*, ed. Ricard Vinyes (Barcelona: RBA, 2009), 569–604.
38 Jeremy Treglown, *Franco's Crypt: Spanish Culture and Memory since 1936* (New York: Farrar, Straus and Giroux, 2013).

6

Imprisoned in everyday life: Sites of violence and social control in Franco's Spain (1936–1950)

Claudio Hernández Burgos

Space, along with time, is one of the fundamental dimensions around which historical knowledge revolves. People move and act in specific places; events have a particular geography; and the processes of change, continuity and evolution traverse settings and locations that are key to understanding them in all their breadth. Space, however, is not an innocent canvas where 'things happen'. On the contrary, it is woven by power relations and takes shape through discourses, policies and actions carried out by multiple agents.[1] For this reason, space is often transformed into an arena of political, social, symbolic and cultural struggles waged by those who battle to define it. But space also constructs and significantly conditions processes and events, thereby surrounding historical actors. In short, space is produced by and a producer of human relations, therefore, it is an essential variable for the comprehension of historical events.[2]

The establishment of the Franco regime and the violence with which it was carried out must also be understood in spatial terms. The dictatorship was not external to the population, nor removed from their everyday lives. In cities, towns and small villages, ordinary Spaniards saw how the 'New State' was built and brought to life through its symbols, institutions, men and policies. Since its birth from the coup d'état of July 1936, the regime understood that a restructuring of national life was necessary. It soon implemented a series of measures aimed at destroying Republican Spain to construct, on its ashes, the Francoist nation. This process of redefinition and regeneration was likewise manifested in spatial terms, since new sociopolitical relations also required new spaces.[3]

Along these lines, this chapter explores the spatial dimensions of the violence and social control deployed by the Francoist state during the years of the Spanish Civil War (1936–1939) and the post-war period (1939–1950). Instead of viewing space as a mere backdrop, it is understood as a central category from which to analyse violent processes and mechanisms of social control. To achieve this, this study is based on documentation from military, state, provincial and municipal archives. Likewise, it makes use of the theoretical and methodological contributions of the *Alltagsgeschichte* and the 'spatial twist', given the emphasis that both approaches place on the constructed nature of spaces and the ability of individuals and social collectives to act on their immediate realities.[4]

The war and the post-war period constitute an ideal chronological framework for considering Francoist violence in spatial terms and connecting it with specific places and locations. In this way, official policies on space will become clear and we will be able to gauge their limits and success, as well as the capacity of individuals to cope with violence and state control mechanisms on a daily basis. Moreover, this will enable us to undertake another of the main objectives of this chapter: to transcend the physical aspects of the violence exerted by the Franco dictatorship and prioritize its most subtle and imperceptible manifestations. Along these lines, these pages address the multiple facets of violence in a broad sense, analysing their social, symbolic and moral characteristics, amongst others. At the same time, and even at the risk of falling into 'overgeneralization', social control is understood here in a non-restrictive way, referring to all those actions and strategies 'that manage to create the bases of governance, regulation and operation of social systems by shaping choices, offering or vetoing opportunities, or marking the thresholds of what is allowed'.[5] Thus, we can gain a more complex perspective on Francoist violence itself and on the devices, measures, regulations and policies used to alter the quotidian spaces that the Spanish encountered every day.

This chapter is arranged around two main axes. The first part explores the Francoist dictatorship's policies regarding space and the role of violence in them. The objective is to demonstrate that space was a complex reality, inhabited by a heterogeneous variety of actors and diverse practices, which is why our view of it must be equally complex. The second part, on the other hand, assesses the Francoist dictatorship's capacity to control everyday spaces, whether from a political, social or moral point of view. In doing so, the multiplicity of agents that traversed these spaces is once again highlighted, as well as their capacity to redefine such spaces daily, turning them into disputed and negotiated realities.

The dictatorship, space and violence

For dictatorships born in interwar Europe, public space constituted an essential focus point. Mass gatherings, parades, demonstrations and political events – along with the symbolism, aesthetics, music and new rhythms that accompanied them – were part of the social and cultural regeneration projects promoted by these regimes. For example, the leaders of Italian fascism defended a totalitarian concept of space and its redefinition according to new parameters. This intention was demonstrated in the grandiloquence of fascist architecture, in the profound transformations undergone by the city of Rome or in the pompous and careful staging that accompanied Mussolini's arrival in each town.[6] Such processes were not exclusive to fascist Italy, but shared many parallels with what happened in other dictatorships. Though not, perhaps, with the same intensity reached in Germany or Italy, the Franco regime also constructed a specific rhetoric regarding spatiality and developed policies aimed at altering the landscape, the streets, public ceremonies and other elements that shaped public life in cities and towns.[7]

The main purpose of colonizing public streets and squares was to snatch them from the enemies and imbue them with a new political, social, cultural and civic style.[8] Violence was thus a supporting element in the occupation of space, manifesting itself in physical and symbolic actions that were visible in the public sphere.[9] In the case of the Franco regime, this process was even more intense due to the bloody nature of the regime's origins. The coup d'état against the Republic was accompanied by an unprecedented spiral of violence that was translated into public space. Arrests, persecutions and executions had specific locations, to the point of becoming, in some cases, significant sites within the collective memory of those who lived through those years.[10] In cities such as Valladolid, for example, sites of executions by firing squad became social gathering points, where part of the community came as spectators to witness the death of their neighbours.[11] Execution and burial sites, such as wells, ditches, forests or ravines, revealed the traces of physical violence in space.[12] During the first weeks of 1936, the civil governor of Salamanca received numerous messages about the appearance of corpses in places and on roads around the different towns of the province.[13] In the towns of Galicia, the appearance of lifeless bodies on the outskirts of villages was 'something typical' in the autumn of 1936.[14] In the same way, police stations, jails, concentration camps and other punishment spaces formed part of the landscape of cities and towns. This was the case of the queues of women who would bring food to their imprisoned relatives. Their presence, exposed to the gaze of all the members of the community, served to publicize these spaces of confinement and punishment and to reinforce their connection to those who bore the stigma of the defeated.[15] Visibility, furthermore, gave additional strength to the violence, beyond its capacity to eliminate political enemies: it made violence a threat, an instrument of control over the population and a catalyst for social cohesion.[16]

These cases demonstrate that the spaces of violence were much more than specific locations, territories and maps drawn up from streets and buildings. Power relations, identities, actors and practices shaped and were shaped by these spaces, so we cannot ignore such elements when analysing them.[17] Adopting a spatial perspective to approach the deployment of violence allows us to broaden our gaze and include other actors, attitudes and actions within the frame, without which our knowledge of the spaces of Francoist violence would be skewed. First, it helps to move the focus beyond the state, to local dynamics within communities.[18] Secondly, it allows us to place other actors on the stage and explore their heterogeneous attitudes and behaviours towards violence. Thirdly, it offers us a concept of violence that is not limited to its physical and bloody dimensions, permitting a closer look at even 'the most subtle forms of coercion' that ran through everyday life.[19] And finally, it enables us to observe the constant process of redefinition and resignification of these spaces marked by blurred and changing boundaries.[20] 'Spaces of violence' were not only those of physical violence, nor of victims and executioners; instead, an analysis of this type must include other elements, actors and dimensions that left their trace in specific locations. By considering violence – and not only administrative or geographical issues – as something that builds and shapes space, we can better study the power relations, the violent practices and the roles of different agents who were part of such processes.[21]

From the field of architectural theory, the concept of 'spatial violence' has been used to interpret the relationship between space and violence. On the one hand, it has been adopted to refer to the various ways in which architecture and urban planning – beyond their aesthetic purposes – have been consciously used by states as a more or less subtle mechanism of violence.[22] On the other hand, and conversely, the concept has served to study the impact of violence on urban space and to gauge the extent to which the latter has been altered by the former.[23] The concept of 'spatial violence' thus offers the relevant analytical potential to study Francoist violence in all its breadth. Specifically, it allows us to evaluate to what extent the Franco regime created spatial policies aimed at governing and controlling the lives of the population in general and marginalizing certain social sectors or individuals in particular.[24] These functions were carried out by prisons, police stations or Falange institutions. The latter were Auxilio Social (Social Assistance) centres. People with the fewest resources – usually those belonging to the defeated sectors – went to these centres when they were forced to accept the charity of the regime to survive. The aesthetics of such facilities represented a humiliation for them. For example, the dining halls inaugurated in the city of Granada in 1938 were decorated with portraits of Franco, the Falangist leader José Antonio Primo de Rivera – assassinated in the Republican zone during the war – and the figure of baby Jesus, 'saved from the flames', in memory of the anticlerical 'fury' of the 'reds'.[25] But no space better symbolized the dynamics of exclusion and inclusion generated in the post-war world than the monuments dedicated to the 'fallen and martyrs of the Crusade'. Around the crosses erected in all the towns of the country, a space was created for the victorious community to gather and commemorate the dead, where there was no room at all for the 'enemies of Spain'.[26] Their role as a symbol of spatial violence was further reinforced by the fact that these monuments were located in visible places where people passed by on a daily basis. As the parish priest of a small town in the province of Granada explained when he blessed the monument inaugurated in the town in 1942, that site should be 'an everyday reference point' for the community, 'a reminder of Marxist barbarism' and 'an eternal sign of the sacrifice and example of the martyrs of the Crusade'.[27]

However, apart from architecture, the concept can be useful for exploring other manifestations of 'spatial violence' in the everyday life of people, in their immediate surroundings, and for examining the specific practices and the various ways through which citizens 'interacted' with violence. In this way, other spaces of violence and social control can be found, such as streets, stations, bars, cafes, houses or brothels, where – beyond physical violence – other elements were visible, for instance, intimidation, coercion, blackmail, and other attitudes and behaviours, in which both the state and unrelated agents participated. Many individuals took advantage of the helplessness of defeated families or those facing legal problems for their own benefit. A woman from Villajoyosa (Alicante) was forced to pay a sum of money to a man who had assured her 'that he would speak to his friends' to change the jail sentence that had been issued to her brother.[28] Even more dramatic was the situation experienced by a resident of Granada in her own home, when an acquaintance accused her of being 'red' and threatened to report her to the police 'if she did not live together with him'.[29] Given that context of instability, in which the authorities were quite receptive to denunciations of any kind, there were no safe havens for the most vulnerable.

The public streets became the main enemy of defeated women in small towns, where they suffered humiliation and explicit punishment. A report indicated that in Galicia their heads were shaved, leaving only a lock of hair 'with a ribbon in the colours of the monarchical flag' and they were then forced to 'sweep the streets'. In La Rioja, two widows of executed Republicans were forced to perform a play, after which they were shaved, given castor oil and marched around town to the laughter of other, right-wing women.[30]

The role of the victors and regime supporters is essential to understanding acts of violence such as those discussed here. The significance of punishment, its visibility in public space and its effectiveness in excluding certain individuals at the end of the conflict can only be explained by analysing intra-community dynamics and the involvement of multiple agents within.[31] Testimonies of those who suffered this violence highlight the extent to which ordinary authorities and neighbours were responsible for their social stigmatization and confirm the hostility they faced in the streets. Antonio Fernández recalls that the local authorities arrested his mother and destroyed her merchandise in the working-class neighbourhood of El Palo (Málaga) due to his father's political background.[32]

Figure 6.1 Public rally with coup plotters addressing people in the small village of Cangas (Galicia, Spain), civil war years. See the Nazi flag at the left corner of the picture. © Histagra Collection / Histagra Research Group.

The children of the 'reds' were also victims of public marginalization. This is what happened to Juan Calvo, when, at just eight years old, he was queuing up to receive a Christmas present like other children his age. The reaction of one of the Falangists in charge of overseeing the process could not have been more forceful: 'Don't give anything to this one, he's a communist.'[33] For the defeated, the public and semi-public spaces of streets and shops became hostile territory: areas of daily intimidation and social exclusion. Faced with this situation, some decided to take refuge in the apparent safety of their own homes. Others, harassed by the authorities and neighbours, made the decision to pack their bags and try to start a new life far from their home towns.[34] Violence had taken over small communities. The public order delegate of the province of Ávila explained it very clearly in a report dated 1937:

> There are towns where the relatives of the victims of red barbarism systemically harass and viciously persecute those who, even having been members of right-wing organizations for reasons against their will, did not suffer the loss of loved ones or their interests. In other cases, resentment or personal revenge leads them to accuse those who are not guilty of any such act of being against the National Cause.[35]

His words acknowledged the workings of the 'punishment communities' made up of victors, victims of revolutionary violence, ex-combatants or widows of the 'fallen' rebels. But, at the same time, they highlighted a more complex picture. The brutal context unleashed by the coup d'état, developed by the war and prolonged for years by victory, created the breeding ground for the spread of various attitudes and behaviours towards violence and multiplied the actors within. Along with the instigators of violence, there were those who interceded, those who saved a neighbour from suffering a penalty or those who, from a certain position, tried to cushion the punishment of those described as 'enemies of the regime'. The prestige of certain members within the community or the occupations they held are critical to explaining why some individuals decided to intervene publicly to prevent bloodshed. The popular memory of communities preserves the memory of acts such as those of a reserve captain from a town in La Rioja who, in the first months after the coup, prevented a group of armed 'outsiders' from arresting several neighbours. The same thing happened in another town in Galicia after the war, where the intervention of a former fighter from the Francoist side prevented acts of violence.[36] Despite being soldiers and ex-combatants, the risk these citizens took was significant, acting in the middle of the street and before the eyes of the community. For this reason, mediation often took place in private spaces, through a call or a letter, with a more tepid attitude and avoiding direct confrontation with the state. This is evidenced by the letter sent by the president of the Ávila Commission for the Seizure of Assets (Comisión de Incautación de Bienes de Ávila) in 1938 to the coup commanders. Faced with the merciless response that could be expected from an authority in charge of seizing the properties and assets of the Republicans, the sender described the work that the commission was carrying out as 'true punishment' and appealed to the 'fairness of the Caudillo' to stop this work because of the 'distressing' situation in which it was leaving many families in the province who 'for the most part did not share the ideas' of their executed or imprisoned relatives.[37]

In spite of everything, within this range of attitudes towards violence, those who 'looked the other way' were more common: the moral onlookers of violence who, for various reasons, decided not to intervene and whose acts have left no documented trace.[38] These behaviours could be linked to fear and the paralysis caused by terror, but they also reflected attitudes of consent or acquiescence. They were the reactions of those who thought that the punished 'must have done something' to deserve it, of those who thought that a little 'heavy handedness' did not hurt, or of those who selfishly decided to have nothing to do with a stranger's fate.[39] All these attitudes reveal a much more complex panorama that requires a closer look. When analysing the daily dynamics of local communities, the heterogeneity of agents and actions increases; the contours of violence broaden; the spaces where violence took place multiply; and the dichotomy between victims and executioners is called into question.[40]

Controlled spaces, spaces of struggle, redefined spaces

The Franco regime's agenda of regeneration was also materialized through the design of a new everyday geography. The dictatorship sought to saturate everyday life with its references, institutions and symbols, monitoring social behaviour and making new power relationships visible. The objective, therefore, was not only to watch over those considered hostile to the regime but also to control the whole of society, ensuring that people's behaviours and lifestyles respected the new rules and regulations.[41] As in the case of physical violence, studying social control as it is linked to space helps to complicate the phenomenon. It allows us to better understand the regime's capacity to penetrate the lives of people, the agents involved in this process and the attitudes of the population towards attempts by the state to shape their day-to-day living.⁴² In addition, it offers us a more complete overview of the daily post-war reality, since those who committed social transgressions and deviations included a heterogeneous mix and were not limited to the political enemies of the dictatorship.

The starting premise of the Francoist regeneration project was the absolute conviction that liberalism, democracy and, specifically, the period of the Second Republic had deteriorated the essence of the Spanish nation, leading it to a war that was seen as inevitable. This degeneration was – from the perspective of the coup plotters – especially visible in the public sphere. The resignification and 'desacralization' of the urban space, symbolized by the changing of street names, the elimination of religious symbols and anticlerical acts, had contributed to creating a 'revolutionary environment' in cities and villages.⁴³ But it had also reached other semi-public places such as schools, cultural centres and even the private sphere, where the 'pernicious' influence of Republican and secular education had disrupted the very essence of family life.⁴⁴ Thus, it should not be surprising that the Franco regime dedicated part of its speeches, policies and legislation to the organization of space and the adaptation of social behaviour to the new reality generated after the war. Public streets and squares, places of culture and leisure, festivities, customs, ways of life, and daily routines and habits were subjected to state scrutiny and control: a task that must be understood as an essential tool for destroying the cultural, symbolic and community framework that supported Republican identity, replacing it with a new national model.⁴⁵

Society as a whole was the target of renationalization. Public space underwent a profound symbolic change. Republican references were eliminated, while the demonstrations, ceremonies, rites, dates and symbols of the Franco regime occupied the street. As with violence, the weight of renationalization fell on the shoulders of the state, but at the daily level, other agents were also involved. In 1937, for example, Antonio Sánchez, director of the Granada Electricity Company, submitted a proposal to the City Council Permanent Municipal Commission to install a luminous sign in the city centre, six metres high and sixteen metres long, with the inscription 'Long live Spain'. The idea was that once the troops led by Franco had taken Madrid, the sign would be lit as a tribute to the army and a daily inspiration for all Granadans.⁴⁶ Similar initiatives featured as key protagonists the dictatorship's supporters or the individuals and collectives that, in one way or another, had sacrificed themselves for the triumph of the uprising. A group of residents in Topas (Salamanca) wrote to the civil governor of the province to request that a street in their town be dedicated to 'The Heroes of the Alcázar of Toledo', killed in defence of the rebel cause.⁴⁷

In June 1938, a widow of a man 'fallen for God and for Spain' wrote to the Minister of the Interior and brother-in-law of Franco, Ramón Serrano Súñer, requesting that crosses be erected 'in all towns' across the country in tribute to 'the sacrifices whose exemplary nature we wish to perpetuate'.[48] No effort was too great to put new cultural references of the 'Spain of Victory' on the urban map. Such thinking must have guided the municipal council of Granada when it decided to withdraw a penalty imposed on a group of men for not complying with the obligatory Sunday rest while constructing the 'cross of the fallen'. In the mayor's opinion, the inspector who had imposed the fine had not understood that, on top of the aforementioned obligations, there were the 'patriotic aims' that justified uninterrupted work on such projects.[49]

Although renationalization policies were not mechanisms of formal social control (in the sense that their opposition or transgression could imply punishment), we can still consider them as informal instruments of social control.[50] A report on Francoist Spain made in 1938 indicated that fines were imposed 'daily' for 'incidents of civilians refusing to salute, stand up or remove their hat in the streets, cafes, cinemas, etc., when national hymns were played'.[51] Carrying out these small acts of resistance was, in a way, a means of fighting for spaces and their meaning. The appearance of 'subversive signs' or leftist and Republican symbols on public roads was probably one of the most frequent examples of this. In January 1938, the small town of Barruecopardo (Salamanca) woke up to a graffiti message in chalk spelling out 'Long live Communism' in the town centre.[52] In May 1946, the authorities of the province of Alicante informed their superiors that flags in Republican colours had been unfurled over the seats of the Ideal cinema.[53] Most likely, these actions were organized by the anti-Franco opposition. However, it is hard to pinpoint the motives that inspired other acts. In 1945, two women from the small village of Venta de los Agramaderos (Jaén) took the red-and-yellow flag fluttering over the entrance of the town's school and threw it to the ground.[54] A few years earlier, in May 1940, two female residents of the town of Cabrillas (Salamanca) were asked by the mayor to explain why they had removed the 'patriotic signs' on the façade of the town hall. Both noted that their actions had not been malicious, but that they had indeed removed the signs because they thought that the façade was 'not very presentable'.[55] We do not know if they were telling the truth or feigning innocence to avoid possible punishment, but the incident highlights the complexity of local dynamics that surrounded space, its social control and its resignification by part of society.

These same complexities are exposed if we analyse the control over morality launched by the Franco regime and its relationship with space. In the first place, because moral control transcends the exceptional and pervades the routines and habitual actions that occur in the realm of everyday life. Second, because the persecution of actions classified as immoral was not exclusively aimed at destroying Republican influence, but could undermine long-standing traditions, customs and community habits. And, third, because moral control affected both the public and the private, highlighting the artificiality of the division between the two spaces. Taking into account, moreover, the enormous range of attitudes and behaviours that could be considered immoral by the regime, we must consider moral control as a key element in the establishment of a certain normativity – particularly regarding gender roles – and as a fundamental platform for regulating behaviours in everyday settings.[56]

As in the political sphere, the initial premise that inspired the discourses and policies aimed at controlling morality was the conviction that Spanish society had undergone an unprecedented process of de-Christianization during the Second Republic. It was quite common for the hierarchies of the Church to affirm in their homilies and pastorals that the secularizing policies and moral laxity of the Republican period constituted one of the fundamental causes of the conflict that began in 1936. 'Our war', stated the cardinal primate of Spain, Isidro Gomá, 'could well be an instrument of the justice of God with which he tried to cleanse us of our collective misery, to reward the good with justice and to give the bad what they deserve'. The 'absence of God', he added, 'has caused the unhinging of our lives and our social customs'.[57] Likewise, the Francoist authorities noted the decline they observed on the moral level. In 1938, the civil governor of Santa Cruz de Tenerife reported with alarm the state of 'public amorality' on the island, stating that it was 'difficult to put back on track'. In his opinion, one of the causes of this situation was the 'influence exerted by the liberal and Marxist period'. Similar impressions were shared by the Huesca authorities, for whom the 'occupation of numerous country estates by the reds' had, amongst other consequences, 'very serious effects on morals'.[58]

In light of this situation, the Franco dictatorship developed a whole project of regeneration and re-Christianization that covered many areas. Social purification of a greater intensity was required in those areas especially afflicted by the 'scourge of Marxism'. This was the case of the towns that had remained in Republican territory during the war, such as, for example, that 'modern Jerusalem' represented by Madrid[59] or cities such as Albacete, where the 'pernicious influence of the International Brigades and the Marxist hordes' had been – in the opinion of the authorities – the main cause of 'moral laxity and prevailing bad habits'.[60] In the latter, the civil governor decided to implement a 'moral sanitation policy', regulating the hours of bars, cafes and taverns, prohibiting the sale of alcoholic beverages after 11.00 pm, exercising 'active surveillance of public decency', punishing 'blasphemy severely' and prohibiting 'unauthorized begging and peddling by children and women'.[61]

Similarly, the intensity of social regeneration was greater in the towns or neighbourhoods considered to be bastions of the Left or hubs of support for Republican ideas. The working-class neighbourhoods of Malaga came to be purified with holy water to cleanse them of the 'traces of Marxism'.[62] Similar initiatives took place in the Granada neighbourhood of the Albaicín. In the words of the archbishop of the diocese, the Albaicín had to be 'redeemed from godless Marxism and its terrible deeds'.[63] To achieve this, acts of atonement were organized, including expiatory processions through the streets and ceremonies to replace crosses and religious niches on the urban map. The inauguration of the restored Cruz de la Rauda in this neighbourhood became a symbol of the new regime's colonization of space. But it was also understood as a mechanism of punishment and social control. The authorities had decided that it was those who had destroyed the cross who should rebuild it, 'thus healing the damage caused to Spain' and making themselves worthy of the 'clemency and sublime prerogative of forgiveness'.[64]

Without a doubt, public space had to be the main reflection of the new morality that was trying to prevail. The political 'eye' of the regime represented by Falangists, civil guards, police or parish priests carefully scrutinized social attitudes and behaviours and did not hesitate to denounce any observed deviations.[65] But moral control went beyond individuals considered 'dangerous' or 'hostile' and involved the whole of society. Hence, other institutions emerged, such as the Municipal Boards of Sanitation and Good Customs (Juntas Municipales de Saneamiento y Buenas Costumbres), which had to account for the 'religious and moral status' of towns, control leisure, repress blasphemy, redirect the behaviour of young people in public places or ensure children's attendance at school. Made up of people of 'good character' belonging to the immediate environment over which they had control, these organizations had functions closely linked to the everyday space of the people, such as the upkeep of façades, cleaning of portals, neighbourhood surveillance, organization of festivities, honouring of local traditions or participation in religious ceremonies.[66] Along with these and other institutions, we must not forget that some ordinary citizens were also willing to keep watch over public morality. This was confirmed by a day labourer from the town of Villena (Alicante) when in the bar of 'Perico el Cafetero' he uttered 'blasphemies against God and other images' in the presence of other customers. One of them went to the authorities and denounced him for this act.[67] The streets and shops were particularly controlled places, but in small communities the lines separating the private sphere were often blurred. After learning that a couple from the town of Loja (Granada) lived together, a neighbour decided to send them a letter reminding them of the advisability of getting married. In Almería, another man decided to denounce two of his neighbours 'for the benefit of morals and the neighbourhood', accusing them of scandalizing people for allowing 'mujeres de mal vivir y de pésima nota' (women of vice and terrible character) to meet at their homes. In that same province, from the town of Roquetas de Mar, the secretary of the Catholic Action organization sent a letter to the *Yugo* newspaper complaining about the moral status of the town and the entry of minors into cinemas to watch 'immoral shows'.[68]

Many agents were involved in inspecting the lives of neighbours, from municipal organizations and political authorities to religious associations and ordinary citizens, including night watchmen or the doormen of buildings.[69] Despite this, and even in the immediate post-war period when control and surveillance were tighter, certain areas not colonized by the regime still remained, such as family units, places of leisure and recreation, festivities or cultural associations.[70] These spaces were subjected to a process of constant resignification driven by attitudes and strategies that sometimes appeared to be forms of resistance, and other times were merely moral or social transgressions. Official authorities and community members did not always agree in their perception of such acts. Attempts to ensure that certain popular celebrations prohibited by the regime persisted, to hold dances without authorization from the authorities or to carry out acts officially considered improper, blasphemous and immoral in the public sphere were all part of these daily struggles for the control of space.[71] Control was in this sense as stifling as it was limited and, consequently, space itself was disputed and negotiated in practice. Everyday spaces had limits and boundaries that were recognizable and recognized, but life within was not experienced exclusively in terms of personal domination and subordination.[72] Intermediate realities, disputes, negotiations, compromises, tacit agreements and digressions were the most common features of these spaces inhabited by ordinary citizens.

Post-war communities as spaces of social control

The physical violence deployed by the Francoist state against its enemies was atrocious and ruthless. It left a traumatic mark not only on the lives of those who experienced it and the lives of their families, but also on specific locations: ditches, mass graves, ravines or prisons that must be included in our analyses.[73] Although not with the same intensity, other memories have survived over the years. The memory of the hunger suffered during the 1940s, the memory of the loss of freedoms, and the officially promulgated memory of 'peace' and 'progress' left by the Franco regime are just a few examples. In this way, the memory of Franco's violence and the spaces associated with it cannot be reduced to physical and bloody manifestations, since other types of violence and various forms of social control were also essential in shaping many individual and collective experiences during the post-war period.

This chapter has tried to contribute to the study of these spaces from the realm of everyday life, where we can better observe the complexities that characterized the relationships with violence, social control and, ultimately, state institutions. Chronologically, this chapter has focused on the analysis of post-war communities. This was the period in which the elimination of Republican space and the establishment of the 'New State' took place, and consequently, when violence and social control were more intense for the population. Despite this, it would be worth examining the evolution of these spaces and the role that violence and social control played in them to deepen our knowledge of phenomena that took place later on. Attempts to organize the rural world through agrarian colonization policies developed during the 1950s, the tightened control of public morality as a result of the expansion of tourism and the arrival of foreign cultural influences, or the violent dispute over certain spaces – neighbourhoods, universities, factories, parishes, etc. – during late Francoism could be areas to explore from these same perspectives. Although alternative spaces and areas of relative freedom emerged in the face of the dictatorship during the 1950s and, above all, the 1960s, we cannot forget the regime's capacity to continue imposing regulations and norms on people's lives, the segregationist intentions that shaped 'developmentalist' policies or the 'return' of violence to the public space in the throes of the dictatorship, symbolized by police charges and states of emergency.[74] Violence, the control of space and the struggle to redefine it were elements that survived Francoism itself.

Notes

1   See Henri Lefebvre, *La producción del espacio* (Madrid: Capitán Swing, [1973] 2013); Edward W. Soja, *Postmodern Geographies: The Reassertion of Space in Critical Social Theory* (London: Verso, 1989).

2   Lefebvre, *La producción*, 14.
3   Nil Santiáñez, *Topographies of Fascism: Habitus, Space and Writing in Twentieth-Century Spain* (Toronto: University of Toronto Press, 2013), 6–7.
4   Barney Warf and Santa Arias (eds), *The Spatial Turn: Interdisciplinary Perspectives* (London: Routledge, 2009); Alf Lüdtke, 'What is the History of Everyday Life and Who are Its Practitioners?', in *The History of Everyday Life: Reconstructing Historical Experiences and Ways of Life*, ed. Alf Lüdtke (Princeton, NJ: Princeton University Press, 1995), 14.
5   Quote taken from Vicente Casals and Quim Bonastra, 'El control del espacio y los espacios de control', in *Espacios de control y regulación social. Ciudad, territorio y poder (siglos XVII–XX)*, ed. Vicente Casals and Quim Bonastra (Barcelona: Ediciones de Serbal, 2014), 9–12. See also Horacio Capel, 'El control social y el territorial como mecanismos de dominación y de regulación', in *Espacios de control y regulación social. Ciudad, territorio y poder (siglos XVII–XX)*, ed. Vicente Casals and Quim Bonastra (Barcelona: Ediciones de Serbal, 2014), 13–18. On the danger of the 'overgeneralization' of the concept of 'social control', see Pedro Oliver Olmo, 'El concepto de control social en la historia social: estructuración del orden y respuestas al desorden', *Historia Social* 51 (2005): 73–91.
6   David D. Atkinson, 'Totalitarianism and the Street in Fascist Rome', in *Images of the Street: Planning, Identity and Control in Public Space*, ed. Nicholas R. Fyfe (London: Routledge, 1998), 13–30; John Agnew, '"Ghosts of Rome": The Haunting of Fascist Efforts at Remaking Rome as Italy's Capital City', *Annali d'Italianistica* 28 (2010): 179–98; Aristotle Kallis, 'The "Third Rome" of Fascism: Demolitions and the Search for a New Urban Syntax', *Journal of Modern History* 84, no. 1 (2012): 40–79.
7   Some examples in Zira Box, 'Paisaje y nacionalismo en el primer franquismo', *Hispanic Research Journal of Iberian and Latin American Studies* 17, no. 2 (2016), 123–40; César Rina Simón, *La construcción de la memoria franquista en Cáceres. Héroes, espacio y tiempo para un nuevo Estado (1936–1941)* (Cáceres: Universidad de Extremadura, 2012); and Carlos Sambricio, 'Urbanism in the Early Years of Francoism', in *Urbanism and Dictatorship: An European Perspective*, ed. Harald Bodenschatz, Piero Sassi and Max W. Guerra (Berlin: Bau Verlag, 2015), 117–34.
8   Diane Y. Ghirardo, '"Città Fascista": Surveillance and Spectacle', *Journal of Contemporary History* 31, no. 2 (1996): 347–72 at 347.
9   Santiáñez, *Topographies of Fascism*, 12.
10 Francisco Ferrándiz, *El pasado bajo tierra. Exhumaciones contemporáneas de la guerra civil* (Madrid: Anthropos, 2014); Zahira Aragüete Toribio, *Producing History in the Spanish Civil War Exhumations* (New York: Palgrave Macmillan, 2017), 177–210.
11 *El Norte de Castilla*, 25 September 1936: 1.
12 Antonio Míguez Macho, 'Un pasado negado. Lugares de violencia y lugares de memoria del golpe, la guerra civil y el franquismo', *Confluenze. Rivista di Studi Iberoamericani* 10, no. 2 (2018): 127–51, at 131–3.

13 Archivo Histórico Provincial de Salamanca (AHPS), 'caja 194, carpeta 2, Expedientes y comunicaciones ordinarias', 1936.
14 Archivo de la Guerra Civil Española (AGCE), 'caja 727, Informe del Servicio de Información Especial sobre Galicia', 1 February 1937.
15 Véase Javier Rodrigo, *Cautivos. Campos de concentración en la España franquista, 1936–1941* (Barcelona: Crítica, 2005); José Ignacio Álvarez Fernández, *Memoria y trauma en los testimonios de la represión franquista* (Barcelona: Anthropos, 2007), 160–3.
16 Helen Graham, *The Spanish Republic at War* (Cambridge: Cambridge University Press, 2002), 117; Lourenzo Fernández Prieto and Antonio Miguez Macho, 'Nomes e voces: balance, preguntas e interpretaciones. Las huellas del golpe de estado en Galicia', in *Otras miradas sobre golpe, guerra y dictadura: historia para un pasado incómodo*, ed. Lourenzo Fernández Prieto and Aurora Artiaga Rego (Madrid: La Catarata, 2014), 80–110; Gutmaro Gómez Bravo and Jorge Marco, *La obra del miedo Violencia y sociedad en la España franquista (1936–1950)* (Madrid: Península, 2011), 72–4.
17 David Harvey, *Cosmopolitanism and the Geographies of Freedom* (New York: Columbia University Press, 2009), 134; Stefan Kipfer, 'How Lefebvre Urbanized Gramsci: Hegemony, Everyday and Difference', in *Space, Difference and Everyday Life: Reading Henri Lefebvre*, ed. Kanishka Goonewardena, Stefan Kipfer, Richard Milgrom and Christian Schmid (New York: Routledge, 2008), 199–200.
18 Claudio Hernández Burgos, 'Les dynamiques locales et quotidiennes de la répression Franquiste (1936–1950)', *Vingtième Siècle* 127 (2015): 197–209.
19 Quote taken from: Slavoj Žižek, *Violence: Six Sideways Reflections* (New York: Picador, 2008), 9. See also Alejandro Pérez Olivares, 'Vigilar y controlar. Espacio público, espacio privado y violencia en el Madrid ocupado (1938–1940)', in *Tiempo de dictadura. Experiencias cotidianas durante la guerra, el franquismo y la democracia*, ed. Gloria Román Ruiz and Juan A. Santana González (Granada: Editorial de la Universidad de Granada, 2019), 63–87.
20 Courtney J. Campbell, 'Space, Place and Scale: Human Geography and Spatial History in Past and Present', *Past & Present* 239, no. 1 (2018): 23–45.
21 Michael Wildt, 'Review of Timothy Snyder's, *Bloodlands. Europe between Hitler and Stalin*', *Kritika: Explorations in Russia and Eurasian History* 14, no. 1 (2013): 197–206, at 205. Available online: http://defendinghistory.com/wp-content/uploads/2013/03/Wildts-review-of-Bloodlands-in-Exlporations-Winter-2013.pdf (accessed 30 June 2020).
22 Andrew Herscher and Anooradha Iyer Siddiqi, 'Spatial Violence', *Architectural Theory Review* 19, no. 3 (2014): 269–77.
23 Freek Colombijn, 'The Production of Urban Space by Violence and its Aftermath in Jakarta and Kota Ambon, Indonesia', *Ethnos: Journal of Anthropology* 83, no. 1 (2018): 58–79, at 59–60.

24 Andy Merrifield, 'Public Space: Integration and Exclusion in Urban Life', *City Analysis of Urban Trends, Culture, Theory, Policy, Action* 1, nos. 5–6 (1996): 57–72.
25 *Ideal*, 1 April 1937; *Patria*, 1 November 1938. For the experience of the defeated in these institutions, see Ángela Cenarro, *La sonrisa de Falange. Auxilio Social en la Guerra y en la posguerra* (Barcelona: Crítica, 2005), 145–74.
26 Miguel Ángel Del Arco Blanco, 'Las cruces de los caídos: instrumento nacionalizador en la cultura de la victoria', in *No solo miedo. Actitudes políticas y opinión popular bajo la dictadura franquista, 1936–1976*, ed. Miguel Ángel del Arco Blanco, Miguel Ángel del Arco and Claudio Hernández (Granada: Comares, 2013), 65–82; Nuala Johnson, 'Cast in Stone: Monuments, Geography, and Nationalism', *Environment and Planning D: Society and Space* 13 (1995), 51–65, at 52.
27 'Inauguración de la Cruz de los Caídos en Villanueva', *Patria*, 1 April 1942: 4.
28 Archivo Histórico Provincial de Alicante (AHPA), 'Gobierno Civil, 02334.001', Parte de Villajoyosa, 22 June 1940.
29 Archivo de la Real Chancillería de Granada (ARCHG), 'Audiencia Provincial, Libro 1096, Sentencia 26', 22 August 1938.
30 The examples in AGCE, Expedientes. Visitas a frentes, Información relativa a distintas áreas geográficas, Servicio de Información especial, 1937; and Carlos Gil Andrés, *Lejos del Frente. La Guerra Civil en la Rioja Alta* (Barcelona: Crítica, 2006), 218–19.
31 Peter Anderson, 'In the Interests of Justice? Grass-roots Prosecution and Collaboration in Francoist Military Trials, 1939–1945', *Contemporary European History* 18, no. 1 (2009): 25–44; and Julio Prada Rodríguez, *La España masacrada, La represión franquista de guerra y posguerra* (Madrid: Alianza, 2010), 200–2 and 361–2.
32 Quoted in Encarnación Barranquero Texeira, 'Mujeres malagueñas en la represión franquista a través de las fuentes escritas y orales', *Historia Actual Online*, no. 12 (2007): 85–94, at 89.
33 Quoted in Santiago Vega Sombría, *La política del miedo. El papel de la represión en el franquismo* (Barcelona: Crítica, 2011), 248.
34 Martí Marín i Corbera, 'Franquismo e inmigración interior: el caso de Sabadell (1939–1960)', *Historia Social* 56 (2006): 131–52.
35 Archivo Histórico Provincial de Ávila (AHPAV), 'Gobierno Civil, caja 95, Informe de la Delegación de Seguridad Interior y Orden Público de Ávila', 1 August 1937.
36 Cases in Carlos Gil Andrés, 'La zona gris en la España azul. La violencia de los sublevados en la Guerra Civil', *Ayer* 76 (2009): 115–41, at 128–9; and Ana Cabana, *La derrota de lo épico* (Valencia: Publicacions de la Universitat de València, 2013), 265.
37 AHPAV, 'Gobierno Civil, caja 95, Escrito de la Comisión de Incautación de Bienes (Ávila)', 16 July 1938.

38   Ernesto Verdeja, 'Moral Bystander and Mass Violence', in *New Directions in Genocide Research*, ed. Adam Jones (Abingdon: Routledge, 2011), 153–67.
39   A testimony in Ian Gibson, *The Assassination of Federico Garcia Lorca* (London: Penguin, 1983), 125–7.
40   Andrés, 'La zona gris en la España azul', 115–16; Antonio Míguez Macho (ed.), *Ni verdugos ni víctimas actitudes sociales ante la violencia del franquismo a la Dictadura Argentina* (Granada: Comares, 2016); Gutmaro Gómez Bravo, *Geografía humana de la represión franquista. Del golpe a la guerra de ocupación* (Barcelona: Cátedra, 2017), 25–8.
41   Pérez Olivares, 'Vigilar', 79–80.
42   Carmen González Martinez and Manuel Ortiz Heras, 'Control social y control policial en la dictadura franquista', *Historia del Presente* 9 (2007): 27–48, at 28.
43   Quote from Juan De Córdoba, *Estampas y reportajes de la retaguardia* (Sevilla: Ediciones Españolas, 1939), 133. On the alterations in public space during the Republican period, see Rafael Cruz, *En el nombre del pueblo. República, rebelión y guerra en la España de 1936* (Madrid: Siglo XXI, 2006), 50–63. See also Michael Richards, *After the Civil War: Making Memory and Re-Making Spain since 1936* (Cambridge: Cambridge University Press, 2013), 100–3.
44   Quoted in Francisco Casares, *25 comentarios* (Tolosa: Unión Gráfica, 1940), 12.
45   Lourenzo Fernández Prieto, 'Represión franquista y desarticulación social en Galicia. La destrucción de la organización societaria campesina 1936–1942', *Historia Social* 15 (1993): 49–65; and Fernando Molina Aparicio, '"La reconstrucción de la nación". Homogeneización cultural y nacionalización de las masas en la España franquista', *Historia y política* 38 (2017): 23–56.
46   Archivo Histórico Municipal de Granada (AHMG), 'Actas de la Comisión Municipal Permanente', 2 November 1937.
47   AHPS, 'Gobierno Civil, caja 191/6, Expedientes y comunicaciones ordinarias', 31 October 1936.
48   Archivo General de la Administración (AGA), 'Cultura, Caja 21/5371, Carta al camarada D. Ramón Serrano Suñer', 19 June 1938.
49   AHMG, 'Respuesta de la corporación a informe de infracción de trabajo en la Cruz de los Caídos', 27 June 1938.
50   On the division of formal and informal social control, see Olmo, 'El concepto de control social', 91.
51   AGCE, 'caja 722, Servicio de Información Especial Estratégico, Boletín de Propaganda del SIEE', 15 March 1938.
52   AHPS, 'Caja 194, carpeta 2, Expedientes y comunicaciones ordinarias, 1938, Aparición de letreros subversivos', 21 January 1938.
53   AHPA, 'Gobierno Civil, 03465.001, Partes e informes, Lanzamiento de banderas en el cine Ideal', 1 May 1946.

54 Quoted in Gloria Román Ruiz, 'La vida cotidiana en el mundo rural de Andalucía Oriental' (MA diss., Universidad de Granada, 2018), 153.
55 AHPS, 'Gobierno Civil, caja 188, carpeta 3, Carta del Jefe local de FET de las JONS de Cabrillas sobre la eliminación de letreros patrióticos', 24 May 1940.
56 Ian Winchester, 'Constructing Normativity: A Historiographical Essay on the Codification and Regulation of Gender and Sexuality in Franco's Spain', *Bulletin of Spanish and Portuguese Historical Studies* 42, no. 2 (2017): 104–19.
57 Isidoro Gomá, *La Cuaresma de España* (Pamplona: Gráficas Bescansa, 1937), 10 and 19.
58 AGA, 'Gobernación, caja 44/2792, Memoria del Gobierno Civil de Santa Cruz de Tenerife', 1938; and 'caja 44/02791, Memoria del Gobierno Civil de Huesca', 1938.
59 Quote from *ABC*, 4 April 1939: 2. See also Olivia Muñoz Rojas, 'Falangist Visions of a Veo-imperial Madrid', *Journal of War and Cultural Studies* 2, no. 3 (2009): 335–52; and Alejandro Pérez Olivares, 'La victoria bajo control. Ocupación, orden público y orden social del Madrid franquista' (MA diss., Universidad Complutense de Madrid, 2017), 333–5.
60 AGA, 'Gobernación, caja 44/02790, Memoria del Gobierno Civil de Albacete', 1939.
61 Ibid.
62 Adela Alfonsí, 'The Recatholization of Málaga, 1937–1966: Church and State in the Spanish Postwar' (MA diss., University of Adelaide, 1998), 60–80.
63 *Ideal*, 16 April 1937: 4.
64 *Ideal*, 27 September 1936. See also Richard Cleminson and Claudio Hernández Burgos, 'The Purification of Vice: Early Francoism, Moral Crusade, and the Barrios of Granada, 1936–1951', *Journal of Spanish Cultural Studies* 16 (2015): 95–114.
65 Ramón García Piñeiro, 'Boina, bonete y tricornio. Instrumentos de control campesino en la Asturias franquista (1937–1977)', *Historia del Presente* 3 (2004): 45–64, at 47; and Conxita Mir, 'Justicia civil y control moral de la población marginal en el franquismo de posguerra', *Historia Social* 37 (2000): 53–72.
66 AHMG, 2403.008, 'Reglamento de Juntas Municipales de Barrio de Granada', 1939. See also González Martinez and Ortiz Heras, 'Control social y control policial', 30–2.
67 AHPA, 'Gobierno Civil, 02334.001, Partes diarios de ocurrencia facilitados por la Guardia Civil, 1939–1940, Acto subversivo en Villena', 21 October 1939.
68 These examples appear, respectively, in ARCHG, 'Juzgado Municipal de Loja, caja 23659, Actos de conciliación', 1946–1947; Gloria Román Ruiz, 'Custodios de la moral. Control socio-moral y sanción popular en el mundo rural altoandaluz durante el franquismo', *Pasado y Memoria*, no. 21 (2020): 131–54; and Óscar Rodríguez Barreira, *Migas con miedo. Prácticas de resistencia al primer franquismo, Almería, 1939–1953* (Almería: Editorial de la Universidad de Almería, 2008), 295–6.

69 For example, Daniel Oviedo Silva and Alejandro Pérez Olivares, '¿Un tiempo de silencio? Porteros, inquilinos y fomento de la denuncia en el Madrid ocupado', *Studia Histórica. Historia Contemporánea*, no. 34 (2016): 301–31.
70 Kyu-Hyum Kim, 'Total War Mobilisation and the Transformation of the National Public Sphere in Japan, 1931–1945', in *Mass Dictatorship and Modernity*, ed. Kyu-Hyum Kim, Michael Schoenhals and Yong-Woo Kim (New York: Palgrave Macmillan, 2013), 117–42, at 123–4.
71 See Cabana, *La derrota de lo épico*, 251–2; Lucía Prieto Borrego, *Mujer, moral y franquismo. Del velo al bikini* (Málaga: Universidad de Málaga, 2018), 47–52.
72 Paul Corner, 'Collaboration Complicity and Evasion under Italian Fascism', in *Everyday Life in Mass Dictatorship: Collusion and Evasion*, ed. Alf Lüdtke (New York: Palgrave Macmillan, 2015), 75–93, at 88.
73 As proposed in Estela Schindel and Pamela Colombo (eds), *Space and the Memories of Violence: Landscapes of Erasure, Disappearance and Exception* (New York: Palgrave Macmillan, 2014).
74 See Inbal Ofer, *Claiming the City and Contesting the State: Squatting, Community Formation and Democratization in Spain (1955–1986)* (London: Routledge, 2017).

7

Memory alephs: The symbolization of violence through places where 'Nothing Ever Happens'

Aldara Cidrás

Memory alephs and the unspeakable

The memory of a civil war's endless violence is the memory of hell. And hell – intangible, ethereal, penetrating – has no place: it occupies all spaces, both public and private. As Mephistopheles revealed to Faust in Marlowe's famous work, hell is *in the entrails*: 'Where we are tortured and remain forever. Hell hath no limits, nor is circumscribed.'[1] Hell, translated into fear, inhabits every street, every house, every body. It is not limited to civil government buildings overtaken by the military or centres of confinement and torture. Necropolitics – of which war is its apotheosis – goes beyond physical spaces, permeating all aspects of people's lives. The memory of the civil war is thus the memory of a place without limits, of a hell that is everywhere.

In this chapter, I will use an analytical approach to study the mechanisms of the symbolization of violence through widespread accounts that gather diverse memories of – and also transcend – the idea of event and place. To describe these mechanisms, I will propose the concept of the *memory aleph*. We will thus see, based on assumptions taken from the Spanish case, two phenomena. The first relates to how the memory of wartime suffering was constructed and transmitted by privileging incidents confined to specific spaces, even when these incidents were not necessarily the bloodiest. The second phenomenon concerns how these events transcended their episodic nature to express the atmosphere of violence and the terror of the entrails: to narrate the unspeakable. In other words, we will study how certain events came to represent the entire conflict, thus enabling its narrative transmission. Moreover, through metonymy, the cities in which such events took place came to symbolize the indelible impression of the violence of the coup and the war in the collective imagination.

In Borges's eponymous tale, the Aleph is 'the only place on earth where all places are – seen from every angle, each standing clear, without any confusion or blending'.[2] Through an exercise in extrapolation, we can take the term and apply it to our aims by suggesting the existence of significative entities that we can call *memory alephs*. A memory aleph is the result of a mechanism of processing and codifying a plural, traumatic memory by unifying diverse accounts linked to places and events. Event and space, inseparably related, transcend themselves and symbolize something much broader than the occurrence or place itself. They act as key markers in the metanarrative that establishes a collective identity, driven by a disseminating agent of that memory. In other words, memory alephs are mnemohistorical figures – to use Jan Assmann's terminology[3] – that capture the process by which certain traumatic events *went beyond themselves* to represent both the *interior* and the *entirety* of the experience of tragedy. This occurs with the peculiarity that, through metonymy and as a way to enable its narrative transmission, the city or the space in which these events took place comes to symbolize all the pain and all the trauma in the collective imagination. As a product of collective memory, alephs are not static, but evolve according to the corresponding *volksgeist* and *zeitgeist* to adapt their function within the framework of a particular community united by mnemonic ties. That is to say, their morphology depends on the time and the social group keeping them alive, as well as on the group's worldview and how it uses its past.[4] Although their purpose is to establish a multifaceted idea in a particular time, as social constructs alephs can be revisited and rethought over the years, and updated based on new needs. Thus, even if it seems contradictory, the way to preserve the memory of a place without limits is to define it. A memory aleph is the place that unites all places, the event that gathers all events. It is not a physical space, but the mark that the signified-symbolization of a signifier-place leaves in the collective imagination, a site of mourning of social *ethos*. A memory aleph is a microcosm of a traumatic past.

In particular, the relationship between memory alephs and the memory sites that Nora discussed in his seminal work is clearly explicit. Although the concept popularized by the French author has often been understood as sites in the physical sense of the word – for example, the wall of a cemetery or a concentration camp – this is only a small part of what Nora included as sites of memory.[5] It is worth referring to the explanation that Nora gives in his prologue to better understand how, far from opposing the concept of *lieux de mémoire*, the aleph draws on and modulates it, acting on the one hand as a very specific mnemohistorical figure within the broad universe of memory sites. On the other hand, if we pay attention to the popularized – and also somewhat distorted – political use of Nora's concept, memory alephs and memory sites coincide in the compression of the symbolic economy of heritage and memory. But they do not allude to the same *significative entity*: even while operating within the same logic of the symbolic, in the aleph, the feature of *spatial representativeness* typical of the *lieu* is diminished, and with it, its corollary of *monumentality*. The *lieu* stimulates memory and fights the forgetfulness of what deserves to be remembered or celebrated: the monument to the distinguished military officer or the unknown soldier commemorate, in their singularity, the heroism that is attributed to all the combatants they represent. The aleph, on the other hand – and although it seems paradoxical – extolls a particular incident and avoids the perpetuation of the memory of singularity: on the contrary, it evokes the experience of shared trauma, of what did not take place precisely because it was ubiquitous. The strength of the aleph does not come from the singularity of the event but from the durability of its imprint, from the depth of the trauma produced by the offence and from the construction of the narrative around it. The aleph sheds light on the social role of memory, but also the institutional management of memory. Its potential to generate a broader historical narrative lies in and is constructed from another level: that of the ability to produce symbolic signifiers, intimately linked to the traces of pain, which enable the expression of the unspeakable.

Case studies: Guernica, Pontevedra, Badajoz and Belchite

The selection of these four case studies, as well as the order in which they will be analysed, responds to specific epistemological aims. Beyond the particular interest of the examples, all of them – with their differences and similarities – paradigmatically represent the multidimensionality of the violent phenomenon, as well as the utility and suitability of the conceptual proposal of the memory aleph. These examples are all characterized by a common element: they are set in small or medium-sized cities – between just under 4,000 and 42,000 inhabitants – which are, moreover, traditionally quiet and peaceful, the kinds of places *where nothing ever happens*. Guernica is the clearest example of the atrocious violence of total and modern warfare, of absolute destruction. Pontevedra, meanwhile, is an example of the omnipresent violence of the rearguard, made singular through the memory of a specific victim as a martyr. On the contrary, Badajoz is the massacre, in which the collective nature of extermination is more powerful than

Figure 7.1 Public rally of the 'Sección Femenina' (Women's Branch of Falange) in the small village of Cangas (Galicia, Spain) with children marching as soldiers, civil war years.

the names of the victims. And, finally, we close the circle with Belchite, another armed conflict, but of less sophisticated warfare than that of Guernica; it is also the only example of an aleph of the war's victors, which in turn allows us to delve into how their memory – uneasy with the fall of the dictatorship – has been reconverted towards a more democratic profile.

Guernica

What is left to say about Guernica, where, as Vicente Talón said in 1970, 'more tons of ink have fallen than bombs'?[6] As part of the northern military campaign, on 26 April 1937, the German Condor Legion and, to a much lesser extent, the

Italian Legionary Air Force – in collusion with the revolting army – carried out an air attack on the Biscayan town of Guernica, located about thirty kilometres from Bilbao. The offensive resulted in the partial destruction of the city, which at the time had a population of approximately 5,000. The number of fatalities has been estimated to be between 100 and more than 1,600, although the general consensus currently puts the figure at around 250 or 300 casualties.[7] Guernica was neither the first bombardment of the war nor the bloodiest of its time. Durango, also located in Biscay, had already been attacked by the Italian Air Force less than a month earlier, with a death toll not much less than Guernica's.[8] However, cases like the attack on Durango had hardly any national repercussions, and none at all at the international level. But Guernica was different. From the first moment it became one of those *événement monstrueux* that Nora discussed in 1972, its name being catapulted into history by the media.[9] Guernica attracted the attention of foreign journalists from the outset and thus, 'in very few days the very name of Guernica had become a more burning subject than the flames of its conflagration'.[10]

Gernika is a place of special symbolism for Basque nationalism. The Gernika tree is found in this historic village: next to this oak tree, since as early as the fourteenth century, individuals with the highest responsibility over the territory – from the ancient Lords of Biscay to the kings of Castile and, currently, the *lehendakari* – swore their allegiance to and respect of the Biscayan *fueros* (regional code of law) and, by extension, the Basque people. In the context of debates surrounding *fueros* in the nineteenth century, its defenders began to promote Gernika as a symbol of Basque self-government within the framework of a *fueros* system, reformed and constitutionalized within the Spanish liberal monarchy. Meanwhile, in 1851, the bard José María Iparraguirre sang and popularized the hymn *Gernikako Arbola*, permanently integrating the Gernika tree into the Basque cosmogony.[11] We can thus understand how, after the air attack on the town in 1937, Basque nationalism added a new layer to the collective imagination around Gernika. The bombing was presented as the clearest manifestation of the Spanish intent on extermination against the natural and traditional attributes of the Basque people, even when the bombardment had not been the first to be carried out in the Basque Country. At the same time, the fact that the tree had not been damaged during the conflict or that a large percentage of the population sympathized with the coup plotters was overlooked. And, although the physical attack had been perpetrated by German and Italian squadrons, responsibility was placed directly on Franco, who was thought to be punishing the Basque *gudaris* (soldiers) for having remained faithful to the Republic.

The multidimensionality of the case of Gernika becomes evident when we examine the role of the Carlists: traditionalists who supported upholding the *fueros* or Basque laws and who, as we know, had sided with the military coup plotters. But as staunch defenders of the *fueros*, the Gernika tree was also deeply symbolic for them. In fact, it was the Carlists who prevented the tree from being cut down by the Falangists once the city had been taken by the rebels, organizing a human ring of volunteers around it. However, with the Carlists' gradual loss of influence in the new Francoist state, such *fuero*-based traditionalism was reduced to a secondary role and merely ritualistic practice, with less ambiguous symbols, such as the annual celebrations in Montejurra. This enabled Gernika, as a site of Basque memory par excellence, to remain in the hands of nationalism.[12]

For its part, Republicanism took advantage of the fact that the bombing of Guernica had been carried out by foreign troops, as well as its international media coverage, to make the attack look like an internationalist struggle against fascism. In this way, Guernica almost immediately became part of the collective imagination of intellectuals and artists in solidarity with the Republican cause, who, in turn, launched a cultural output that materialized in every possible way, giving shape to the symbolism of Guernica. The most universally known of all these cultural manifestations is the oil painting created in 1937 by Pablo Picasso. *Guernica*, commissioned by the Republican government to be exhibited in the Spanish pavilion during the Paris International Exposition that same year, earned the following words from the then-prime minister Juan Negrín: 'The presence of the mural painted by Picasso is the propaganda equivalent for the Republic to a military victory on the front.'[13] In other words, the painting was thought of as an instrument of war on the discursive level, as a propaganda weapon as important as any military victory. This reveals not only the awareness that existed of the role of foreign propaganda in modern warfare, but also the Republic's early interest in constructing its account of resistance and martyrdom in the face of fascist horrors, using *Guernica* as a symbol. Moreover, *Guernica* is a symbol whose strength resonates in its ability to represent the harshness of war itself, whatever war it may be. In this way, *Guernica* was successfully constructed as a universally recognizable anti-war symbol and, through this symbol, Guernica has transcended as a city and event to become a memory aleph that is not only Basque or Spanish, but global. It has no borders: '[Guernica] is both Reims and Hiroshima.'[14]

The power of the Republic's discourse, intrinsically linked to Picasso's mural, would not decline even after its defeat in 1939. Quite the contrary: it would reach a mythical dimension by establishing a parallel between the expatriation of the Republican government in exile and *Guernica*, also 'exiled' to the Museum of Modern Art in New York. Exile, the suspension of the territorial nature of the nation, acts as a metaphor for the democracy and freedom stolen from Spain, but which would one day be recovered – a construct reinforced by Picasso's prohibition on the painting being moved to Spain during the dictatorship.[15] The culmination of this narrative was reached, finally, after Franco's death: in parallel, the country began its transition to democracy and arrangements were made to bring *Guernica* to Spain for good. Neither process was free of difficulties. But finally, in September 1981, the painting arrived for the first time in Madrid – 'not returned [...] something that had never been in Spain could hardly return to Spain'[16] – representing the end of the dictatorship and the political instability of the following years that crystallized in the coup d'état on 23 February 1981. Until 1995, the painting was protected by bulletproof glass, the epitome of the fragility of Spanish democracy. Currently, *Guernica* is in the Reina Sofía Museum in Madrid, freezing in time what was and never should have been, and what could have been and never was.

At the time, Basque nationalism did not attempt to incorporate *Guernica* in its national imaginary. It was not the symbol of its aleph. Faced with Negrín's flattering words, the painting met with deep rejection amongst those responsible for the Basque government as early as 1937, when the work was exhibited in Paris: rejection because Pablo Picasso was not amongst the Basque government's candidates for creating the work, as well as because the painting, too abstract, did not contain any explicit reference to Guernica beyond the name. The contempt that the work aroused both in the Basque commissioner, José María Uzelai, and in the *Lehendakari*, José Antonio Aguirre, was captured by the Basque nationalist press with statements as visceral as those of Uzelai when he said that Picasso, with his work, '[was] shitting on Guernica, on the Basque Country, on everything'.[17] However, with the arrival of democracy and *Guernica* in Spain, the permanent location of the painting in Madrid began to raise questions, as the work, due to its subject matter, could be considered the heritage of the Basque people. Nearly thirty years after its arrival in Spain, all requests for *Guernica* to return either temporarily or permanently to Guernica – with the slogan '*Guernica* Gernikara', or in other words, '*Guernica* to Gernika' – have been turned down due to the fragile state of the work, with claims that the move could have irreversible consequences. Nonetheless, it is still significant how different interpretations of the same aleph have finally converged on the same material object promoting its memory. Even the *abertzale* left – patriotic, of a pro-independence nature – has ended up accepting part of the Spanish narrative attached to Guernica.

Proof of this can be found in the setting of the *Acuerdo para un escenario de paz y soluciones democráticas* (Agreement for a scenario of peace and democratic solutions) or the Gernika Agreement (2010), where a wide range of Basque sovereignist political forces, including the independence movement, publicly asked ETA for a permanent ceasefire. During the event, held in the secondary school of the historic town, Picasso's painting presided over both the stage and the lectern. We thus see how, despite Basque nationalism's traditional identification of Gernika exclusively with the tree and the inalienable freedoms of the Basque people, Basque nationalism has ended up incorporating the most typical symbol of the narrative of Spanish Republicanism, assimilating its pacifist meaning. However, although there has been a convergence, to a greater or lesser extent, of the symbols of each narrative – that of Republicanism and that of Basque nationalism – the double significance of this memory aleph remains unchanged: for the former, the bombing of Guernica continues to represent the integrity of the Republic against the horrors of fascism; for the latter, Gernika is etched into nationalist social memory as one more example of the constant attacks on the freedoms of the Basque people.

Pontevedra

Pontevedra, capital of the Galician province of the same name, had just over 33,000 inhabitants in 1936. When the coup took place on 18 July, the military members stationed in the city sided with the insurrectionists. As a result, and despite the immediate civil mobilization of numerous political and social forces loyal to the legitimacy of the Republic, the coup plotters officially assumed local power on 21 July 1936. However, the rapid seizure of the city and the lack of a nearby war front – Galicia remained in the rearguard throughout the war – did not stop the new powers from unleashing brutal eliminationist violence against the civilian population.

Although outside the city limits, the memory of Pontevedra in 1936 is closely related to that of the San Simón islands, a small and uninhabited archipelago located in the Vigo estuary and about sixteen kilometres from the capital. The islands, which had served as a pilgrimage destination in the Middle Ages, a home to Franciscan monks in the modern era and a leper colony from the mid-nineteenth century, were used as a penal colony from 1936 to 1943. Following the coup d'état from 18 July, the areas controlled by the coup plotters began to fill up with an immense number of prisoners, until no room was left in conventional jails and makeshift prisons. Other spaces were then hurriedly prepared to serve as concentration camps, including the San Simón islands. In 1937, more than 1,200 inmates – most of them detained pre-emptively and without sentencing – lived on an island measuring about 270 by 130 metres on its main axes, which gives an idea of the harsh living conditions on San Simón. Even so, in 1938, by express orders of the Director General of Prisons, Máximo Cuervo, it was decided that the prison should be adapted as a concentration camp for prisoners over sixty years of age, due to the 'suitability of the climate' for them. More than 1,000 prisoners were then transferred from all over Spain to San Simón, bringing the total number of inmates to 2,500 and making survival on the island practically unbearable.[18]

In addition to San Simón and Pontevedra, the parish of A Caeira – belonging to the small town of Poio, bordering Pontevedra – would play a key role in the Galician account of the civil war, for reasons that we will see later. However, it is worth mentioning now that these three places form a kind of triangle of Galician memory of the coup violence. This is probably because most of the people who were arrested after the coup's victory in the capital ended up being transferred to the penal colony. But above all, it is due to the symbolism that the city of Pontevedra represents – and surpasses – through the figure of a very specific man: Alexandre Bóveda.

Alexandre Bóveda Iglesias was a well-known politician of the Galicianist Party and one of the most recognized faces of Galician nationalism, along with Alfonso Daniel Rodríguez Castelao, considered the father of Galicianism. Bóveda moved for professional reasons to Pontevedra in 1928, where he started a family and, as the collective memory recounts, led an *exemplary* life.[19] It is in this city where he met Castelao and other intellectuals linked to Galicianism, and, in 1930, he was invited to collaborate in the development of a draft bill for the Galician Statute of Autonomy. From this year on, his political role grew exponentially, as he co-founded the Galicianist Party (1931) and actively proselytized for the Statute of Autonomy until the campaign prior to the plebiscite, on 28 June 1936. With the military base of Pontevedra in favour of the coup on 18 July, control of the city government was seized and Bóveda, amongst others, was arrested and brought to justice. On 14 August 1936, a military court sentenced him to the death penalty, accusing him of having participated in the resistance to the uprising. In the summary trial, Bóveda said a few words in his defence that would turn him into a historical emblem of Galician nationalism:

> My natural homeland is Galicia. I love it fervently; I would never betray it. If the court understands that for this dear love the death penalty should be imposed on me, I will receive it as one more sacrifice for my homeland. I did my best for

Galicia and would do more if I could. If I can't, I would even like to die for my homeland. Under its flag I wish to be buried, if the court judges that I must be.[20]

On 17 August 1936, Alexandre Bóveda was executed by firing squad in A Caeira at the age of thirty-three. The death of Bóveda would become a fundamental episode within Galician nationalism, while he would be consecrated as a martyr for the national cause. Castelao, who managed to go into exile in Argentina thanks to his being in Madrid at the time of the coup, and as a leading figure of Galician nationalism until his death in 1950, would be the main person in charge of managing Bóveda's memory on a political level. As a multifaceted artist, he would introduce the figure of Bóveda into the collective imagination through various forms, the most important of which would be a painting – just as in the case of the Republican account of war and Picasso's *Guernica*. During the civil war, Castelao published several collections of engravings, such as *Galicia Mártir* or *Atila in Galicia*.[21] Both collections, made in Valencia in 1937, are reminiscent in many ways of Goya's drawings of the Spanish War of Independence (1808–1814), which were also reprinted in 1937 in the same city. In 1945, already in Buenos Aires, Castelao would adapt one of these engravings into an oil painting: *A derradeira leición do mestre*, based on engraving number six from *Galicia Mártir*. Both the engraving and the painting represent the same image of a man killed in a ditch and, beside him, two children crying. Like *Guernica*, nothing in the two-tone image indicates where the scene is taking place. It could be any bombing; it could be any execution: it could be anywhere in Spain. This all-encompassing nature makes the works – and the events they reproduce – universal. However, the 'teacher' that Castelao refers to is no schoolteacher, as we might think from seeing the children or the caption that accompanies the image: 'The teacher's last lesson.' The teacher, perfectly characterized and recognizable, is Alexandre Bóveda. The message that *A derradeira leición* transmits lends Bóveda a Christ-like aspect in a nationalist tone, under the idea that he died for his love of Galicia, and all Galicians should learn from what Bóveda has taught them. The moral and political example of the executed man make him a secular saint. His killing was not an end, but a necessary sacrifice for the liberation of the Galician people, the symbol of an upcoming resurrection that Castelao himself hinted was near in the caption of the adjacent engraving: 'It is not corpses that are buried but seeds.'[22] But, just as *Guernica* reached the peak of its own metanarrative when it was permanently brought to Spain in 1981, symbolizing the return of democracy to the country, *A derradeira leición* still remains in Buenos Aires, a metaphor for how Galicia has not yet achieved its national liberation.[23]

The undeniable power of this pictorial support in the discursive account of Galician nationalism and independence was followed by many other initiatives. Works such as *Alba de Groria* (1948), also by Castelao, or the hagiographic biography *Vida, paixón e norte de Alexandre Bóveda* (1972) by Xerardo Álvarez Gallego – Bóveda's brother-in-law – deepened the mythology of the executed man. Similarly, in an initiative supported by Castelao himself in the Galician Centre of Buenos Aires, since 1945 the anniversary of Bóveda's killing on 17 August has been commemorated as the *Día de Galiza Mártir*, in memory of all those who sacrificed their lives for the Galician homeland during the civil war. Although public tributes of this kind were banned in Spain during the dictatorship, this did not stop some from carrying out private tributes, such as leaving flowers on Bóveda's tomb in the San Amaro cemetery in Pontevedra. The emotional, intimate nature of these acts gained a political and activist dimension from 1977, when public – but unofficial – yearly ceremonies on 17 August in Pontevedra began to commemorate the Galician victims of the dictatorship.[24] In 1996, at the request of the Alexandre Bóveda Foundation and financed by popular subscription, a monument was placed at the site where Bóveda was executed to serve as a physical reminder of memory and to combat fears of forgetting.[25] Since then, acts for the Día de Galiza Mártir have been held there, turning the site of memory into one of those pilgrimage sites that are fundamental to the elaboration of any national narrative.

It is worth highlighting how the political tool designed by Castelao to canonize Bóveda has been successful and how its cultural production has fed the imagery of coup terror in Galicia, replacing history as a discourse.[26] Of the victims of violence perpetrated between 1936 and 1939, only a small number were Galicianists. However, nationalism has been able to monopolize and instrumentalize the memory of the civil war in Galicia, penetrating the collective imaginaries of even non-nationalists, who have assumed its narrative. In this way, through the meta-event of the killing of Alexandre Bóveda, Pontevedra – and its ramifications, such as San Simón or A Caeira – has been enshrined as a memory aleph of the coup violence in Galicia: the blood of the martyr had watered his land and, upon it, the seeds of national freedom would be reborn.

Badajoz

'I have just witnessed such a spectacle of devastation and dread that it will take time to fade from my eyes.'[27] With those words, the Portuguese journalist Mário Neves described on 15 August 1936 the brutal massacre of civilians that he had witnessed the previous night in Badajoz. On the 17th, he continued: 'I want to leave Badajoz, whatever the cost, as quickly as possible and solemnly promising myself that I will never return.'[28]

Badajoz, an Extremaduran city of about 42,000 inhabitants in 1936, is the provincial capital where the implementation of agrarian reform had the greatest impact during the Republican period. After the coup broke out, the Civil Guard of Badajoz declared itself in revolt twice: on 22 July and on 6 August. Part of the army officers were also sympathetic to the uprising, but the attitude of the pro-Republican commanders and the loyalty of other law enforcement agencies prevented the coup plotters from seizing local power. This gave Badajoz – unlike, for example, Pontevedra – nearly four weeks to prepare to defend itself against the imminent uprising, during which time the main right-wing figures of the city were jailed in the provincial prison. Although the capture of Badajoz would mean that the rebel army could connect the territories under its control in the north and in the south of the country, it was a risky bet strategically, as it represented a deviation from the final objective: Madrid. However, controlling Badajoz was necessary to ensuring that the rearguard was *disinfected*, one of the main unmoveable goals of the coup leaders. Thus, the column of troops coming from Seville, conquering and looting all towns in its path, reached Extremadura in early August. On the 7th, land and air bombing of the city began in order to undermine the morale of the civilian population and the military personnel stationed there, clearly showing the disparities between the defensive and offensive forces. Some people managed to escape by crossing the border with Portugal – just six kilometres from the city – but the Salazar dictatorship immediately returned them to the coup plotters. After a brief resistance, Badajoz fell on 14 August. Rebel troops entered the city under the command of Lieutenant Colonel Juan Yagüe – who would go down in history as 'the butcher of Badajoz' – and began a savage and systematic political purging of civilians with help from local Falangists. Residents were killed in cold blood and in broad daylight on the streets, or taken to makeshift detention centres, such as the bullring. Their belongings, taken.[29] Corpses piled up all over the city. One of the darkest chapters of the coup and the Spanish Civil War took place in the Badajoz bullring: armed in the stands with rifles and machine guns, coup troops killed an undetermined number of civilians trapped in the arena of the bullring. Some authors mention hundreds, although most say the number of fatalities was in the thousands. Whatever the exact figure, the number of deaths was such that between the 16th and 17th, cremation pyres were lit in front of the municipal cemetery, burning for hours and filling the city with a putrid stench, with smoke visible from several kilometres away.³⁰ In the words of the American journalist Peter Wyden, what happened in Badajoz '[was] something of a preview of Auschwitz'.³¹

As would happen later in Guernica, the presence of foreign correspondents in Badajoz allowed the international media to cover the massacre. Their testimonies all show the cruelty of the eliminationist practices inflicted on the civilian population, and they were the ones to give the first figures of the victims of the Badajoz massacre: between 600 and 4,000 people. Most of these victims, as we have seen, would have been killed in the bullring. Subsequent studies have shown that the total figure is probably much closer to the latter than to the former, which means that around 10 per cent of Badajoz's population was decimated during the capture of the city.³² Amongst the material produced by reporters, the images taken by René Brut stand out for their brutality, showing piles of charred corpses throughout the city. The Republic used the testimonies of journalists and the circulation of Brut's images to internationalize the conflict, but although it did horrify the public, it was not very successful in galvanizing support. In a lesser way, in the country's interior, the events of Badajoz were used as an excuse for violence against right-wingers in Republican Spain, such as the executions carried out in Madrid's Modelo prison by anarchist militiamen on 22 August. For their part, all the journalists who covered the capture of Badajoz would personally suffer later retaliation.³³ However, their contributions enabled the Badajoz massacre to find its place in the collective memory as an iconic reference to mass murder. Badajoz brought the threat of fascism into reality in August 1936. However, as we already know, eight months later the Republic would turn the bombing of Guernica into the axis of its story of resistance, leaving the case of Badajoz in the background.

For their part, the perpetrators counterattacked at the propagandist level, denying the high numbers of victims. The only exception would be Lieutenant Colonel Yagüe himself, who, according to correspondent John T. Whitaker's version, assured the journalist that 4,000 people were killed during the takeover of the city:

> Of course we shot them. ... What do you expect? Was I supposed to take 4,000 reds with me as my column advanced, racing against time? Was I expected to turn them loose in my rear and let them make Badajoz red again?³⁴

But aside from Yagüe's alleged statements, the dictatorship's official version was always to lower the victims to a few hundred people and justify its action as a response to a presumed *red terror*. From then on, they also regulated the presence of journalists in captured cities and put in place a system to filter documents that would grow in time and, ultimately, prevent current investigators from obtaining more reliable data on executions. It is on this basis that the Franco regime built a denialist account of the Badajoz massacre, calling it a 'legend', ignoring its existence or treating it as a mere military operation of no importance. Starting in the 1960s, some voices of Francoist historiography – in line with the regime's discourse in the 'XXV Years of Peace' campaign – began to treat what had happened in Badajoz differently, alleging that excesses had been committed by both sides in Badajoz due to the lack of control during the first months of the war, and that it was thus better to forget the past.

The arrival of democracy has allowed and encouraged the multiplication of investigations into the victims of the coup and the civil war, including in Extremadura. However, in 2000, the municipal corporation chaired by the Popular Party authorized the demolition of the old bullring that had served as a concentration and extermination camp in order to proceed with the construction of a conference centre. A few years later, in 2009, the local government of the Popular Party ordered the re-walling of the city cemetery: a place where victims had been shot during the war, and where the indentations of bullets in the wall were still visible. Even though both initiatives provoked heavy criticism amongst historians and associations for the recovery of historical memory, they were carried out in the end. Thus, Badajoz lost its most notorious physical sites of memory, believing that the voices of the past can be silenced with bricks. The place that, eighty-four years ago, raised awareness around the world of the horrors of fascism is today in danger of being nothing more than a hazy memory, probably alien to much of the population. This demonstrates, once again, that without a disseminating agent to take responsibility for their transmission, memory alephs can cease to fulfil their function and fall into oblivion.

Belchite

Unlike the previous examples, at the core of a peripheral nationalist and/or Spanish Republican narrative, the case of Belchite is special: it is an aleph of the collective Francoist imaginary, which joins other deeply rooted cases such as the Alcázar of Toledo or Paracuellos, and shares the objective of magnifying the feats of the coup plotters in what they called the 'national crusade'. It therefore falls within what François-Xavier Nénard and David El Kenz conceptualized as a 'perpetrator memory site'.[35]

At the time of the coup, Belchite, about fifty kilometres from Zaragoza, was a small rural community of about 4,000 inhabitants. Traditionally conservative, left-wing Republicanism had been gaining ground since the early 1920s, without provoking any conflict that could foreshadow what would happen after the coup. Belchite was, in short, a 'town like any other in the Spanish countryside'.[36] However, the town would experience up to three waves of violent purging – carried out, chronologically, by rebel troops, Republicans and rebels once again – in just a year and a half from 18 July 1936 due to the porosity of the nearby war front. The first of these waves would take place in the same summer of 1936, when between 100 and 300 people were killed by the coup plotters after they seized local power. A year later, in August 1937, Belchite was surrounded by Republican troops in an attempt to move the Ebro front to the west. The rebel troops managed to resist the attack for a month thanks to Italian-German air reinforcements and the belief that they would receive the reinforcement of more troops soon. However, on 6 September, the few surviving soldiers stationed there broke through the Republican siege to flee to Zaragoza, leaving a large number of civilians in the town. Initially seen as a shameful retreat, what was initially known as 'the Belchite disaster' was quickly renamed by the coup administration as 'the heroic feat of Belchite'. Taking advantage of the anniversary and the similarity of the feat with that of the Alcázar, all the tools were put in place to spread the propaganda message that the incipient Francoist state wanted to transmit: the defeat of Belchite had been, in reality, a moral and strategic victory, and the massacre of the troops, a heroic sacrifice for the country.[37] This is the genesis of the Belchite myth. In this way, the Aragonese town became a strategic target above the military level, so its recapture was urgent. The rebel troops achieved their mission in March 1938, when they regained control of the military base, and the third and final wave of violence was unleashed on Belchite: far more atrocious and systematic than the previous ones, seeking to cut short any possible attempt at resistance.[38]

With the reconquest of Belchite, the mythomaniac Francoist discourse was reactivated, and Franco himself played a fundamental role: on 11 March, he travelled to Belchite to rally the troops that had just 'liberated' the town and promised that, over the ruins of Belchite, 'a beautiful and spacious city will be built as a tribute to its unparalleled heroism'.[39] This promise – almost tangible, as it came from the mouth of the Caudillo himself – encouraged the mayor of Belchite to request that the town be renamed 'Belchite de Franco', a change that was effectively approved in October 1939.[40] However, such a city was never built *on* the ruins of Belchite. Aware of the power of the image of the skeleton of the town, Franco decided that New Belchite would be built a few metres from the original, keeping the ruins as a physical memory of 'red barbarism' and immortalizing Old Belchite as a kind of martyr town. Its sacrifice had to be fully capitalized on. In the outskirts of the future town centre, a concentration camp was created to facilitate slave labour for the construction of the new town. The construction, begun in 1940, would not be completed until 1954, forcing local inhabitants to survive in very poor conditions for more than fifteen years. While streets were named and celebrations were held throughout Spain in honour of Belchite, the material reality of the town's residents was ignored.

The production-dissemination of the Francoist myth of Belchite took shape through an important propaganda campaign in the press and in military literature, which repeated and established the narrative within the dictatorship's frame of reference. Added to this was a ritualized worship of death in the physical space of the ruins, with commemorative acts and annual funerals, which merged the religious with the political-military. In such events, ex-combatants were given a preferential place for the Homeric transmission of the account. However, the passage of time led to a fall in the commemorative frenzy, especially from the end of the Second World War. There was a small upturn in 1962 with the twenty-fifth anniversary of the heroic deed, an event with which the myth of Belchite was reactivated and that served to briefly revalidate support of the dictatorship in the new sociopolitical context, but it did not last long. The failure of the generational transmission of the Francoist epic achievement at Belchite demonstrated how the sublimated dialectic of the account had ceased to work once the draftees of the war had lost their social hegemony.[41] The Belchite feat did not offer the same political benefits as it had during the war and post-war period, while the stagnation of the referential and legitimizing frameworks of the dictatorship had made them obsolete in the face of the dynamic social changes of late Francoism. When the hierarchy between the collective receiving the account and the agent transmitting memory breaks down, the aleph ceases to be operational.

Belchite is an example of a military disaster redefined and transmitted as a heroic event. The potentiality of the Aragonese town was that it was an ordinary place where something extraordinary had happened, and for that very reason it could reflect the essence of all places in Franco's New Spain, characterized by the tireless fight of its brave and virtuous men. Belchite was the example of the valiant *Hispanic-Imperial race*. However, just as the Francoist frame of reference was declining in tandem with the stagnation of the dictatorship, Belchite ceased to fulfil its function: a fact that did not prevent it from continuing to be a paradigmatic example of a city devastated by war. Names of barracks, streets, and so on, were gradually emptied of signifiers, acting as vestiges of a past time whose resonation was increasingly blurred in the collective consciousness. Even so, Belchite is also an example of the readaptation of a symbol and shows the fundamental role that public institutions play in managing traumatic pasts. Recently, we have witnessed a reconversion of this victimizing aleph into an aleph of democratic memory. This paradigm shift became more acute as of 2010 with the updating of the street map of New Belchite, which replaced street names evoking the dictatorship with others more in line with the country's new democratic reality. On the other hand, the ruins of Old Belchite have been turned into a cultural heritage site and tourist attraction, promoted as a destination that exemplifies the dire consequences of war. This shows us, once again, the range of possible transformations that a memory aleph may undergo according to the interests of the entity in charge of its narrative.

A new map of the memory alephs

In the present chapter, I have taken the paradoxical condition of the collective memory of this traumatic past as a starting point for delving into its catalytic mechanisms. We have seen how places without limits are delimited in order to be transmitted. How the unspeakable has the most discursive strength. How what cannot be verbalized is what most needs to be told. I have highlighted the way in which the account of the Spanish Civil War has been generated and transmitted around discursive axes in which certain cities hold a preferential place. These cities, which metonymically symbolize a specific traumatic event, have served to materialize the unspeakable and to overcome the limitations of narrative transmission – in particular, its inability to tell *the whole*. Specifically, I proposed a term to designate these mnemohistorical figures: memory alephs, conceptually inheritors of Nora's *lieux de mémoire*, but introducers of new nuances. The aleph, which operates in the collective imagination, is the construct of the memory of what did not take place because it was ubiquitous. The atmosphere of terror, the fear, the humiliation marked on bodies, inscribed in the entrails. And not only the traumatic event of a place, but that of all places affected by the violent macro-context. We then looked at how in this process of reinterpreting the past, fundamental in the construction of the metanarrative of a collective identity, small and medium-sized urban spaces – places like any other – transcended themselves and became icons of something greater, going beyond limits of any kind. It is the extraordinariness of the banal: the places where nothing ever happened became mirrors of hell. Quiet towns and cities, but where the unimaginable suddenly came to life.

We believe that this new theoretical-analytical perspective can offer profoundly enriching results and open up new avenues for study. One of the future prospects enabled by this new line of research is the creation of a new map of the Spanish Civil War, far from territorial representations of the conflict as an overlapping of fronts or areas controlled by one side or the other. A new map of the memory alephs that articulate the collective mentalities towards the conflict. A network of microcosms from the traumatic past. And, ultimately, a new way of (re-)thinking about the central episode of the Spanish twentieth century, examining the contrasting and paradoxical diversity of its memories from within its core.

Notes

1 See Christopher Marlowe, *Doctor Faustus and Other Plays* (1592, Reprinted with notes and introduction, Oxford: Oxford University Press, 1995), B-Text, section 2.1, lines 121–2.
2 Jorge Luis Borges, *The Aleph and Other Stories, 1933–1969* (New York: E.P. Dutton, [1949] 1978), 23.
3 Jan Assmann, *Moses the Egyptian: The Memory of Egypt in Wester Monotheism* (Cambridge, MA: Harvard University Press, 1997), 9.
4 Maurice Halbwachs, *On Collective Memory* (Chicago: University of Chicago Press, [1925] 1992), 46–51.
5 Pierre Nora, 'General Introduction: Between Memory and History', in *Realms of Memory: Rethinking the French Past*, vol. 1, *Conflicts and Divisions*, ed. Pierre Nora (New York: Columbia University Press, [1984–1992] 1996), 14–15.
6 Vicente Talón, *Arde Guernica* (Madrid: Editorial San Martín, 1970), 287.
7 Josep Maria Solé i Sabaté and Joan Villarroya, *España en llamas. La Guerra Civil desde el aire* (Barcelona: Temas de Hoy, 2003), 91.
8 Ibid., 79. The authors say that the number was no less than 250 victims, the majority of them—as in Guernica—civilians.
9 Pierre Nora, 'L'événement monstre', *Comunications*, no. 18 (1972): 162–72. For Nora, the 'monstruous events' are those that are made viral, absorbed and blurred by the media, which 'have a monopoly on history'.
10 Pierre Vilar, 'Foreword', in *Guernica! Guernica! A Study of Journalism, Diplomacy, Propaganda and History*, ed. Herbert R. Southworth (Berkeley: University of California, 1977), xi.

11 Ludger Mees, 'Guernica/Gernika como símbolo', *Historia Contemporánea* 35 (2007): 532.
12 Ibid., 549.
13 Elena Cueto Asín, *Guernica en la escena, la página y la pantalla: evento, memoria y patrimonio* (Zaragoza: Prensas de la Universidad de Zaragoza, 2017), 23.
14 Vilar, 'Foreword', xii.
15 Ian Patterson, *Guernica and Total War* (Cambridge, MA: Harvard University Press, 2007), 175.
16 Santiago Amón, 'Un grabado llamado "Guernica"', *ABC*, 11 September 1981: 3.
17 Mees, 'Guernica/Gernika', 543–4.
18 Evaristo A. Mosquera, *Catro anos a bordo dunha Illa. Memoria dun preso en San Simón, ou un estraño xeito de vivir a nosa guerra civil* (Vigo: A Nosa Terra, [1984] 2006).
19 Evidence of this is in the interviews of the HISTORGA collections: 479–86, 657–62, 664, 673, 675, 676, 772–4, 777–9, available online: https://www.terraememoria.usc.gal (accessed 8 June 2020).
20 Xerardo Álvarez Gallego, *Vida, paixón e morte de Alexandre Bóveda* (Vigo: A Nosa Terra, [1972] 1996), 229.
21 Alfonso R. Castelao, *Galicia mártir. Estampas por Castelao* (Vigo: Galaxia, [1937] 2018) and Castelao, *Atila en Galicia. Estampas por Castelao* (Vigo: Galaxia, [1937] 2018).
22 Marie-Pierre Bossan, *Memoria da guerra civil en Galicia. O caso de Pontevedra* (Santiago de Compostela: Fundación Luís Tilve, [1998] 2019), 98.
23 On 2 October 2018, *A derradeira leición do mestre* arrived for the first time in Galicia for the exhibition *Castelao maxistral*, displayed in the City of Culture of Galicia, Santiago de Compostela. On 3 March 2019, the exhibition ended and the work returned to Argentina.
24 Bossan, *Memoria da guerra*, 100.
25 Ibid., 102.
26 Cueto Asín, *Guernica en la escena*, 13.
27 Mário Neves, *La matanza de Badajoz. Crónica de un testigo de los episodios más trágicos de la Guerra Civil Española (Agosto de 1936)* (Badajoz: Editora Regional de Extremadura, 1986), 43.
28 Ibid., 59.
29 Francisco Espinosa, *La justicia de Queipo. Violencia selectiva y terror fascista en la II División en 1936: Sevilla, Huelva, Cádiz, Córdoba, Málaga y Badajoz* (Barcelona: Crítica, 2005), 133–5.
30 Neves, *La matanza de Badajoz*, 60.
31 Peter Wyden, *The Passionate War: The Narrative History of the Spanish Civil War, 1936–1939* (New York: Simon & Schuster, 1986), 138.

32 Francisco Espinosa, *La columna de la muerte. El avance del ejército franquista de Sevilla a Badajoz* (Barcelona: Crítica, 2003), 233–38.
33 Ibid., 212.
34 John T. Whitaker, *We Cannot Escape History* (New York: MacMillan, 1943), 113.
35 François-Xavier Nénard and David El Kenz (eds), *Commémorer les victimes en Europe (XVIe–XXIe siècles)* (Seyssel: Champ Vallon, 2011).
36 Stéphane Michonneau, *'Fue ayer'. Belchite: un pueblo frente a la cuestión del pasado* (Zaragoza: Prensas de la Universidad de Zaragoza, 2017), 12.
37 Ángel Alcalde, 'La "gesta heroica" de Belchite: construcción y pervivencia de un mito bélico franquista (1937–2007)', *Ayer* 80 (2010): 196–201.
38 Michonneau, *'Fue ayer'*, 42–53.
39 Ibid., 89.
40 Ibid., 60.
41 Alcalde, 'La "gesta heroica"', 209–12.

Part Three

Sites of Memorialization and Conflict

8

Memory on the walls: Violence, memory and the forgetting of sites of violence during the transition to democracy after Franco's death[1]

Iria Morgade Valcárcel

In this chapter I will approach the study of two sites of violence located in the northwest of Spain, in Galicia, which were used as concentration camps from 1937. In particular, I will analyse the graffiti left by prisoners on the walls during their captivity. This chapter argues that the action of drawing and writing on the walls, and the result – drawings that have remained, more or less hidden, with a greater or lesser degree of degradation – constitute actions of memory in themselves. Thus, an examination of the fate of these drawings, their preservation or obscurity, yields more global insights on the treatment of memory in Spain in recent decades.

Oia and Camposancos, the history of two places

This is the history of two buildings and the drawings that prisoners made on their walls. This is the history of the prisoners, of those killed, of their families, of those who tried to recover everything that terror had tried to silence under kilos of lime. We begin in two concentration camps, set in two historical buildings, with a history that seems to weave them together, linking them from the past to the present.

The monastery of Santa María de Oia and the Camposancos college, separated by only fifteen kilometres, have broad similarities and also notable differences. Both are located in the northwest of the peninsula, Galicia, very close to the border with Portugal, in the Baixo Miño region.[2] Both were used by the rebels after the 1936 coup as concentration camps. Constructed in places where nature and solitude were the only companions of its inhabitants, designed for reflection, meditation and even defence, their walls were testimony to hunger, torture and death. On their walls, in both buildings, the prisoners drew while they waited. Their history, but above all their present, takes us to the debate on sites of memory.

During the years after its use as a concentration camp, the building in Camposancos, an area located in A Guarda, a small town in southern Galicia, housed the Jesuit college Santiago Apóstolo. A former student, Juan Castro, would remember decades later the moment when he and his classmates secretly discovered the forbidden rooms of the building, those where the drawings of the prisoners still remained intact.[3] The use of the building as a school in the 1940s returned it to its original function, for which it had been built at the end of the nineteenth century by the Jesuit order. But the remoteness of the place led the college to move in 1916. The facilities were then occupied by the Portuguese Jesuits. This fact would link it to the events of the Oia monastery.

The monastery is a unique place in many ways. First, it is the only Cistercian monastery located next to the sea. It is also unique for its monk-artillerymen, who were in charge of the defence of the coast against privateers and pirates in the seventeenth century.[4] Following Mendizábal's confiscation, after passing through various owners, it was rented to the Portuguese Jesuits in 1910 until they were expelled in 1932.[5] The Jesuits were similarly expelled from the Camposancos college, in accordance with the Republican constitution that declared certain religious orders dissolved.[6] Paradoxically, the college and the monastery, which were under the Republic's custody, would later be used by the authorities as a place of confinement, torture and death of thousands of Republicans. But these authorities would be the coup plotters, who, from July 1936, established a hitherto unknown system of terror and extermination in the areas under their control, such as Galicia.

The coup d'état perpetrated by part of the army quickly triumphed in Galicia. Baixo Miño, the district where the school and the monastery are located, would be one of the last places in Galicia to be taken by the rebel troops. Many fled to the mountains or tried to flee to Portugal. Others decided to remain in their villages, believing that their lives would not be in danger. This was the case of Brasilino Álvarez, the mayor of A Guarda, and Juan Noya, the deputy mayor. The atmosphere had been intensifying with searches and arrests until the fearsome date of 10 August, when Captain Teresa of the Civil Guard met with right-wing men from the town at the Santa Tecra parador. It was time to carry out the 'blacklist', the killing of the neighbours who were already detained in the Jesuit school.⁷ The brothers Ángel and Antonio Domínguez Pacheco had arrived days before, with the walls still bare. They were two of the five selected from the blacklist for execution that same day. Decades later, their brother, Manuel Domínguez, would recall coming across the van that took them from Camposancos to the nearby Sestás cemetery, where they were shot. They were the first, many more followed. Another case was the anarchist Manuel Noya. He spent his life in the tailor shop. But it was not just another shop. Between needles, looms and chalk, the smoke of cigars with books and political gatherings lingered until dawn. Manuel was the most important cadre of the National Confederation of Labour (CNT) in town – a cultured man, everyone would say later. An intelligent man who had foreseen what was going to happen. That is how he had warned his brother, Juan, and the mayor himself days before. They must hide. But his hiding place was of little use to him. On 24 August he was handed over to a group of Falangists. After a long journey of beatings and torture, they arrived at the beach of San Xián, near Oia. Before shooting him, they castrated him and put his genitals in his mouth.⁸

Manuel did not return to sit in his tailor shop, making a new suit, discerning the future of the working class. Manuel was removed from his place to be taken elsewhere. He had been identified as the enemy, and as such was transferred to a new space, created solely for his destruction. Facing the sea.

The sand on the beach, the hills surrounding the town cemetery, the walls of the college and the stone of the monastery are the new sites of violence created after the coup of July 1936. Very different from sites of war. These are the sites shaped by a new type of violence – state-led, en masse and genocidal.⁹ The plan was clear: part of the population, considered subhuman and carrying the terrible red gene, had to be exterminated. Among the strategies used to achieve this, in addition to killing, was the infliction of humiliation and harassment, which would leave them powerless, unable to rebel against the New Spain. In Galicia, a territory in which the coup triumphed from the outset, there was no war. There, the genocidal practices that would configure a new reality were rehearsed, and among them would be the concentration camp system.¹⁰

The Domínguez brothers were confined in a place they might have known well: the Jesuit college of Camposancos. This building served as a prison in the first phase of the development of the coup plotters' penitentiary system.¹¹ At the same time, and even though dozens of camps began to operate from the same month of July in the areas under the plotters' control, it would be from 1937 onwards when a network of camps becomes official through the creation of the Inspection of Concentration Camps of Prisoners. The camps functioned as a classification system where the prisoners were divided into four groups. Groups C and D would receive the harshest sentences of life imprisonment or death.[12]

The transformation of the college from a place of provisional confinement to a concentration camp took place in close relationship with the destruction of the Northern Front at the end of 1937. The taking of Asturias and Cantabria marked the beginning of a new phase, in which the coup plotters had to manage thousands of prisoners in an estimated 300 camps across the territories under their control.[13]

In the civil registry of Oia's town hall, after the death certificate of Manuel Noya, killed on San Xián beach, there are the death certificates of the prisoners in the concentration camp of the Oia monastery. Using these documents, a list of twenty-four prisoners who died between February and May 1939 was compiled.[14] All were registered as deaths due to illness. But through the analysis of another much less conventional registry, two more victims would be added to this list.[15]

The handwriting is uneven, but the engraved message is perfectly distinguishable. We are in the cloister of the monastery. The partitions on which the drawings have been made were possibly built by the Portuguese Jesuits at

Figure 8.1 Exhibition of inscriptions and drawings by prisoners from the concentration camp in the Monastery of Oia (Galicia, Spain), 2019.
© Histagra Collection / Histagra Research Group.

the beginning of the twentieth century. The handwriting is uneven, perhaps due to the poor quality of the lead used to write. The message is surrounded by many other messages. The sketch of a woman's body is visible nearby. Below are two calendars, and two days, special for someone: 'Day 13, Day 14'. Another phrase can be read above, which is beautiful: 'The month of May, the month of freedom.' But we stop at that message with the uneven handwriting, which is crucial, transformed into a historical source of information with its reading: 'Eugenio Blanco arrived here on 12-2-39 and left for the [sic] semetery on 18-4-39.'[16]

The death of Eugenio Blanco was not reported in the civil registry of Oia with those of the other twenty-four men. Eugenio had written several times on the brick walls; perhaps some of the hundreds of anonymous drawings were his as well. He was eighteen years old. He told us himself through the walls. He also wrote, on an unknown date: 'Concentration camp of war prisons (Santa Maria de Oya) Vigo (province) Pontevedra.' And as a brutal metaphor of what it meant to draw, and also of the power that the guards had to take those spaces of freedom away from the prisoners, Eugenio's handwriting appears crossed out. Just below we can read:

Long live Franco.

We are in 1939, and the Francoist troops have taken control of Catalonia. The end of the war is near, and Spain has become one big concentration camp.[17] The monastery of Oia functioned as an initial classification camp where prisoners were divided according to their categories. For this reason, thousands of prisoners were crowded there, awaiting classification. Many relatives came to the small village, bringing with hope the *avales* or guarantees[18] that could save them, those that the Classification Commissions of the camps needed to be able to exonerate the prisoners. Eduardo Pérez, an altar boy in the monastery church, remembers the story of a married couple that had arrived with the guarantees the same day that their son was buried after dying of starvation.[19] Eduardo himself recalls: 'In Oia people were not shot, they only died of hunger and disease.'[20]

Two different terms come to identify the camps of Oia and Camposancos: hunger and execution, respectively. The Camposancos camp was known as 'the gates of hell' since that was where the number one military court of Asturias was established. A total of thirty-one courts martial were documented. The end result was the execution of 156 death sentences and 143 life sentences amongst other shorter sentences.[21] Camposancos was thus another place where inmates waited, in many cases until their execution. This is explained on the walls, on which prisoners wrote the letters that they would send to their relatives, if they could. In the 'I love you's' addressed to Jonas or Candelas, individuals who would never read the messages that still remained, decades later, etched into the solitude of the school walls.

In Oia and A Guarda, inmates speak who hardly knew how to write, while painters and poets also express themselves; in both, the prisoners' youth can be glimpsed in drawings of cowboys and racing cars.[22]

Prisoner drawings as places of memory

> One more year in a civic reunion we approach this mass grave where 53 Republican patriots sleep their last sleep, who dreamed of a more just and humane world, who offered their lives in defence of the noblest ideals of social justice.[23]

This fragment was written and spoken by Juan Noya Gil on 1 November 1984, at the reunion that, like every 1 November since at least 1976, brought together residents of A Guarda, in front of the mass grave in the Sestás cemetery, where some of the prisoners shot in the Camposancos concentration camp were buried. Perhaps his last name, Noya, sounds familiar from the beginning of this chapter. Juan was the brother of Manuel Noya, brutally killed on the beach of San Xián, near the Oia monastery.

There had always been flowers at the mass grave. Already during the dictatorship, neighbours threw carnations, at the risk of being seen. It was a clandestine but collective gesture in remembrance of the prisoners of the camp. But the social relevance that the grave acquired leads us to think that its meaning went beyond the tribute to those who were buried there, becoming a place of homage to all those killed by the coup plotters and Francoists. This assertion is based on events that took place at the grave beginning in 1976. That year, Juan Noya decided to buy the land where the grave was located. The idea, which he would spearhead in the following years, was to dignify the site with the construction of a small monument. In 1976, after the death of dictator Francisco Franco, Noya had just returned from exile. In that same year, Juan wrote his memoirs where he told his story, that of his brother Manuel and others such as Manuel Domínguez: the brother of the first men on the 'blacklist' to be killed, taken from the Camposancos prison in July 1936 and also shot near the Sestás cemetery.[24] It is they, Juan Noya and Manuel Domínguez, with families marked by brutal violence, who would lead the movement to bring dignity to the mass grave of the Camposancos prisoners in the 1970s, which was finally inaugurated in 1986. Former prisoners of the camp and relatives of the executed Asturians were present for the inauguration. Many of them would repeat this trip to Galicia periodically, transforming it into a ritual of homage and remembrance.

A similar pilgrimage also took place to the nearby monastery of Oia. In Oia, there had not been a neighbourhood movement to dignify the burial place of the prisoners. Nor was there anything to indicate the past of imprisonment and terror in the monastery itself, which after the civil war had gone through various owners, most of them using it as their private home. Still, visits from prisoners were common. In 1984, the same year in which Juan Noya gave a speech of homage at the foot of the Sestás mass grave, José Oliveira arrived at Oia on a cold and rainy day, like many of the days he remembered spending there almost forty years earlier. 'Let me in, please, because I was imprisoned here when I was eighteen,' José asked the owners of the monastery. He regrets not having found the cemetery where the prisoners who died of hunger and disease were buried. He knew it still existed because another Catalan family had gone to it. 'The family told him that visits must be common because on the graves of his former companions there were fresh flowers.'[25]

> We got closer, and by the light of some matches we began to read names written on the wall. The writing was a kind of urgent epitaph. One said: 'To those of you who read this, know that we die for freedom.'[26]

Practically at the same time that the memoirs of Juan Noya were published, an Asturian journalist, Juan Antonio Cabezas, brought forth his memoirs, in which he recounted his experience in the Camposancos camp. The above quote refers to his stay in the Tui prison, where he spent one night as he was transferred from the Cedeira camp to the Camposancos camp. Inmates had also left their memories written on the walls of that prison, with the urgency of a transfer that often led to death. In this way, the walls were a last link with life, which had become a continuum of prisons and concentration camps. In recent years, various cases have been documented in Spain, such as the graffiti in the San Cristobal fort in Navarre, the site of one of the largest concentration camps, known for the escape of hundreds of prisoners, which ended with mass executions in 1938.[27] Studies have also been carried out on graffiti in the prisons of Cangas de Narcea (Asturias) and the castle of Castelldefels (Catalonia), amongst others.[28] The testimonies of two prisoners demonstrate the dire situation in Oia:

On 1 May 1939, my brother Antonio became ill due to diarrhoea [...]. On 16 May 1939 at 3 in the morning he ceased to exist in my company alone, after 67 hours of painful and terrible agony.

When a man wrapped himself in his blanket, sat in a corner and did not move, not even to eat, we already knew that he would die [...]. They would stay close to the corner and from there they would not move until they fell to the side, dead.

The first was written by Julián Hernández Angosto in his diary.[29] The second was told by José Oliveira to a journalist in 1984 when he visited the monastery in search of his memories.[30] Oia prisoners died from severe diarrhoea and fainting after trying to satiate their hunger by pulling seaweed from the beach next to the monastery. The prisoners were surrounded by their own excrement as they moved, desperate, returning again and again to eat what would end up killing them.[31]

Like other examples of fascism, in the Spanish case, the fascists considered their enemies to be subhuman. And they were treated as such. The concentration camps were part of the extermination plan carried out after the 1936 coup. The ultimate objective: to eliminate the enemy part of the population – the anti-Spain – understanding that the only way to defeat it, to make it disappear, was by killing or re-educating through exploitation and humiliation.[32] This fascist re-education was carried out in the concentration camps and prisons, which would thus manage to eliminate men and women to mould them into the values of national-Catholic identity. In this dehumanized context, the prisoners of Oia, as well as those of Camposancos, turned to the walls in search of lost humanity, beauty, art or love.

Extracting the victims from the space of their daily lives by taking them to detention or execution sites constitutes a fundamental spatial element in Francoist genocidal practice.[33] The prisoners of Oia, Camposancos, and dozens of jails and camps that were extirpated from their houses, their towns and their families resort to the walls, perhaps to make them their own. To flee from genocidal spatiality, to resist horror. In this way, we understand the act of writing on the walls on the basis of three interrelated issues.

In the first place, as an act of rehumanization in the face of dehumanization. Imagine the prisoners of Oia, suffocated by death and hunger. Faced with that, a glance at the walls that surrounded them might have returned them to their hometown, like that graffiti depicting the bridge of the Catalan town of Martorell.[34] Writing and drawing turns them back into people, brings them once again to intellectual activity, fleeing from that subhuman life that surrounds them.[35]

Secondly, the act of writing must be understood as an act of resistance, of rebellion against authority. In this attempt to rehumanize, they rebel against the authority that wants them to be an animal. By appropriating the walls in which they are imprisoned, that space of violence to which they have been taken becomes their own.[36]

They draw their dreams, they shout against their executioners, they create poetry or they simply write their names, when they arrived and when they left. And that act connects us with the third issue: graffiti as an act of memory. As mentioned above, part of the experience of the victims of coup violence is their removal from daily spaces and forced transfer to other spaces. These spaces, in many cases, are unknown to their relatives. Whether they are taken to their execution or to be imprisoned, the unknown location of the place is one more part of the terror strategy itself. Thus, suffering did not end with killing, but continued for the relatives whose loved ones' whereabouts were unknown.

Before their execution by firing squad, many of the victims wrote their names, trying to fight against the forgetting and forced disappearance systematically carried out by the executioners. An act against forgetting, an act of memory that we could almost say constitutes the 'first act of memory'. Because it is the victims themselves who write their name, in the first list of victims – the one etched onto the walls of camps and prisons.

Eighty years later, those lists, those original acts of memory, survive as an invaluable historical source. In Camposancos, since the 1980s, a site of memory in the Sestás cemetery paid tribute to the victims of the concentration camp; in contrast, the school itself remained abandoned for decades, along with the school's drawings. In the early 2000s, former students and various neighbours who were aware of the drawings would speak to José Ballesta and Miguel Anxo Fernández, two film-makers from the province who, attracted by the history of the concentration camp, decided to make a documentary about it.[37] After discovering some of the drawings behind a layer of lime, they carried out an intervention consisting of cleaning and documenting the etchings. A real estate company, Valery Karpim, decided to collaborate in the process. At that time, it was interested in buying the building from the Jesuits to open a luxury hotel.

In Oia, curiously, and adding to an already intertwined history, a company had also decided to buy the monastery with the intention of building a luxury hotel and housing development. But unlike in Camposancos, where the deal did not go ahead, in the monastery, after an arduous bureaucratic and technical process, the first results of the restoration work began to see the light of day. Drawings were rediscovered in Oia by Javier Costas, Lucía Álvarez and Lorena González, who in 2017 decided to carry out the exhaustive documentation and analysis of the drawings. At the same time, and since its acquisition, the property's owners had been working to conserve the drawings, securing the areas where they were found until the building's complete restoration in 2019. The restoration followed National Heritage guidelines but was supported by private financing alone, that of the monastery itself, without the interest or participation of any public institution.

Thus, in November 2019, an inauguration was held for the first permanent exhibition of the Oia monastery. At 'The prisoners of the monastery. Memories of the Spanish Civil War', visitors can see the inscriptions and drawings of the camp's prisoners. In the Jesuit school, completely abandoned for more than fifteen years, the graffiti is still on the walls today. Some examples survive, while many others are probably already missing.[38]

The situation of the Oia and Camposancos drawings – some restored through a private initiative, others abandoned due to inaction – exemplifies the situation of dozens of places with prisoner graffiti in Spain. A limited minority of the graffiti has been protected, such as that of the Montjuic castle in Barcelona, and very few have been given a public or memorial purpose, for instance, the concentration camp of Castuera (Extremadura). Many of these etchings have been abandoned or ruined, forgotten, for example, the graffiti in the buildings of Madrigueras (Castile-La Mancha), destroyed in 2005. And examples of protected etchings have usually been protected in a fragmentary and limited way, as in the case of the graffiti of the Kentura forts (Euskadi), with an archaeological intervention by the Basque government.[39]

To understand this diverse and heterogeneous issue, we must frame it in a global process: the treatment of coup violence and Francoist violence in Spain from the Transition to the present.

The evolution of the public policies of memory during the Spanish Transition

The monastery of Oia was a place of slow and agonizing violence, while the Camposancos school was a place of rapid violence, marked by bullets in mass shootings. Memory sites have been defined as those spaces, physical or symbolic, in which memory takes refuge, where it crystallizes.[40] Also called memorials, they could be places that have been resignified to protect the memory of what happened there.[41] The resignification of sites of violence is highly linked to transitional justice and the duties of memory. According to international law, after a period of human rights violations, the state, as the ultimate entity responsible for what happened, has the responsibility to implement a series of political, legal and symbolic measures that fight against impunity, based on the right to truth, justice and reparation for the victims.[42]

Under these parameters, the protection and resignification of sites of violence is carried out in various countries. One example is Argentina, where the trial of Memory, Truth and Justice took place in relation to crimes against humanity carried out by the state itself between 1976 and 1983. In 2011 the enactment of law number 26,691[43] declared as 'Sites of Memory of State Terrorism' those that functioned as clandestine centres for detention, torture and extermination, guaranteeing their preservation and diffusion due to their testimonial value and their contribution to judicial investigations related to crimes against humanity. At this point, one might wonder what is happening in Spain? Are policies implemented to guarantee the public and memorialist use of sites of violence?

Two years after the death of dictator Francisco Franco, while Juan Noya was taking his first steps on the road to building the Sestás memorial, Law 46/1977 was enacted. Known as 'the 1977 Amnesty Law', it absolved all acts of political intent 'classified as crimes and misdemeanours carried out prior to 15 December 1976 and those carried out between that date and 15 June 1977 in which a motive to restore public liberties or to vindicate the autonomy of the peoples of Spain can be observed'.[44] Thus the law granted amnesty to two very different types of actions. On the one hand, actions carried out by the coup plotters when they rebelled against Republican democracy, and on the other hand, actions carried out by those who first defended that democracy and those who later opposed the dictatorship. In this way, acts of genocide were equated with acts of war, thus consolidating the discursive construction from the dictatorship years of a 'war between brothers' that placed equal guilt and responsibility on both sides.

The Camposancos memorial was inaugurated in August 1986, five years after the failed military coup on 23 February 1981. A dove of peace occupies a central place in the memorial. Underneath it reads 'Your sacrifice was the seed for a better and more just society.' Other sites of violence were similarly resignified during the first years of democracy throughout Spain. In most cases, this was at the initiative of the victims' relatives; some had the support of local or regional institutions. This was the case of the Fossar de la Pedrera, in Barcelona, a mass grave where thousands of those shot in Barcelona had been buried during the civil war. There, the association of relatives of the victims managed to have the place rehabilitated with the participation of the city council and the Generalitat. The memorial is a fundamental symbolic place.[45]

Twenty years after the inauguration of the Sestás memorial, the doors of the Jesuit college were opened. Ballesta and Fernández entered to make their documentary. It was 2006, in the middle of a period of memorial action; a few years before, a social movement had emerged with the exhumation of mass graves by relatives of victims who denounced the situation of injustice and neglect of the victims of 'Francoist repression'. Their actions reached their peak in that year, when their demands crystallized into institutional responses. The most anticipated legislative measure was promulgated at the end of 2007, popularly known as the 'Historical Memory Law' since it was the first norm that dealt with the treatment of Francoist crimes.[46] Its detailed analysis reveals an argumentative and strategic line that continues the discourse born during the dictatorship and strengthened during the transition.

In the first years after the coup plotters' victory, the interpretation of what happened revolved around a Christian crusade against the 'reds', a subhuman species that needed to be defeated and eliminated. This was modified at a later stage, when the Franco regime adapted the discourse to the international context, hiding similar lines of reasoning and distorting what had happened to present the past as a civil war, where two sides had fought in an irrational way.[47]

The violence carried out by the coup plotters obeys the logic of a genocidal process. In this process, the last phase is the denial of the fact itself. The victims are killed, buried in unknown places and finally all evidence of their killing is covered up – thus eliminating it from the official memory as well.[48] This denialist phase is evidenced in the Amnesty Law that eliminated any possibility of complying with the basic postulates of transitional justice. But, in what sense can we say that the 2007 Historical Memory Law continues the state of denial? As an example, let us look at the following paragraph:

> This Law aims to contribute to healing wounds that are still open in the Spanish and to give satisfaction to the citizens who suffered, directly or in the person of their relatives, the consequences of the tragedy of the Civil War or the repression of the Dictatorship.

This description of the events once again removes planned violence, different from the violence of the war itself, from the official memory. In addition, the 1977 Amnesty Law is not questioned, nor the imprescriptibility of crimes against humanity; the new law is limited to an act of reparation for the victims outsourced through subsidies and subcontractors, which clashes head-on with the consensual definition in international law on transitional processes and state responsibility.[49] As for the spaces of violence, it only promotes the withdrawal of Francoist symbolism from public spaces. Moreover, the measures were paralyzed with the economic crisis of 2008 and the change of government that in 2013 completely abolished their expenditure.[50]

For the memorialist collectives, the norm was considered insufficient, and they initiated a lawsuit requesting judicial protection for the pursuit of the truth. But, although at first a judge is declared competent to process a case in the context of crimes against humanity, the judicial system itself blocked any possibility of this in the following years, taking refuge once again in the Amnesty Law. The memorial movement then took its demands to the international level, seeking there the justice that the Spanish state had denied it for decades.[51]

On 14 April 2010, the so-called 'Argentine lawsuit' – lawsuit 4591/2010 for genocide and crimes against humanity committed between 17 July 1936 and 14 June 1977 – was initiated in Buenos Aires. Since the first phases of the investigation to the present, the Spanish state's response to the requests of the Argentine justice system has obeyed a clear strategy of blocking, by delaying the actions requested or even denying them. The arguments once again refer to the discursive framework already analysed: the defence of the Amnesty Law and the statute of limitations of the crimes.[52]

A certain counterpoint to this situation can be found in the measures agreed upon in some autonomous communities. A paradigmatic example would be the Catalan law that establishes the institution called Memorial Democratic, which defines the transition to democracy as a reform process initiated from the institutional legality of the Franco dictatorship and that contemplates the dissemination of democratic heritage and spaces of political memory through the Network of Memory Spaces.[53] Similar policies have been developed in other autonomous communities, such as Navarre, the Basque Country, Andalusia or the Valencian Community, with the implementation of measures for the conservation of sites of memory, while incorporating the fight against impunity or the promotion of the investigation of crimes into their discourse.

This difference in the treatment of the issue may be due to the willingness of territorial governments to acknowledge the demands of local memorialist associations or due to the existence of differentiated party systems, in which regionalist or left-wing political currents (critical of the development of the Transition) have notable influence.

Final reflections

> It is about those buildings in whose walls our memories remain, pure nostalgia, in the form of the most varied inscriptions: drawings, calendars, poetry, prose, signatures ... nostalgia.

This fragment is part of a letter written by José Betriu.[54] In the letter, he recounts his visit to the monastery of Oia, forty-five years after his imprisonment there. 'I hasten to clarify that these lines are not going to open old wounds, or create literature about our war.' His statement reminds us of many others that were spoken or written by victims or relatives during the Transition years. They had to justify their act of remembrance of their experiences, their suffering, over which a supposedly reconciliatory silence had been imposed.[55] José addresses his writing to his companions who had also been imprisoned in the monastery, and who 'wrote on the walls'. He does so with emotion, because during his visit the owner had explained his intention to preserve the inscriptions, 'recognizing them as a sanctuary for us'.

'Come closer to our sanctuary' writes José. This is what the former prisoner of the monastery calls the graffitied walls. There seems to be something deeply moving that makes the victims return to the places where they suffered such terrible violence, years and decades later. Like a trip to their deepest memories, in search maybe of some answers, of the healing of traumas, perhaps as a process of mourning the loss of friends or one's own pain. The ex-prisoners of Oia did this in that long and constant pilgrimage, retracing their steps to find themselves again in front of the fierce sea that lashes the foundations of the monastery. The ex-prisoners and the relatives of those shot in Camposancos do the same, returning regularly to A Guarda since the inauguration of the memorial. 'We have a place to return to,' says Honorino Palacios with restrained tears. His brother was among those executed in the camp.[56] Every summer they stop in front of the memorial; they have no grave, they never had his body. They have his name on the tombstone that the neighbours built in 1986. It was brought about by people like Juan Noya and Manuel Domínguez, whose brothers were killed in the first days after the coup; the memorial is also their place.

Other relatives did not arrive in A Guarda until the filming of the documentary. Ballesta remembers the moment when the son of one of those killed entered the Camposancos college for the first time:

> They were filming one more scene, one of those walks around the school, the surrounding air tense, which seemed to express with its heaviness what had

happened there. The decayed walls, of as many shades as years had been in the most absolute solitude ... He arrived, looked at them and smiled. 'Don't worry, you keep working.' He was a man of few words, rough in appearance, used to living on little, away from the noise of towns and cities. They kept filming, the walls spoke, with their silence, of terror [...] they were so expressive [...]. Ballesta could not say how much time had passed, suddenly he came out of his state of concentration and looked at the man. Kneeling, perhaps leaning against one of those walls, he cried like a child. Touching the last place his father had been.[57]

Ballesta remembers this moment as a fundamental experience for his own deep understanding of what happened, of understanding the unique force that sites of violence have to transmit their story to the people who visit them: 'you are feeling the physical sensation that those people experienced'.

Space can become even more crucial when it contains primary historical sources, such as etchings made by prisoners. There is consensus among researchers in considering the high archaeological and historical value of such drawings and writings as a source through which to understand the daily life of prisoners, but also to investigate the identity and number of people who went through the concentration camps. Eugenio Blanco is an example of the latter. There is no other source documenting his presence in the monastery. Eugenio Blanco, his uneven handwriting, remains intact today under the glass of the monastery's exhibition. He would not exist were it not for his own action, before he died, which survives eighty years later.

In this way, places such as the monastery of Oia, the Camposancos college and so many other places throughout the geography of Spain have within their walls the power to become three different spaces at the same time. First, they are spaces of reparation: that place to which the victims return, looking for themselves, looking for others. Finding in their drawings the sanctuary of their own suffering. Secondly, they are essentially a living historical archive, with their most relevant sources engraved on the walls. Finally, and closely related to the above, they are potentially a space for collective learning. There is the air, there is that same salty wind that the prisoners felt, there is the damp cold of the stone walls, but above all there are the testimonies of the victims and even the executioners. What better space for new generations to come to know and understand the dynamics of the coup in its entirety?

Today it is still civil society, through collectives and memorialist associations, that has understood this and acts to achieve it. The action continues to be collective, not public. The Spanish state, the central government ultimately

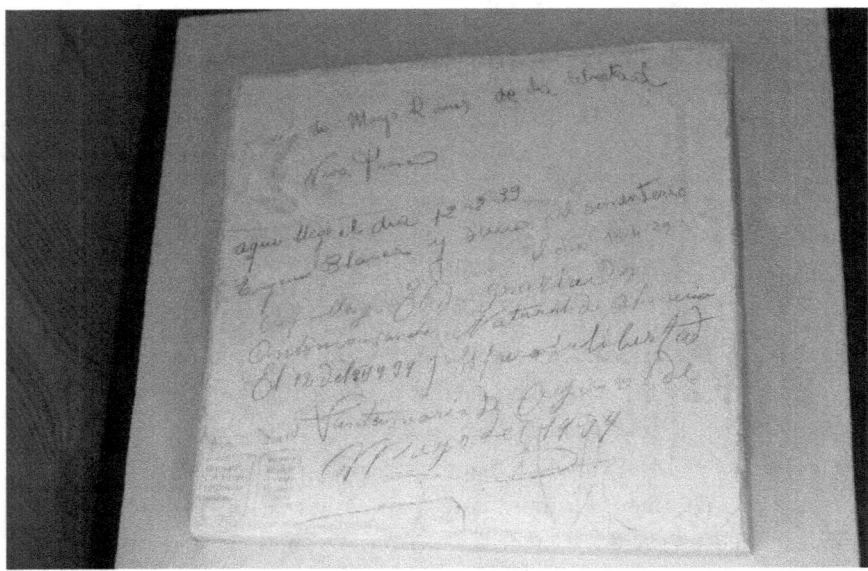

Figure 8.2 Detail of inscriptions and drawings by prisoners from the concentration camp in the Monastery of Oia (Galicia, Spain), 2019. © Histagra Collection / Histagra Research Group.

responsible for the violation of human rights, continues on its denialist course, without following a path towards a global policy of justice, truth and reparation – essential to successfully meeting the fundamental demands of a democratic society.

Notes

1 Special thanks to Javier Costas, José Ballesta, Xoán Martínez, Inma Riu and Josep Miret.
2 The Baixo Miño region is made up of several municipalities, including A Guarda and Oia, where the Camposancos college and the monastery are located, respectively.
3 José Ballesta and Ángel Rodríguez, 'Camposancos: Una imprenta de los presos del franquismo', *Complutum* 19, no. 2 (2008): 199.
4 Javier Costas, 'Santa María de Oia enclave de interés estratégico-militar', *Glaucopis. Boletín de Estudios Vigueses* 17 (2012): 25.
5 Carmen Manso, 'El monasterio de Santa María La Real de Oia. Estudio Histórico-artístico', *Cuadernos de Estudios Gallegos* 49, no. 115 (2002): 10–15.

6   *Boletín Oficial del Estado* (BOE), 24, 610, 24 January 1932.
7   Marcelino Laruelo, *La libertad es un bien muy preciado* (Gijón: Trea, 1999), 20; Ángel Rodríguez, 'A represión franquista na Guarda e Camposancos', in *O Miño, unha corrente de memoria. Actas das Xornadas sobre a represión franquista no Biaxo Miño*, ed. Xosé María Álvarez Cáccamo (Ponteareas: Alén-Miño, 2008), 215.
8   Laruelo, *La libertad es un bien muy preciado*, 77.
9   Antonio Míguez, 'Un pasado negado. Lugares de violencia y lugares de memoria del golpe, la guerra civil y el franquismo', *Confluenze. Rivisti di Studi Iberoamericani* 10, no. 2 (2019): 131.
10 Antonio Míguez, *La genealogía genocida del franquismo. Violencia, memoria e impunidad* (Madrid: Abada Editores, 2014), 99; Carlos Hernández, *Los campos de concentración de Franco* (Barcelona: Penguin Random House, 2019), 77.
11 Xose Manuel Suárez, 'Campos de concentración e prisións en Galicia (1936–1940)', in *A represión franquista en Galicia: actas dos traballos presentados ao Congreso da Memoria, Narón, 4 a 7 de decembro de 2003*, ed. Enrique Barrera, Eliseo Fernández, Xosé Manuel Suárez and Manuel Santalla (Ferrol: Asociación de Cultural Memoria Histórica Democrática, 2003), 110.
12 Laruelo, *La libertad es un bien muy preciado*, 102.
13 Carlos Hernández, *Los campos de concentración de Franco* (Barcelona: Penguin Random House, 2019), 72; Domingo Rodríguez Teijeiro, 'Los espacios de reclusión franquistas en Galicia. Análisis de la población reclusa (1940–1950)', *Minius: Revista do Departamento de Historia, Arte e Xeografía* 16 (2008): 248.
14 Carlos Meixome, 'Da toma dos ineses ao campo de concentración de Oia. Notas para un estudo de represión franquista no Val Miñor (1936–39)', in *O Miño, unha corrente de memoria. Actas das xornadas A Represión Franquista no Biaxo Miño*, ed. Xosé María Álvarez Cáccamo (Ponteareas: Alén-Miño, 2008): 56.
15 Javier Costas, Lorena González and Lucía Álvarez, *Con otra mirada. Horror de la Guerra Civil Española en el monasterio de Oia 1936–1939* (Oia: Concello de Oia, 2019), 52.
16 Ibid., 53.
17 Javier Rodrigo, *Cautivos: campos de concentración en la España franquista, 1936–1947* (Barcelona: Grupo Planeta GBS, 2005), 41.
18 A series of documents prepared about a person to justify their good behaviour, which would serve as the basis for their classification in the camps.
19 Carlos Meixome, 'Da toma dos ineses ao campo de concentración de Oia. Notas para un estudo de represión franquista no Val Miñor (1936–39)', in *O Miño, unha corrente de memoria. Actas das xornadas A Represión Franquista no Biaxo Miño*, ed. Xosé María Álvarez Cáccamo (Ponteareas: Alén-Miño, 2008), 69.
20 Javier Costas, Lorena González and Lucía Álvarez, *Con otra mirada. Horror de la Guerra Civil Española en el monasterio de Oia 1936–1939* (Oia: Concello de Oia, 2019), 109.

21   Laruelo, *La libertad es un bien muy preciado*, 83.
22   The writings and drawings described were studied by Costas, González and Álvarez, *Con otra mirada*, 37–87; on the Monastery of Santa María de Oia, see José Ballesta and Ángel Rodríguez, 'Camposancos: Una imprenta de los presos del franquismo', *Complutum* 19, no. 2 (2008): 200–11.
23   Speech written by Juan Noya, provided by José Antonio Uris Guisantes.
24   Juan Noya, *Fuxidos: memorias de un republicano gallego perseguido por el franquismo* (Caracas: Casuz, 1976).
25   Carmen Parada, 'Un catalán visita en Santa María de Oia, el lugar donde estuvo prisionero en la guerra', *La Voz de Galicia*, (1984): 24.
26   Juan Antonio Cabezas, *Asturias, catorce meses de guerra civil* (Madrid: G. Del Toro, 1975), 205.
27   L. Herrasti, C. Martín, and F. Ferrándiz, 'Escrito en la pared. Mensajes ocultos en los grafitis', in *El fuerte de San Cristóbal en la memoria: de prisión a sanatorio penitenciario*, ed. Etxebarria y Pla (Navarra: Aranzadi y Txinparta, 2014), 314.
28   In Belén G.Hidalgo, 'Cangas busca recuperar los dibujos de los calabozos hechos por represaliados', *El Comercio*, 7 November 2019; Alfonso López, *Las Brigadas Internacionales en Castelldefels* (Castelldefels: Ayuntamiento, 2015), 345.
29   Diary provided by the researcher Javier Costas, who received it from the niece of the diary's writer, Inma Riu Hernández. The brother, Antonio, died in the camp.
30   Carmen Parada, 'Un catalán visita en Santa María de Oia, el lugar donde estuvo prisionero en la guerra', *La Voz de Galicia*, 4 April 1984: 24.
31   Costas, González, and Álvarez, *Con otra mirada*, 59.
32   Rodrigo, *Cautivos*, 4; Hernández, *Los campos de concentración de Franco*, 99.
33   Míguez, 'Un pasado negado', 131.
34   Information provided by Javier Costas Goberna in his archives.
35   F. Figueroa, 'El grafiti carcelario: causas y procesos funcionales a la sombra de Lombroso', *Vegueta. Anauario de la Facultad de Geografía e Historia* 19 (2019): 80.
36   Herrasti, Martín, and Ferrándiz, 'Escrito en la pared', 314.
37   José Ballesta and Miguel Anxo Fernández, *Memorial de Camposancos* (Auga Morna: Grupo Creativo, 2007).
38   The property continues to belong to the Jesuits. Although it is considered a site of historical heritage, no institution has carried out any formalities for its possible conservation.
39   On the Montjuic castle, see https://ajuntament.barcelona.cat/castelldemontjuic/es/activitats/noticies/el-castillo-presenta-el-nuevo-espacio-de-acogida-y-los-grafitos-de-los-calabozos (accessed 30 June 2020). On the Castuera camp, see Antonio López and José Ramón González, 'Cartas prisioneras. Vida cotidiana y últimas voluntades en el campo de concentración de Castuera', *Vegueta. Anuario de la Facultad de Geografía e Historia* 19 (2019): 255. On Madrigueras, see Antonio

Selva, 'Los graffiti de la iglesia de Madrigueras', *Revista Cultural Albacete* 4 (2005): 17. On Kentura, see Josu Santamarina and Xabier Herrero, 'Grafitis de guerra. Un estudio arqueológico de los fortines republicanos de Ketura (Araba/Álava)', *Revista Internacional de la Guerra Civil (1936–1939)* 8 (2019): 191.

40 Pierre Nora, *Pierre Nora en Les Lieux de mémoire* (Montevideo: Ediciones Trilce, 2008), 53.
41 Míguez, 'Un pasado negado', 136.
42 UN Human Rights Commission, 'Conjunto de principios actualizados para la protección y la promoción de los derechos humanos mediante la lucha contra la impunidad' (E/CN.4/2005/102/Add.1, de 8 de febrero de 2005).
43 Available online: https://web.archive.org/web/20170330191313/http://www.jus.gob.ar/derechoshumanos/red-federal-de-sitios-de-la-memoria.aspx (accessed 30 June 2020).
44 'Ley 46/1977'. In BOE, no. 248, 17 October 1977.
45 Ricard Conesa, 'David contra Goliat. Memoria, reconciliación y espacio público en la Barcelona de los ochenta', *Historia, Trabajo y Sociedad* 9 (2018): 82.
46 'Ley 52/2007', BOE, no. 310, 26 December 2007.
47 Antonio Míguez, *La genealogía genocida del franquismo. Violencia, memoria e impunidad* (Madrid: Abada Editores, 2014), 140; Lourenzo Fernández and Antonio Míguez, 'Os verdugos no golpe de estado de 1936. Quen matou a Antonio Azarola?', in *Golpistas e verdugos de 1936. Historia dun pasado incómodo*, ed. Lourenzo Fernández and Antonio Míguez (Vigo: Editorial Galaxia, 2018), 79.
48 Ibid.
49 Javier Chinchón, *El tratamiento judicial de los crímenes de la Guerra Civil y el franquismo en España: una visión de conjunto desde el Derecho Internacional* (Bilbao: Universidad de Deusto, 2012), 110.
50 Ibon Uría, 'Memoria histórica: de 6 millones a 0 euros', *Infolibre*, 8 July 2007. Available online: https://www.infolibre.es/noticias/politica/2013/07/08/el_niega_dedicar_solo_euro_las_victimas_del_franquismo_guerra_civil_5627_1012.html (accessed 30 June 2020).
51 Iria Morgade and Bruno González-Cacheda, 'La internacionalización del movimiento de la memoria: el caso de la querella argentina', in *Actas del XIII Congreso*, ed. Asociación Española de Ciencia Política y de la Administración (2017), 25.
52 Iria Morgade and Bruno González-Cacheda, 'Camiño a Bos Aires: unha ollada ao proceso de internacionalización do movemento da memoria', *Tempo Exterior* 40 (2020): 125–45.
53 'Ley 13/2007', BOE, no. 284, 27 November 2007.
54 José Betriu, 'Santa María de Oya, Campo de concentración', *Diario de Terrasa*, 28 November 1984.

55 Iria Morgade, 'Rosa Branca. Accións colectivas da memoria na transición: vítimas sen verdugos', in *Golpistas e verdugos de 1936. Historia dun pasado incómodo*, ed. Lourenzo Fernández and Antonio Míguez (Vigo: Editorial Galaxia, 2018), 420.
56 Quote from the documentary, see Ballesta and Fernández, *Memorial de Camposancos*.
57 Fragment inspired by the testimony of José Ballesta (interview with José Ballesta, 21 January 2020, Cangas do Morrazo, by Iria Morgade. Fondo sonoro no arquivo persoal da autora.).

9

Discourses and public policies on memory: The narrative construction of the violent past in the Basque Country (1936–2020)

Erik Zubiaga Arana

On 3 May 2018, the terrorist organization Euskadi ta Askatasuna (ETA, Basque Homeland and Freedom) issued a statement announcing the definitive end of its 'political activity'. The announcement came after a trajectory of more than half a century that had left a tragic total of some 850 victims killed, 2,500 injured, 80 kidnapped, thousands of cases of extorsion, and attacks of various kinds against property and people, as well as an ingrained culture of violence and hatred that fuelled the group's actions and the dehumanization of its victims.[1] This definitive renunciation was largely thanks to successful police and judicial action against the group, greatly accelerated since 2001, such as the immediate arrest of commandos and leaders, which pushed the group into a situation of extreme structural weakness. But it was also due to factors such as the rising mobilization of citizens against ETA, the emergence of new forms of international terrorism and growing internal dissent against the use of murder because it was deemed strategically useless.[2]

As is often the case after the end of long processes of violence, in the Basque Country a series of opposing narratives are currently proliferating – unequal in terms of objectives, rigour and social projection – regarding the violent past. This past is not exclusively limited to ETA terrorism (1959–2018), but also incorporates periods such as the Spanish Civil War (1936–1939) and the dictatorship (1939–1975), as well as the victims of extreme right-wing groups (1975–1982) and para-police terrorism, such as the GAL (1983–1987).

In general terms, these accounts occupy two broad parallel spaces, which sometimes also intersect. On the one hand, there are academic works that are the product of historical research: increasingly abundant and exhaustive, these works gradually cover the existing historiography gaps on the subject, but their social diffusion is limited, so their findings do not always transcend public debate. On the other hand, there is another series of discourses, generally outside of academia and mainly supported by memory narratives, which is established by different political associations and institutions whose primary objective is memory and its management (memory policies), more than the rigorous interpretation of the fact itself. In essence, they are the ones with the greatest means available to intervene in opinion and in public space. In this chapter, I will try to present the main narratives and public policies of memory constructed around the different phenomena of political violence in the Basque Country (and in the whole of Spain) from the Spanish Civil War to the present, while also addressing the most significant public debates in this regard.

The war of 1936

As in the rest of Spain, the 1936 war in the Basque Country was a fratricidal war that pitted Basques against Basques. It could not have been otherwise in a territory characterized by broad political plurality. The Spanish right, represented mainly by Carlism and monarchist Alfonsism; Basque nationalism, represented mainly by the deeply religious and traditionalist Basque Nationalist Party (PNV); and the Left, with a strong presence of Socialists and Republicans, had competed electorally on an equal footing until July 1936, when a sector of the army, in an armed uprising, decided to violently break the constitutional legality then in force.[3]

The evolution of the coup in the Basque Country reflected the complex and varied panorama of politics and identity that characterized Basque society at the time: Álava, with the exception of a small area in the north, was soon in the hands of the Francoist rebels. Gipuzkoa surrendered two months later, after quelling the initial attempt at uprising thanks to the prompt response led by the anarchists, and experienced the intense revolutionary process before surrender.[4] And Biscay, where there was no coup or revolutionary outbreak due mainly to the skill of the political and military commanders loyal to the constitution, maintained a relatively stable political and social order, violently broken on several occasions, until the Navarre brigades occupied Bilbao on 19 June 1937 after several months of harsh conflict.[5]

The repression carried out by the coup plotters in Álava killed 228 people, mostly supporters of left-wing political groups. Eighty-six per cent of whom were extrajudicially killed in 'sacas' – removals organized by patrols of Requetés and Falangists – during the so-called hot terror in the first hours. Before this, Republican violence had left a total of forty-seven killed in the province.[6] Around the same time, the 'spontaneous' violence of leftists also killed 248 people in Gipuzkoa. Similar situations occurred in Bilbao in September and October 1936 and in January 1937, when crowds violently killed more than 200 'right-winger' prisoners under the pretext of the Francoist air raids suffered during those days. In total, 569 people lost their lives as a result of rearguard violence in the province.

The repression led by the plotters also left a total of 604 fatalities in Gipuzkoa, 86 per cent of whom correspond to extrajudicial killings, and 636 in Biscay, the majority (90 per cent) executed after court-martial sentencing. After the fall of Bilbao, most of the military contingents, including many civilians, fled to Cantabria in a general atmosphere of defeatism, evidenced by the constant trickle of uncontrolled desertions. Finally, approximately 30,000 combatants, mostly assigned to battalions of Basque nationalism, surrendered in the coastal town of Santoña (Cantabria) on 25 August 1937, after an agreement reached between Juan Ajuriaguerra, a prominent leader of the PNV, and the Italian Fascist military commanders of the Flechas Negras.[7] It is estimated that a total of 111 Basque combatants were executed in Cantabrian territory.[8] It should be noted that the consequences of Francoist repression in the Basque Country, in terms of killing, were far from the figures of the majority of other Spanish regions, where repression was significantly more intense.[9]

In the post-war period of repression and social control, the Franco regime initiated an intense policy of memory aimed at the remembrance of the war and its deaths. The 'fallen' coup plotters became the pillar on which to establish a set of measures officially intended to combat 'time and forgetting' and to consecrate 'the martyrs of the Movement'. This particular policy of remembrance, in a first phase that lasted until the 1950s, exclusively honoured the victors of the war. There was no Spanish town that did not have at least one monument in memory of the 'fallen'. References to the war flooded the public space through new street names and the erection of crosses, busts, plaques and various other monuments.[10]

Besides pursuing the legitimation of the military coup, this policy of public space launched by the new state sought the cohesion of its ranks and, at the same time, the perpetual stigmatization of the defeated.[11] It was a memory of the war based on a discriminatory Spanish nationalist vision, integrated into an instrumental and combative reading of history that connected the coup against the Republic with medieval crusades. This circumstance did not impede the new regime from assuming and promoting some regional discourse and its traditions, including those of the Basque Country, insofar as they remained subordinate to the exaltation of the Spanish nation.[12]

The political cultures that made up the defeated side also developed their particular account and memory of the war. In the Basque case, these memories were far from synchronized, especially among Basque nationalists and leftists. Despite forming a coalition government during the war and fighting together on the front lines, the mutual hostility between many *gudaris* (combatants loyal to the PNV) and militiamen (left-wing combatants) resulted in numerous confrontational situations. This was not surprising, given that these antagonistic political cultures had been confronting each other dialectically since their very origins in the late nineteenth century.

Since the immediate post-war period, Basque nationalism developed an account of the war that fundamentally revolved around the same idea: the

Figure 9.1 Monolith in memory of victims of terrorism and violence (San Sebastián-Donostia, Spain), 2007. © Histagra Collection / Histagra Research Group.

Basque people – always identified with Basque nationalists, heroically defended by the *gudaris* – had been singled out as victims by the Spanish invasion.[13] This narrative would subsequently achieve great social projection in the Basque Country, due to the lack of a strong and refuting alternative narrative from the leftist forces, amongst other reasons. For instance, the bombing of Guernica (26 April 1937) was presented by Basque nationalism as the greatest example of the Spanish exterminating intent against traditional Basque essences.[14] The reports by British journalist George L. Steer, a direct witness of those events, replicated that image of the Basque people as particularly subjugated by Spanish fascism.[15]

The Francoist rebel air force bombed more than thirty towns in Biscay, causing even more fatalities on some occasions; however, none of these spaces has acquired the relevance of Guernica, which was turned by Basque nationalists into the site of war remembrance par excellence.[16] Picasso's 1937 painting *Guernica*, commissioned by the government of the Republic, gave that attack even more significance. On a smaller scale, though also carrying certain social relevance, there are other sites of violence such as former battlegrounds, including Mount Intxorta (Elgeta, Gipuzkoa), Peña Lemona (Biscay) and the defensive line that protected Bilbao and its adjacent municipalities, which are currently the subject of exhibitions and guided tours. On the contrary, most other sites of violence, such as places of confinement or execution – many of them redefined or no longer in existence today – continue to be pushed into the background socially, if not completely ignored.

In any case, since the immediate post-war period, Basque nationalism has passed a distorted narrative of the war down through the generations, via the most intimate social circles of family and friends. In general terms, this account, presented in the Basque nationalist context, omitted references not only to the fratricidal nature of the war but also to the plurality of Basque society, the scope of the repression in the whole of Spain, the initial doubts of the PNV before the coup as well as the final outcome of the war in the Basque Country.[17]

ETA, the 'new gudaris'

Created in 1959, ETA assumed and adapted much of the Basque nationalist community's anguished and victimizing memory to give meaning to its own existence and actions, which ETA considered necessary in light of the passivity it attributed to the PNV in defence of the 'Basque people'.[18] The search for historical legitimacy meant that many nationalist references to the war were exploited[19] by the terrorist group to establish a logical line of continuity between the war of 1936 and the context of the 1960s, although the origins of the secular conflict were sometimes traced to an even more distant past.

ETA gradually assumed – not without internal controversies – the idea of the use of violence as inevitable to forging the nation. The terrorist organization defended the inevitability of 'armed struggle' until the end of its days. It argued that the adoption of such a measure was justified as a response to external issues, thus minimizing the responsibility of the voluntary and reasoned individual decision to use murder as a tool to achieve political ends. Julen Madariaga, a historical leader of ETA, said in 1964 that 'our policy of defending ourselves from the violence of the tyrannical occupier through violence has not been chosen by us, the Basques; they have imposed it on us. We are only applying the very just right to legitimate defence.'[20] One of the group's last statements insisted on that same idea, the inevitability of violence: 'we did not go looking for war. The conflict was brought to us at home.'[21]

Somehow, this Providence-like reading of history – in which the subject is not the owner of its decisions, and there is a tendency to claim to genuinely represent the national will – shared certain foundations with the discourse that the Francoist rebels used for forty long years to justify the military uprising against the government of the Republic; the subsequent repressive policy directed against the internal enemies of the national community (the so-called anti-Spain); and the public policies of commemoration carried out during the dictatorship. This is reflected in the 'explanatory note' of the Causa General of 1940:

> The National Uprising was inevitable, and it emerged as the supreme reason of a people at risk of annihilation, in anticipation of the imminently threatening communist dictatorship. When it took place on 18 July 1936, this legitimate defence movement led by General Franco […].[22]

On 7 June 1968, ETA claimed its first victim. Two gunmen of the group killed Civil Guard traffic officer José Pardines in cold blood in the Gipuzkoan town of Aduna, initiating an escalation of violence that would not stop until the declaration of the 'permanent ceasefire' of terrorism in October 2011.[23] The existence of fatalities was part of the action-reaction-action strategy designed by the organization in the spring of 1965. As the Franco regime's response to the group's actions became more violent and indiscriminate, the more possibilities there would be to mobilize and gather support in a society 'made drowsy' by the Franco regime. Growing labour conflicts and the progressive escalation of terrorism made the Basque Country, this time indeed, the focus of Francoist repression in Spain.[24] The Basque people, a synecdoche for the Basque nationalist community, were depicted as the favourite victim of the Franco regime both inside and outside the Basque Country.[25]

The collective victimization of the Basque people that ETA encouraged acquired even greater social projection with the Burgos trial in 1970. This conveyed the idea that (Spanish) repression was suffered not as a result of being an activist for a particular ideology, but as a result of being a member of the Basque community.[26] Years later, various ETA members of the time acknowledged that during their militancy, they had been imbued by a desire for sacrifice that had more overtones of political-religious fundamentalism than traditional nationalist values.[27] In other words, they recognized that they had developed ideological foundations and practices that resembled the national-Catholic premises that they claimed to be fighting against. According to Martín Alonso, these were characterized by the following aspects: the creation of a suffering 'we', the hostile representation of the enemy, the belief in the inevitability of violent confrontation, the designation of a vanguard of struggle, the natural assumption of violence, a concept of the fallen as martyrs and conviction in the saving power of violence.[28] Mario Onaindia himself, sentenced to death in the Burgos trial, was surprised by these concomitances upon reading the works of José Antonio Primo de Rivera, founder of the Spanish Falange, while serving a prison sentence for belonging to ETA.[29]

The handling of the memory of Francoist repression carried out during the Transition has been (and still is) the subject of a heated debate. In general terms, while some scholars maintain that there was not a pact of forgetting but one of remembrance instead, others blame the Transition for confusing reconciliation with forgetfulness and argue that it even built a hegemonic account of denial and impunity.[30] In the Basque case, the dominant discourse resulting from the Transition institutionalized the narrative that had been forged since late Francoism, where the Basque Country was presented as a collective and resistant victim of a conflict imposed from outside.[31] Francoism was presented as a foreign element to the Basque body, without roots in the territory. The natural heirs of Basque sociological Francoism, who had consented, with greater or lesser enthusiasm, for so many years to the dictatorship, were first erased from the social imaginary and later 'crushed' by the terror campaign implemented by ETA against the representatives of the right in the Basque Country. The group killed twenty-seven civilians accused of sympathizing with the Franco regime between 1976 and 1983, practically eliminating their presence in public space.[32] The exceptional circumstance of being subjected to a spiral of silence, a product of the fear caused by the suffocating terrorist pressure, made it extremely difficult for right-wingers to disseminate their political project affiliated with the Spanish democratic right, and to possibly challenge the hegemonic account of the time.[33]

The most significant reminders of the war and the dictatorship in the public space were suppressed in most Basque towns after the constitution of the first democratic city councils in April 1979. In Bilbao, for example, almost eighty street names referring directly or indirectly to the war were eliminated, including 'January 4th Street', which was a reminder of the victims of the tragic events that occurred that day in the prisons of Bilbao.[34] However, some references were kept after being previously resignified, such as references to relevant battle sites. Likewise, along with all the new memory policies implemented by democratic institutions, ETA continued its particular war against the monuments associated with the Franco regime.[35] No one rebuilt those destroyed tombstones and memorials dedicated to the 'fallen'. In this way, the Franco regime gradually lost all symbolism of memory instituted after the war, to the point of disappearing from the memory of the Basques. They, in turn, had been converted by the new hegemonic account into the genuine representatives of anti-Francoism, thanks in large part to the activity of ETA, the crushing of the Right and the institutionalization of a suffering Basque 'we'.[36]

Contemporary narratives

The collective affiliated with radical Basque nationalism, which has historically supported ETA, is currently seeking to adapt to the new situation of the absence of terrorism. While assuming the 'suffering caused' by ETA, the discourse of this collective avoids the explicit condemnation of the group's crimes, as it frames them within a global armed confrontation between ETA and the Spanish state during the last sixty years that caused 'pain and suffering' on both 'sides'.[37] This narrative deliberately ignores explosive issues, such as the fact that 95 per cent of ETA's killings were committed after Franco's death. The anti-Francoist nature of ETA's struggle continues to be accentuated, although historiography has already demonstrated that its anti-Francoism was purely incidental.[38] ETA continued to act, with much greater brutality if possible, in the context of democracy, confirming that the group's ultimate objective was to attack the Spanish state, whether it took the form of a dictatorship or parliamentary democracy.

In essence, this narrative continues to be an updated version of the message that ETA has been transmitting since the end of the dictatorship to justify its existence and crimes. Thus, the violence practised by ETA is generally presented as a reactive response in defence of the 'Basque people' – always understood as a recognizable natural entity – compared to 'Spain', identified as an aggressor and annihilator of 'Basqueness' in a historical conflict dating back to ancient times.[39]

The foundation Euskal Memoria, created in 2009, is one of the institutions that works most tirelessly to disseminate the narrative of the 'two types of violence' described above.[40] To this end, it draws up lists of fatalities attributed to the Spanish state (the French state has also been included). In addition to the Basque victims of Francoist retaliation – who adhered to various ideologies – and the killings committed by extreme right-wing and parapolice terrorism between the end of the 1970s and the mid-1980s (which historiography estimates at sixty-two),[41] the lists include deaths such as those that were the result of manipulating explosive devices as well as others caused by suicide, natural illness, traffic accidents or even physical disappearances, for instance that of ETA political-military (ETApm) member Eduardo Moreno, otherwise known as Pertur – though not proven, the most corroborated indications about the cause of Pertur's disappearance point to the ETA organization itself. This clumsy increase in the number of victims attributed to the 'Spanish side' is intended to convey an equalizing idea of the two types of violence, balancing responsibilities in some way, and consequently minimizing the centrality of ETA in the recent violent past.

On the other hand, thanks to the determined commitment of regional and municipal institutions, in recent years the Basque Country has become, together with Navarre, the autonomous community with the largest number of memorials dedicated to the reprisals of the Franco regime.[42] Between 1987 and 2017, a total of thirty-five monuments were built for this purpose, the majority (85 per cent) erected since 2006, in the wake of social movements that emerged after the exhumation of thirteen bodies in Priaranza del Bierzo (León) in 2000 and the Law of Historical Memory of 2007.[43] Along with these constructions, monuments have also been erected in tribute to the dedication and courage of Basque fighters who died in combat against the Francoists.

At times, the monuments and plaques suggest that all or the vast majority of the war's fatalities fought for the Basque nationalist cause, while other political persuasions and identities that defended legality in the Basque Country remain hazy.[44] This is the case in the last inscription that accompanies the considerably large cross located on Mount Sabigain (Biscay), a former battle site, in which only the courage of the *gudaris* is mentioned, when Basque socialist and communist battalions, and even some Asturian detachments, also fought in those conflicts.[45] Another notable aspect of the public memory policies promoted in the Basque Country is the striking absence of references to the victims in the area controlled by the Republicans. Their suffering is not explicitly mentioned in the plaques erected in memory of the victims of the war, nor in the other public memory policies. It is as if these politically motivated killings had never taken place, even though some of the most significant personalities, such as mayors or deputies, are among the 936 victims.[46]

On the contrary, in recent years, the Basque government has been promoting different policies for the search and identification of disappeared persons as a result of war violence, as well as the removal of Francoist symbols, to the point of eliminating most vestiges in memory of the 'fallen' erected during the dictatorship. In line with the Historical Memory Law, city councils, which are ultimately the ones with authority over the matter, have progressively eliminated references to the Franco regime that were still present in the public space. The elimination of these symbols, many in a clear state of abandonment, is generally carried out without drawing excessive social attention; however, on other occasions, mostly at the initiative of radical Basque nationalism, a whole ceremony is prepared to give meaning to this collective's particular account of history, enabling them to make political gains in the present.[47] One example in this regard is the action and message that a youth group affiliated with radical Basque nationalism published in 2019 on social networks. Upon taking down a column located in Ondarroa (Biscay), built in honour of the residents of the town who had died serving on the Francoist side during the war, they stated: 'We are the generation that is going to defeat fascism. […] We will fight fascism everywhere as we did in 1936. They will not come through Euskal Herria!'[48]

Basque institutions, like other state institutions, have gradually devoted greater attention to the victims of ETA terrorism since the rise in memory movements and social awareness of the victims triggered after the kidnapping and subsequent killing of Miguel Ángel Blanco in July 1997, a 28-year-old councillor for the Popular Party (PP) in the town of Ermua (Biscay).[49] Until then, for a long time, the victims of terrorism had little social and political presence. Currently, the Basque Country has approximately ten artistic pieces dedicated to the victims of ETA, half of them located in the three Basque provincial capitals.[50]

These tributes do not always fit in harmoniously with the rest of the monuments erected in memory of the retaliation of the Franco regime. Sometimes, as in the case of San Sebastián, where they are separated by a few metres, the idea of opposing memories is misleadingly transmitted: as if some (the victims of ETA) were the consequence of the others (the victims of Francoism).⁵¹ Historically, Basque public space, especially in towns where radical nationalism is strongly present, has been occupied by graffiti and posters with both slogans of support for the group and its members as well as explicit messages of intimidation against multiple individuals and collectives. Even today, when that scene has practically disappeared, news occasionally still appears about vandalism carried out against tributes to ETA victims. However, social and political support for attacks of this kind has been declining, to the point that even the top leader of the Basque nationalist left, Arnaldo Otegi, showed public disapproval of a recent attack on the plaque commemorating the killing of Gregorio Ordóñez, a city councillor of the PP in San Sebastián.⁵²

The conflicting management of memory

Likewise, over the last decade, both the regional and national governments have set up institutions based in the Basque Country to preserve the memory of the victims of the various contemporary phenomena of violence that have occurred on Basque soil (and in the whole of Spain): the Gogora Institute for Memory, Coexistence and Human Rights, set within the framework of the Basque government and based in the National Historical Archive of Euskadi, in Bilbao, created in November 2014; and the Memorial Centre for Terrorism Victims (CMVT) based in Vitoria and promoted by the government of Spain, launched in 2016. Both centres share some general objectives, such as the need to preserve a memory of the violent past and to increase the visibility of the victims; however, there are profound differences related to the way in which this traumatic legacy is managed.

The first major difference between the two bodies lies in the chronological range and in the scope of action. The CMVT exclusively covers the victims of the different terrorist groups that have operated in Spain from 1960 to the present, such as the various branches of ETA, far-right and far-left organizations, and the GAL, as well as Islamist terrorism. ETA terrorism is featured the most prominently, due to the greater impact of its activity; approximately 60 per cent of the total fatalities of terrorism in Spain correspond to ETA and its related groups (a figure that rises to 92 per cent in the Basque Country).⁵³ In contrast, Gogora not only covers forms of terrorism after the 1960s, but also handles public policies related to the Spanish Civil War, the Franco dictatorship and police abuse. In this sense, Gogora goes far beyond the common norm of other regional laws enacted in terms of historical memory, which focus exclusively on the victims of Francoist retaliation.

The mission of managing memory is also different; each centre offers different answers to the question of what to remember and why. Gogora, for example, is in favour of reflecting a multifaceted account of memories of the suffering and violation of human rights as a result of the multiple forms of violence that have taken place in the Basque Country during the last eighty years.[54] The cornerstone of this account is the unjust suffering caused by various types of violence, and the memory, therefore, is primarily aimed at stitching the fractured community together. Thus, for the sake of community reconciliation, a narrative of a series of violent phenomena is transmitted that, ultimately, ends up strengthening the historical account constructed by Basque nationalism in which the Basque people are presented as a collective victim.[55]

An illustrative example of this is one of the highlighted activities organized by Gogora, called Plaza de la Memoria, which travelled through different Basque towns for three years (2016–2019). The exhibition featured multiple testimonies on an equal level that referred to different episodes of violence from 1936 to 2010, with the aim of constructing 'the puzzle of collective memory'.[56] In reality, behind initiatives of this type, there is no discernible will to understand the key factors that enabled the development of each form of political violence, since issues such as the intent of the perpetrators, the social support they amassed and the responses of citizens to the crimes are hardly addressed. Academic historians have already warned that the accumulation of memories without contextualization or interpretation does not permit an exhaustive understanding of victimization processes – which are, in the end, those that serve to identify and better prevent future analogous episodes.[57]

For its part, the Memorial Centre (CMVT) also promotes the need to build a collective memory of the victims; however, in this case, the defence of that memory is inexorably linked to the political significance of each victim. This positioning is unequivocal, as can be seen in the 2011 law to establish the Centre, which explicitly mentions the search for

> knowledge of the truth, attending to the real causes of victimization and contributing to an account of what happened that avoids moral or political equidistance, value ambiguities or neutralities, that collects with absolute clarity the existence of victims and terrorists, of who has suffered harm and of who has caused it [...], without any justification of terrorism and the terrorists.[58]

To achieve these goals, the CMVT has a museum in Vitoria – scheduled to open at the end of 2020 – which will house a permanent exhibition and aims to incorporate diverse activities. Likewise, it will have a documentation centre specialized in terrorism and its victims, equipped with primary sources on victims' associations, pacifist movements, judicial and police reports, and documents related to terrorist organizations, amongst others, that will be available for use by academic researchers.[59] The first investigations developed and promoted by the centre, most of them in collaboration with university groups, are already bearing fruit in the form of conferences and the publication of various reports, journals and books.[60] Thus, in addition to the intention to preserve the democratic and ethical values of the victims through acts of remembrance and activities of various kinds, the centre has a clear vocation to contribute to the search for historical truth through historiographic methods that enable rigorous knowledge of the forms of terrorism that have acted in Spain. The CMVT considers this the best way to raise awareness in society as a whole about the ideas of 'the defence of freedom and human rights and against terrorism'.[61]

Figure 9.2 Sculpture in memory of Francoist repression victims (San Sebastián-Donostia, Spain), 2014. © Histagra Collection / Histagra Research Group.

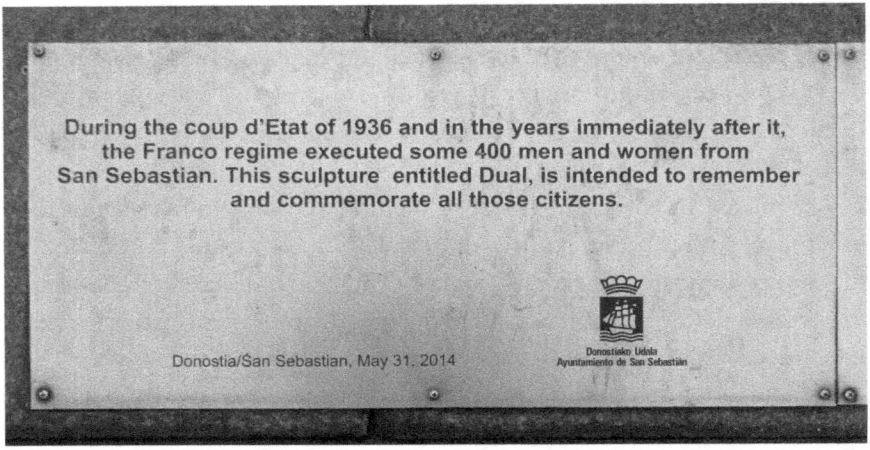

Figure 9.3 Plaque in English. Sculpture in memory of Francoist repression victims (San Sebastian-Donostia, Spain), 2014. © Histagra Collection / Histagra Research Group.

The treatment of the memory of political violence continues to cause controversy among different Basque political groups. Not all of them share the same objectives in this regard, as evidenced by the construction of two memory centres in the Basque Country with non-matching strategic policies. Recently, for example, a bitter debate has risen around the publication of the 'Herenegun' pilot didactic materials, prepared by the Basque government's Human Rights Secretariat to explain the phenomena of political violence that occurred in the Basque Country between 1968 and 2018, and destined for use in secondary schools.[62] Be that as it may, the management of public memory, as this chapter has attempted to demonstrate, is constantly being built and rebuilt in a conflictive context that varies depending on the conceptions and political interests of the moment. Historiography, as until now, will continue to travel its path, with greater or lesser success, covering new fields of knowledge and participating in public debate. However, this circumstance does not offer us certainty about the future. Only time will tell which of the competing accounts will achieve greater social and political penetration in the future, as well as whether the memorials that have been erected will attract the interest of future generations – or if, on the contrary, they will simply become decorative structures devoid of meaning.

Notes

1 'ETA anuncia su disolución', *El País*, 3 May 2018. Available online: https://elpais.com/politica/2018/05/03/actualidad/1525336524_523980.html (accessed 18 May 2021); Rafael Leonisio, Fernando Molina and Diego Muro, *ETA's Terrorist Campaign: From Violence to Politics, 1968–2015* (London: Routledge, 2017). The 'permanent ceasefire of armed activity' was announced on 20 October 2011, see 'ETA pone fin a 43 años de terror', *El País*, 20 October 2011. Available online: https://elpais.com/politica/2011/10/19/actualidad/1319056094_153776.html (accessed 18 May 2021).

2 Florencio Domínguez, 'Las claves de la derrota de ETA', *Informe del Centro Memorial de las Víctimas del Terrorismo* 3 (2017): 1-63. Antonio Rivera, 'Una paz donde no hubo guerra. El final del terrorismo en el País Vasco', *Vínculos de Historia* 7 (2018): 115-31.

3 José Luis De la Granja, *República y guerra civil en Euskadi. Del pacto de San Sebastián al de Santoña* (Oñate: IVAP, 1990).

4 Pedro Barruso, *Violencia política y represión en Guipúzcoa durante la guerra civil y el primer franquismo 1936–1945* (San Sebastián: Hiria, 2005).

5 Juan Pablo Fusi 'La Guerra Civil en el País Vasco: Una perspectiva general', in *La Guerra Civil en el País Vasco 50 años después*, ed. Universidad del País Vasco-Euskal Herriko Unibertsitatea (Bilbao: UPV-EHU, 1987), 49.

6 Gogora, *Primera fase del Informe base de violaciones de derechos humanos en Euskadi durante la Guerra Civil y el Franquismo: Víctimas mortales durante la Guerra Civil y el primer franquismo 1936–1945* (Bilbao: Gobierno vasco, 2019). Available online: https://www.gogora.euskadi.eus/contenidos/informacion/gogora_dokumentuak/es_def/Informe%20violaciones%20DDHH%20en%20Euskadi%20Guerra%20Civil%20y%20Franquismo%20CAST%20(azke....pdf (accessed 18 May 2021). Gómez puts the number of victims of rebel-led repression in Álava at 193, see Javier Gómez, *Matar, purgar, sanar. La represión franquista en Álava* (Madrid: Tecnos, 2014), 339-45 and 347.

7 Fernando De Meer, *El partido nacionalista vasco ante la guerra de España 1936–1937* (Pamplona: EUNSA, 1992), 534-35.

8 Gogora, *Primera fase del Informe base*.

9 Santiago Vega, *La política del miedo. El papel de la represión en el franquismo* (Barcelona: Crítica, 2011), 336; Francisco Espinosa, 'Sobre la represión franquista en el País Vasco', *Historia Social* 63 (2009): 59-75.

10 Zira Box, *España, año cero: la construcción simbólica del franquismo* (Madrid: Alianza, 2010).

11 Miguel Ángel del Arco, 'Las cruces de los caídos: instrumento nacionalizador en la cultura de la victoria', in *No solo miedo. Actitudes políticas y opinión popular bajo la dictadura franquista*, ed. Miguel Ángel del Arco (Granada: Comares, 2013), 65-82.
12 Fernando Molina, 'Afinidades electivas. Franquismo de identidad vasca, 1936–1970', in *Imaginarios nacionalistas durante el franquismo*, ed. Xosé Manoel Núñez-Seixas and Stéphane Michonneau (Madrid: Casa de Velázquez, 2012), 155-75.
13 Paloma Aguilar, 'The Memory of the Civil War in the Transition to Democracy: The Peculiarity of the Basque Case', *West European Politics* 21, no. 4 (1998): 88–109.
14 Roberto Muñoz, *Guernica. Una nueva historia* (Barcelona: Espasa, 2017).
15 George Lowther Steer, *The Tree of Guernica: A Field Study of Modern War* (London: Hodder and Soughton, 1938).
16 Jesús Casquete, Santiago de Pablo, José Luis de la Granca, and Ludger Mees, *Diccionario ilustrado de símbolos del nacionalismo vasco* (Madrid: Tecnos, 2012), 407-16.
17 Gaizka Fernández, 'Mitos que matan. La narrativa del conflicto vasco', *Ayer* 98 (2015): 213-40.
18 Fernando Molina, 'Lies of Our Fathers: Memory and Politics in the Basque Country Under the Franco Dictatorship, 1936–68', *Journal of Contemporary History* 49, no. 2 (2014): 296–319.
19 Jesús Casquete, *En el nombre de Euskal Herria. La religión política del nacionalismo vasco radical* (Madrid: Tecnos, 2009).
20 Fernández, 'Mitos que matan', 230.
21 'ETA: "El reto es construir un proyecto popular entre todos y para todos"', *Naiz*, 27 March 2016. Available online: https://www.naiz.eus/es/hemeroteca/gara/editions/2016-03-27/hemeroteca_articles/eta-el-reto-es-construir-un-proyecto-popular-entre-todos-y-para-todos (accessed 18 May 2021).
22 Luis Castro, *Héroes y caídos. Políticas de memoria en la España contemporánea* (Madrid: Catarata, 2008), 204.
23 Gaizka Fernández, 'A sangre fría. El asesinato de José Antonio Pardines (y sus antecedentes)', in *Pardines. Cuando ETA comenzó a matar*, ed. Gaizka Fernández and Florencio Domínguez (Madrid: Tecnos, 2018), 89-90.
24 Between 1968 and 1970 alone, 3,218 people were arrested. The 1960s in the Basque Country was also a decade of a new wave of immigrants, the urban transformation of cities, profound economic development and growing labour unrest, which completely modified the political, social and economic reality of the Basque Country. Juan Pablo Fusi, 'Los años 60: Los años de ruptura', in *Euskadi 1960–2011. Dictadura, Transición y Democracia*, ed. José Luis de la Granja and Carmelo Garitaonandia (Madrid: Biblioteca Nueva, 2017), 40.
25 Luis Castells and Antonio Rivera, 'Las víctimas. Del victimismo construido a las víctimas reales', in *El peso de la identidad. Mitos y ritos de la historia vasca*, ed. Fernando Molina and José A. Pérez (Madrid: Marcial Pons, 2015), 265–305.

26 Antonio Rivera, 'Violencia vasca: Una memoria sin Historia', *Libre Pensamiento* 88 (2016): 70-7.
27 Text of Eduardo Uriarte, Teo, see Eduardo Uriarte Romero, 'Cuando era joven', 24 February 2017. Available online: http://www.arovite.com/es/cuando-era-joven/ (accessed 18 May 2021).
28 Miguel Alonso, 'Estructuras retóricas de violencia política', in *Violencia política: historia, memoria y víctimas*, ed. Antonio Rivera and Carlos Carnicero (Madrid: Maia, 2012), 122-48.
29 Mario Onaindia, *El precio de la libertad: memorias, 1948-1977* (Madrid: Espasa, 2001).
30 Antonio Míguez, 'Un pasado negado. Lugares de violencia y lugares de memoria del golpe, la guerra civil y el franquismo', *Confluenze. Rivista di Studi Iberoamericani* 10, no. 2 (2018): 127-51; Santos Juliá, 'Echar al olvido. Memoria y amnistía en la transición', *Claves de razón práctica* 129 (2003): 14-24.
31 José Antonio Pérez and Raúl López, 'La memoria histórica del franquismo y la Transición. Un eterno presente', in *El peso de la identidad. Mitos y ritos de la historia vasca*, ed. Fernando Molina and José Antonio Pérez (Madrid: Marcial Pons, 2015), 243-46.
32 Gorka Angulo, *La persecución de ETA a la derecha vasca* (Córdoba: Almuzara, 2018).
33 Francisco José Llera and Rafael Leonisio, 'La estrategia del miedo. ETA y la espiral de silencio', *Informe del Centro Memorial de las Víctimas del Terrorismo* 1 (2017): 9-55.
34 Jesús Alonso 'La evolución de la memoria de la Guerra Civil en el espacio urbano de Bilbao: una mirada comparativa', *Cahiers de civilisation espagnole contemporaine* 5 (2009). https://doi.org/10.4000/ccec.3000.
35 Fernando Molina, 'Intersección de procesos nacionales. Nacionalización y violencia política en el país vasco, 1937-1978', *Cuadernos de Historia Contemporánea* 35 (2013): 76-9.
36 Ibid.
37 Diego Muro, 'The Politics of War Memory in Radical Basque Nationalism', *Ethnic and Racial Studies* 32, no. 4 (2009): 659-78; Antonio Rivera, 'Una paz donde no hubo guerra. El final del terrorismo en el País Vasco', *Vínculos de Historia* 7 (2018): 125-26; Luis Castells, 'La triada salvífica: sufrimiento común, reconciliación social, teoría del conflicto', in *Naturaleza muerta. Usos del pasado en Euskadi después del terrorismo*, ed. Antonio Rivera (Zaragoza: PUZ, 2018): 51-7; Gaizka Fernández, 'Se ha reescrito un crimen. Cómo el nacionalismo vasco radical cuenta la historia de ETA', in *Naturaleza muerta. Usos del pasado en Euskadi después del terrorismo*, ed. Antonio Rivera (Zaragoza: PUZ, 2018), 197.

38 Luis Castells, 'La paz y la libertad en peligro. ETA y las violencias en Euskadi, 1975–1982', in *Nunca hubo dos bandos. Violencia política en el País Vasco 1975–2011*, ed. Antonio Rivera (Granada: Comares, 2019): 84; José Antonio, Pérez, 'Historia (y memoria) del antifranquismo en el País Vasco', *Cuadernos de Historia Contemporánea* 35, (2013): 41–62.
39 See the group's statement in June 2006. Available online: https://e00-elmundo.uecdn.es/documentos/2006/06/comunicado_eta.pdf (accessed 18 May 2021).
40 Fernández, 'Se ha reescrito un crimen', 196–8.
41 Raúl López, *Informe Foronda* (Madrid: Catarata, 2015), 149.
42 Núria Ricart, 'Monumentos. Memoria y espacio público. 2007–2017', in *Diez años de leyes y políticas de memoria 2007–2017*, ed. Jordi Guixé, Jesús Alonso and Ricard Conesa (Madrid: Catarata, 2019), 147.
43 Jesús Alonso, *Memorias de piedra y de acero. Los monumentos a las víctimas de la Guerra Civil y del franquismo en Euskadi 1936–2017* (Guernica: Gernikako Bakearen Museoa Fundazioa, 2017), 302–3.
44 For another example in this regard, see Erik Zubiaga, *La huella del terror franquista en Bizkaia. Jurisdicción militar, políticas de captación y actitudes sociales* (Bilbao: Universidad del País Vasco-Euskal Herriko Unibertsitatea), 278.
45 Alonso, *Memorias de piedra,* 153.
46 Gogora, *Primera fase del Informe base*; José Manuel Azcona and Julen Lezamiz, 'Los asaltos a las cárceles de Bilbao el día 4 de enero de 1937', *Investigaciones históricas: Época moderna y contemporánea*, 32 (2012): 217–36; Pedro Berriochoa, 'Franquistas guipuzcoanos tempranos', *Cuadernos de Alzate. Revista vasca de la cultura y las ideas* 50–1 (2018): 231.
47 The demolition of the cross on the Biscayan mountain of Gaztelumendi is another illustrative case. See 'La edil herida en el derribo de la cruz de Larrabetzu es operada de las piernas', *Cadena SER,* 19 July 2017. Available online: http://cadenaser.com/emisora/2017/07/10/radio_bilbao/1499678174_499643.html (accessed 18 May 2021).
48 'Un grupo de personas derriba en Ondarroa un monumento franquista', *El Periodico,* 14 January 2019. Available online: https://www.elperiodico.com/es/politica/20190114/derribado-monumento-franquista-ondarroa-7245582 (accessed 18 May 2021); 'Varios desconocidos derriban una cruz franquista en Ondarroa', *El Diario.es,* 14 January 2019. https://www.eldiario.es/norte/euskadi/Varios-desconocidos-derriban-franquista-Ondarroa_0_857064994.html (accessed 18 May 2021).
49 José Antonio Pérez and Víctor Aparicio, 'La mirada del Otro en el País Vasco. Historiadores, instituciones y víctima de la violencia política', in *Naturaleza muerta. Usos del pasado en Euskadi después del terrorismo*, ed. Antonio Rivera (Zaragoza: PUZ, 2018), 102.

50 Numbers provided by the Fundación Miguel Ángel Blanco, see 'Mapa de las Víctimas del Terrorismo'. Available online: https://www.fmiguelangelblanco.es/actividades/por-la-memoria/mapa-las-victimas-del-terrorismo/ (accessed 18 May 2021).
51 Castells, 'La triada salvífica', 55-7.
52 'Otegi dice que "no comparte" el ataque a la placa de Gregorio Ordóñez', *El País,* 3 February 2020. Available online: https://elpais.com/politica/2020/02/03/actualidad/1580733282_466086.html (accessed 18 May 2021).
53 Rául López, *Informe Foronda,* 9.
54 The work developed by the Aranzadi Society of Sciences also falls within this framework.
55 Antonio Rivera, 'Dos focos para una memoria de la violencia vasca: Centro Memorial e Instituto Gogora'. in *El pasado siempre vuelve. Historia y políticas de memoria pública,* ed. Julio Ponce Alberca and Miguel Ángel Ruíz Carnicer (Zaragoza: PUZ, 2021), 247-71. I thank the author for kindly providing access to the text.
56 Gogora, 'Plaza de la Memoria: Presentación'. Available online: https://www.gogora.euskadi.eus/plaza-memoria/-/plaza-de-la-memoria-presentacion/ (accessed 18 May 2021).
57 Antonio Rivera, *Nunca hubo dos bandos. Violencia política en el País Vasco 1975–2011* (Granada: Comares, 2019).
58 'Ley 29/2011, de 22 de septiembre, de Reconocimiento y Protección Integral a las Víctimas del Terrorismo'.
59 Gaizka Fernández and Raúl López, 'Retos del relato. El Centro Memorial de las Víctimas del Terrorismo', *Studia Historica. Historia Contemporánea* 37 (2019): 63.
60 Center for the Memory of the Victims of Terrorism Foundation, 'Publicaciones'. Available online: http://www.memorialvt.com/publicaciones/ (accessed 18 May 2021).
61 Center for the Memory of the Victims of Terrorism Foundation, 'Inicio / Presentación'. Available online: http://www.memorialvt.com/memorial-presentacion/(accessed 18 May 2021).
62 *El Diario Vasco,* 13 November 2019.

10

From the courts of Buenos Aires to the walls of Guadalajara: The Argentine Lawsuit against crimes of the Franco regime as a transnational space of memory

Marina Montoto Ugarte

Since the French historian Pierre Nora introduced the concept of *lieux de mémoire* within the social sciences in 1984, an enormous academic corpus has developed to account for the relationships between space – physical or imaginary places – and the processes of social and collective memory. In general, the concept refers to a significant entity (material or non-material) that is transformed by the will of different agents (individual, collective or social) and the work of time into a symbolic element of the memorial heritage of a community.[1] Although at first, places of memory were conceived to reflect the commemorations of communities within the framework of the nation state, the concept gradually became more nuanced and opened the way towards an understanding of these 'places of memory' based on the multifaceted and conflictual nature of the struggles and disputes over memories,[2] developing in turn new categories such as 'sites of memory', 'spaces of memory', 'commemorative actions', 'dates of memory' or even 'places of non-memory'.[3]

But all these lines of research and work are united by the fact that this place, space, date or event *is the element from which* the processes of appropriation, dispute and re-elaboration of memories about it emerge. From this basis, could an active international criminal trial that re-elaborates the recent past of a country be conceived of as 'a place of memory'? More specifically, could the Argentine Lawsuit against Franco-era crimes – an international criminal case initiated in 2010 in Buenos Aires with the aim of investigating possible crimes against humanity committed by the regime of dictator Francisco Franco in Spain

(1936–1977) – be a place of memory? According to a strict interpretation of Nora's definition, we would have to say no, since these criminal proceedings are in fact a means or a space where different narratives dispute the events, dates and places of memory of the Franco regime, such as the Battle of the Ebro, the Carabanchel Prison or Ventas Prison, the Valley of the Fallen, the Prisoners' Canal or 3 March 1976.

In this sense, all these names refer to events, places, dates or actions that are fundamental milestones of the Spanish Civil War (1936–1939), the Franco regime or the Transition to democracy, therefore, they are objects of dispute over the meanings of the past in Spain. The Battle of the Ebro is a famous battle of the civil war. The Carabanchel and Ventas Prisons were the prisons that housed prisoners and political prisoners, respectively, during the dictatorship. The Valley of the Fallen is a national-Catholic mausoleum built with forced labour that until a few months ago housed the remains of the dictator, and which currently contains more than 33,000 bodies of 'martyrs and fallen' from the Francoist side, but also Republican soldiers whose bodies were taken there without the consent of their families.[4] The Prisoners' Canal or Canal of the Lower Guadalquivir is an extensive irrigation construction in southern Spain that took twenty years to build; it is estimated that 10,000 prisoners were forced to work there under extreme conditions. The date of 3 March 1976 commemorates the Vitoria massacre, where the Francoist police killed five people and injured hundreds more during a general strike in the city.

But if we think of the Argentine Lawsuit against Franco-era crimes as a *social space*[5] that, in recent years, has been home to the struggles over the meanings of the past in Spain and has produced new memories and accounts about this past, then yes, we can talk about this lawsuit as a key place of memory for the victims of the Franco regime. On the one hand, the lawsuit has enabled Spanish plaintiff associations to appropriate human rights discourses, practices and knowledge to rework the recent past of political violence in Spain, establishing a foundation for the construction of the 'victim of Francoism' category of identity in Spain. On the other hand, these proceedings have (re)produced a specific transnational space or corridor, articulated around different *round-trip journeys* between Spain and Argentina, taking the cities of Buenos Aires and Madrid as fundamental enclaves.

Based on my ethnographic research,[6] this chapter develops the idea of the Argentine Lawsuit as a transnational space of memory. To flesh out *the spatial* dimension, this exercise begins from the analysis of three specific physical places, which became fundamental symbolic anchors in the legal proceedings.

First, the 'Ronda de la Dignidad' (Circle of Dignity), in the Puerta del Sol square in Madrid, reflects the reappropriation process carried out by the Franco regime victims and lawsuit plaintiffs, modelled after the March of Mothers of Plaza de Mayo in Buenos Aires, and based on a transnational circulation of practices, discourses and aesthetics linked to human rights. Secondly, the importance of the role of judicial headquarters in the processes of identifying the plaintiffs as 'victims' will be analysed, which will take us both to the Federal Courts of Comodoro Py in Buenos Aires and to other Spanish judicial headquarters where testimonies and other milestones of the proceedings have been collected, such as the National High Court in Madrid. The third place corresponds to the civil cemetery of Guadalajara, a small provincial capital one hour from Madrid, where a court order led to the exhumation of fifty men and women killed in the fall of 1939 and buried without dignity, providing an example of the exhumations of mass graves as places of memory in modern Spain.[7]

Before entering into the analysis as such, it should be noted that the Argentine Lawsuit encompasses many other places: airports, consulates and embassies, meeting venues of the victim groups, and places where activities and workshops have been carried out to promote the lawsuit. However, priority has been given to places related to the processes of public action and collective denunciation carried out by the victim platforms and organizations supporting the lawsuit; therefore, spaces that have been most important for internal activism and militancy have been set aside.

The next two sections offer a brief socio-historical introduction on the emergence of the debate 'for the recovery of historical memory' in Spain: its main causes, characteristics and particularities as well as its most important milestones, up until the culmination in the Argentine Lawsuit. In the second part of the text the three physical enclaves that have been selected will be discussed.

From the Spain of reconciliation to the 'struggles for historical memory'

The emergence of the victims of the Franco regime in Spanish political and social space is relatively recent, especially given the time that has elapsed since the end of the Franco dictatorship (1977). It is during the Transition to democracy and the constitution of a new political architecture in post-Franco Spain that the powerful imaginary of national reconciliation has produced, amongst other things, this particularity. Specifically, the political process incorporated a reading that branded the Spanish Civil War as a human and fratricidal drama, in which the whole of society was guilty, and the two sides were viewed with equidistance. During those years (1973–1986), the real trauma of the war was articulated – a feeling of fear incorporated after forty years of daily political repression, in a climate of strong social mobilization – as well as the horizon of European normalization and standardization, to 'turn the page'. In other words, a public discourse was generated that was sustained by the need to not look to the past,[8] or to only do so with the exclusive purpose of forgetting and forgiving, in an environment of definitive 'reconciliation'. In reality, it was not so much forgetting as an imperative of privacy and silence around the memories of the defeated and the victims of retaliation,[9] placing them on the margins and outside public debate, precisely as the condition for the democratization of the country. This social framework of hegemonic memory was crystallized in the so-called Amnesty Law of 15 October 1977.[10] The law not only amnestied the events of the war but also all the violence perpetrated by the coup plotters and the Francoist state from 1936 to 1977. This dominant discourse of the Transition was consolidated throughout the 1980s and 1990s as the framework of common sense through which the majority of citizens had access to interpret recent events in their collective past.

At the turn of the millennium, new associations of the relatives of victims emerged within the context of strong public debate. At that time, there was a demand above all for reparation for those killed by the Franco regime during the war and the first years of the dictatorship, executed without trial and buried in mass graves and ditches throughout the entire peninsula. Nearly all those corpses continued – and continue – to be buried underground, under the responsibility of no specific jurisdiction. This sudden movement was promoted, mostly but not only, by the grandchildren of those victims. Between 2000 and 2006, significant media interest was generated in what it meant for the country to find out about the existence of these mass graves, the location of hundreds of them and the demands for exhumation, in parallel to this different memorialist associations in the country were constituted and the processes of unpacking the legal concept of the 'disappeared', through which this type of crime, coming from international criminal law, was retranslated by these collectives.[11] In addition, other issues began to enter the political agenda in later years, although with less impact: Republican exile after the war and its consequences; the reality of the forced labour carried out by political prisoners during the dictatorship in the construction of roads, railways and canals; sexual violence against Republican women; the demands of political prisoners during late Francoism against the demolition of the Carabanchel Prison, or the conspiracy of babies stolen by the Franco regime from poor or morally 'fallen' Republican women. This melting pot of new demands and subjects appeared in the first decade of the 2000s in a scattered and fragmented way, emerging as a 'movement for historical memory'.[12]

These social demands saw their own institutional translation in Law 52/2007 'by which rights are recognized and expanded, and measures are established in favour of those who suffered persecution or violence during the civil war and the dictatorship', more commonly known as the 'Historical Memory Law'. The law was promoted by the Socialist Party, which was in government at the time. Although it represented important steps towards meeting the demands of memorialist associations – amongst them, the improvement of different economic rights; a declaration of reparation and personal recognition of victims of the war and the dictatorship and their relatives; and the ordering of the removal of Francoist plaques, statues and monuments – the law had great limitations. The trials and sentences of the dictatorship were not annulled; no definitive proposal was given on what to do with the Valley of the Fallen;

Figure 10.1 Resignification of public spaces carried by social movements of memory (A Coruña, Spain), 2007. © Histagra Collection / Histagra Research Group.

and no consideration was given to the establishment of a truth commission or judicial investigation of the violence suffered by the population, all of which gave the impression that a legal and symbolic break with the Franco regime had not been achieved. One of the most problematic limitations was the *model of subcontracting human rights*[13] with respect to exhumations: the state allocated a certain budget to memorialist associations without establishing clear timelines or guidelines, and the associations found themselves competing with each other for grants. In 2011, the arrival of the Popular Party to the government led to the suppression of any funds earmarked for this purpose, so in practice the law was not executed. It was in this context of frustration that the Argentine Lawsuit began.

The opportunity of the Argentine Lawsuit

Lawsuit 4591/2010 was filed in Buenos Aires on 14 April 2010 in the National Criminal and Correctional Court No. 1 of Buenos Aires on Comodoro Py Street, by different Argentine human rights associations and the Association for the Recovery of Historical Memory (ARMH), a Spanish association linked to the relatives of those who were killed in mass graves. The lawsuit was filed through the framework of universal jurisdiction, which allows other countries to investigate human rights violations that occurred at another time and in another place.[14] However, this case did not acquire real relevance until 2012, when the Spanish Supreme Court definitively blocked the only inquiry initiated in Spain on possible human rights violations committed by the Franco regime between 1939 and 1952. This inquiry is famously known as the 'Garzón case' in reference to the surname of the National High Court judge who processed the criminal investigation. Baltasar Garzón had already become well known among international law courts when he prosecuted the Argentine and Chilean dictatorships a few years earlier, paradoxically from Spain. The Decree of 27 February 2012 of the Supreme Court closed this case and, therefore, the possibility of judging the crimes of the Franco regime in Spain, as they were considered prescribed crimes and amnestied by the Amnesty Law.[15] With this block to investigating in Spain, all eyes fell on that small lawsuit filed in Buenos Aires.

Thus, between 2012 and 2016, the Argentine Lawsuit gradually became a major international criminal case. This lawsuit was also the only one against the entire period of Francoism, because unlike Garzón's, it incorporated all forms of violence perpetrated by the regime, from the coup, the civil war and the dictatorship to the Transition (1936–1977). In those early years, more than 300 individual and collective complaints and denunciations were filed by victims' associations, individual relatives and political organizations – these data are collected on the State Coordinator of Support for the Argentine Lawsuit (CEAQUA) website.[16] The CEAQUA operated, in turn, as a unifying force for all these associations of historical memory and groups of plaintiffs, victims of Francoism of all kinds, who came together for the first time within the same lawsuit: former tortured political prisoners; relatives of disappeared persons, of stolen babies, or of forced labourers; victims of exile, child abuse, sexual violence, etc. At the time, the most powerful historical memory associations of the Spanish territory were at its core: ARMH, La Comuna Association of Former Prisoners and Political Prisoners, Historical Memory and Justice, CGT-Memoria, and so on.

The criminal investigation has involved comings and goings between Spain and Argentina. This has enabled the transnational circulation of people and documents – but also discourses, practices and aesthetics – linked to the legal proceedings and the framework of human rights. Firstly, Spanish associations have travelled to Buenos Aires to file complaints, bring reports or give statements, which has connected them with the human rights organizations in Argentina and their repertoires of action. Secondly, the judge, in addition to meeting the lawyers and plaintiffs in Buenos Aires, made a trip to Spain in May 2014 to take statements from several older witnesses who could not travel and to obtain more documentation. Thirdly, this same judge has processed statements taken by videoconference via letters rogatory, ordered the first two exhumations that were carried out under a court order in Spain (Guadalajara, 2016 and 2017) and brought charges against up to twenty people – some already deceased – who were related to the regime, including ex-officials of the bodies and forces of the Francoist state, ex-ministers of the dictatorship and a doctor.[17]

There have been key places and spaces in the process of these comings and goings, such as the Ronda de la Dignidad in Sol, the Comodoro Py court in Buenos Aires and other judicial headquarters in Spain, and finally, the Guadalajara cemetery, where the two exhumations were carried out under judicial order. Each of these three places has served in a different way as a setting, space and device in the processes of constructing *victim of Francoism* as a collective identity in the face of public opinion. Let us look at each one carefully.

The Ronda de la Dignidad in Sol as a device at a halfway point

The Puerta del Sol square in Madrid – like other central squares in capitals and large cities – is itself a place of memory.[18] It combines the short- and long-term memory of collective actions, such as protests or political demonstrations, that have taken place there throughout the nineteenth and twentieth centuries, along with its urban purpose and daily use as a space for crowds, transit, and local and tourist consumption, in the epicentre of one of the most important commercial areas of the city. Therefore, Sol is already a significant space linked to citizen protest for different communities that reappropriate public space; a place that at the same time *vomits* thousands and thousands of tourists from the Metro exits each day, who do their shopping, take a photo with the statue of the Bear and the Strawberry Tree, or go to eat at the famous pastry shop La Mallorquina. Adding to the complexity, the building in the square currently occupied by the Presidency of the Government of the Community of Madrid is the former headquarters of the General Directorate of Security, a centre of torture and repression of thousands of people during the Franco dictatorship; this fact is unknown to the majority of Madrid's citizens since the Government of the Community of Madrid has repeatedly refused to mark it as a place of memory.

The Ronda de la Dignidad is a practice that takes place in this dense public space, every Thursday at 8.00 pm. It emerged as a result of the mobilizations in 2010 in support of Judge Garzón and against the 'impunity of Francoism', and continues to organize itself through the 'Platform against the impunity of Francoism'. During the first years of the Argentine Lawsuit (2012–2015), given that many of the plaintiff collectives had been or continued to be part of this platform, the Ronda was used as a place to share news of the proceedings, bring lawyers or Argentine human rights associations during their visits to Spain and publicize the lawsuit. Above all, it was a place for participants to articulate their demands through denunciation and public mobilization in front of the rest of society.

The Ronda basically consists of a reappropriation of the famous Ronda de las Madres y Abuelas (Circle of Mothers and Grandmothers) of the Plaza de Mayo in Buenos Aires.[19] Some references to this reappropriation are explicit. For example, the decision was made to hold the Ronda at the same time as the Buenos Aires circle: every Thursday – in Buenos Aires at 3.00 pm and in Madrid at 8.00 pm – taking into account the time difference. In Madrid, participants walk slowly in a circle around the square, in small groups, just as the mothers and grandmothers of Buenos Aires. In this way, the Ronda de la Dignidad in Sol reflects the appropriation of the human rights framework by groups of Franco regime victims and plaintiffs. In this regard, until that moment many of the actors and collectives that joined the lawsuit and participated in the Ronda had never stated their demands in those terms: many did not even consider themselves 'victims (of Francoism)'; some of them came from militant backgrounds and referred to themselves as 'members of the resistance' or 'heroes'; the relatives of stolen babies used more diffuse discourses linked to the pain of mothers and the imaginary of the family; many relatives had discovered a history of family repression only a few years earlier; and others never thought that the acts they had suffered could be indictable.

On the one hand, the framework of human rights was incorporated and used by these associations due to the enormous legitimacy it holds in the public space.[20] Here, the work of lawyers Ana Messuti and Carlos Slepoy as *human rights translators*[21] was key, as they translated transnational ideas and practices linked to humanitarian law as a way of facing local demands, and vice versa. On the other hand, within the international frameworks of 'truth, justice, reparation and guarantees of non-repetition', the more concrete demand for 'justice' enabled the plaintiff collectives to overcome their fragmentation in pursuit of a common objective: judicial initiative. This common issue made it possible to transcend the individual demands of each association, coordinate the work of the platforms to support the lawsuit and unite the participating plaintiff collectives through this demand for justice expressed in the Ronda.

In the comments made during the Ronda in Sol, the groups chanted slogans such as 'WATCH OUT, WATCH OUT, WATCH OUT IT'S COMING, UNIVERSAL JUSTICE FROM LATIN AMERICA!' or 'IN THAT HOUSE THEY TORTURED, IN THAT HOUSE THEY KILLED', indicating the former General Directorate of Security. They also used key signifiers in the struggles for human rights in Argentine territory, such as the slogan 'NEITHER FORGET NOR FORGIVE.' Some of these chants reconstructed the transoceanic flow of learning and reappropriations of symbolic and aesthetic practices of memory: from Argentina to Spain.[22] In this regard, during the Ronda, the groups of victims and their families made large banners or individual signs with black-and-white photographs of those killed and made to disappear during the first years of the dictatorship. Many of them are taken from wedding portraits of the 1920s or 1930s and cropped so that only the faces are seen, resembling the passport photos of the Argentine disappeared. At the same time, as Bergerot points out, 'the black-and-white photos shown in Sol are mostly of men, with war uniforms and sepia tones'.[23] Without other signs or tools nearby to assist society in the interpretation of these images, the photos ultimately give the impression that these demands belong to the past, failing to generate much mutual understanding among passers-by.

On this note, there are multiple local characteristics or particularities of the Ronda in its re-elaboration of human rights that are worth analysing and that distinguish it from the Buenos Aires Circle of Mothers and Grandmothers in its effectiveness in addressing Spanish citizens. In this sense, the participants in the Ronda tend to be older – most of them over sixty years old – and, as I have mentioned, they usually come from backgrounds of political and clandestine militancy in leftist parties. In this way, chants about universal justice are accompanied by whole stanzas of the 'Himno de Riego', a Republican song in which the call 'to win, win or die' is shouted, with fists raised in a revolutionary imaginary that is far from the repertoires of collective action of the present. Coinciding with messages about 'imprescriptible crimes', the Ronda is filled with red flags, pins and badges of communist parties or leaders, some accused of human rights violations and not at all transversal within the civic Spanish imaginary, such as Joseph Stalin or Mao Zedong.

All these particularities may explain why there has been little capacity, beyond anecdotal encounters or disagreements – such as the weeks in which the Ronda coexisted with the anti-austerity 15-M 'Indignados' camp in Sol between May and June 2011 – for 'involving the younger generations of Spanish society, of articulating their demands with other popular movements and addressing citizens as a matter that concerns them regarding the democratic quality of the country'.[24] Returning to the idea that 'a place is constituted precisely in the tension between its enunciative dimension and its interpretive dimension',[25] one can see how the Ronda in Sol did not end up embedding itself into the popular struggles of those years and did not know how to address social groups beyond those strictly affected. At present, this has remained as something limited to the strictly militant sphere, which allows us to analyse how memory practices circulate from different transnational spaces and hybridize with other local discourses and assemblages, producing new realities and particular subjectivities.

Comodoro Py and the Spanish National High Court: The judicial institution as recognition or grievance

In the interviews with the plaintiffs who have gone to Argentina to file a complaint and confirm legal testimonies, the image of Judge Servini receiving them in her office on the third floor of the Federal Courts building on Comodoro Py Avenue, in the city of Buenos Aires, appears repeatedly. For them, the fixed gaze of the judge, the hearing of their testimonies, the photograph on the stairs of the building and the hugs between the plaintiffs' broken sobs in the hallways of the courts have been some of the most important moments within the process of filing a lawsuit and turning to the Argentine justice system. In this sense, for the vast majority, testifying before the judge was the first time that they had given statements as 'victims' in an official judicial headquarters, since in Spain they have never received a response from such institutions. A press article thus reflected their feelings after the first testimonies in Buenos Aires:

'For the first time the witnesses see on a printed page what they think, what they witnessed, what they experienced. And for the first time there is also a document stating that the victims are victims and the torturers are criminals,' Spanish lawyer Eduardo Ranz Alonso told Efe.[26]

In an interview, a plaintiff described the collective emotions and feelings that the group had shared the days they testified before Judge Servini in Comodoro Py:

When we went [to Argentina], of course people went with great emotion. You saw them go out [...] I imagine that I went out like that, but of course I didn't see myself, but you saw the others and they were people who went from laughing to crying constantly. Everyone said, 'I've just gotten rid of a burden.' I remember [another plaintiff], when he left he hugged us all and said 'I just left a backpack [...]', also as I go to see another companion, [another plaintiff] was hugging a secretary there sobbing [...] the two [...] incredible, right? Feeling heard, it was already something.[27]

The plaintiffs' access to the Argentine justice system produced milestones that had never before happened in Spain: tests, identifications, expert reports, exhumations, databases of DNA tests, indictments and testimonies were all carried out. During all these procedures, the plaintiffs had access for the first time to *an institution* that classified, named and treated them as victims. In this sense, in the trial, the judiciary, as a 'neutral' institutional authority,[28] exercised enormous symbolic effectiveness: both when classifying and, therefore, establishing the events and the subjects involved in them, as well as producing rituals of institutional and social recognition by deploying highly performative modes of classification.[29]

This symbolic efficacy had two fundamental effects. The first was the standardization of groups of victims based on a single legal category of 'victim of crimes against humanity and/or genocide': the Argentine magistrate's admission of a very diverse range of complaints through this legal tool permitted the incorporation of subjects, relatives and affected persons with different trajectories. The class action suit had the ability to *undo the singular* and 'each of the individuals in question could, if necessary, be treated as a member of a category that could be replaced by any other member of the same category without resulting in a modification of the structure of the relationship'.[30] In other words, each particular claim, each 'victim type', each repressive act or each history of violence, united from the beginning by the lack of reparation or recognition by the Spanish state, became equivalent as the consequences of a systematic violation of human rights. The photographs of everyone all together in Comodoro Py, the hugs, are displays and gestures that embody that community formed around the category of 'victim of Francoism'.

The second effect was found in the reparative function of the mere fact of being heard as victims by an institution. It was access itself to justice, not the execution of justice, that led to reparation. Here, reparation – contrary to the meaning that is usually found in the literature on victims or transitional justice, often referring to financial compensation – refers to reparation in a political sense: that the subjects, upon feeling part of the political community as full members once again, experience this type of moral sentiment. In other words, it is the official, institutional and legal hearing, something that has not been possible in Spain yet, which offers the plaintiffs reparation as victims of the Franco regime.

From another point of view, the latter point allows us to reflect on the effectiveness of *symbolic spaces* and not merely physical ones, since the interviews showed that this reparative dimension was experienced both by the plaintiffs who had testified in person in Argentina, and those who had done so in the consulates by videoconference or who had met with the judge in the Spanish courts during her trip to Spain. All of them underline *the presence* (physical or online) *of the judge*: how she was dressed, the questions and comments she made, and the secretaries who went with or accompanied her. In the same way, they describe the room, the official documents, the cameras that recorded them, the videoconference screens, the microphones, the tables and the established places where each person should sit. All these details serve to describe with greater strength and realism the social ritual of production of an institution, an official body, which is listening to them and recognizing them as victims for the first time.

At the same time, this reparative dimension was articulated with a strong feeling of injustice regarding the Spanish institutions. In some way, it was as if the listening and the accompaniment of Argentine officials increased the feeling of grievance towards the plaintiffs' institution of reference: that of Spain, an institution that has not addressed or treated them as victims except on rare occasions. In some way, the Argentine Lawsuit became a *comparative mirror* of the injury that they and their relatives continued to experience, caused by the Spanish state. To delve into this further, let us travel 10,000 kilometres once again, from Comodoro Py to the headquarters of the Spanish National High Court in Madrid.

The National High Court (AN) was created in the middle of the Spanish Transition, in 1977. It was established at the same time that the Public Order Court (TOP) – the judicial body in charge of trying political crimes during the dictatorship – was abolished, and to investigate crimes of terrorism, in the context of the terrorism of Euskadi Ta Askatasuna (ETA), reducing the pressure on the judges and courts that carried out their jurisdictional function in the Basque Country. Currently, the Criminal Chamber of the National High Court has jurisdiction over the following matters: crimes against certain high institutions of the state, organized crime, fraud that affects the national economy, terrorism, extraditions and international justice.

The headquarters of the National High Court is located in a wealthy neighbourhood in the centre of Madrid. When high-profile cases are underway – which often happens, given the nature of the crimes tried by the Court – the building is usually guarded by the police and besieged by journalists. As the National High Court is on a narrow street, the groups that gather in front of it are usually limited to a part of the road that is on the corner of the major avenue Paseo de la Castellana. When in 2013 the Argentine authorities demanded the extraditions of former Francoist officials Antonio González Pacheco and Jesús Muñecas Aguilar – accused of torture in the lawsuit – the National High Court had to indicate whether it would extradite the accused or not. By chance, Judge Servini was taking statements from a group of victims in Buenos Aires on the same days (10 and 11 December 2013) that the National High Court summoned the accused to take their statements before deciding on their extradition. At the Madrid courthouse where the former Francoist police officers were testifying, a small group of plaintiffs who had not gone to Argentina to testify held a demonstration on the street corner. According to many of the attendees, the police officers who were guarding the courthouse pushed them until they were thrown off the pavement; when one of the plaintiffs protested the aggression, a policeman replied 'tell that to Garzón', referring to the judge mentioned at the beginning of this chapter.[31] The officials of the forces and bodies of the Francoist state, on the contrary, were protected by the National Police, which allowed them to cover themselves up and exit through other doors, they even made some improvised gestures of support.

In other words, while in Comodoro Py they were dealt with, listened to and treated as victims, in the National High Court they were answered with indifference – an offence compared to the treatment received by the accused – if not with violence. A few months later, in April 2014, the National High Court ruled against the extradition, making it clear that Spain does not judge the crimes of the Franco regime nor does it allow other countries to do so in the name of universal justice. Two years later, in October 2016, the Spanish Attorney General issued an internal order to judges not to collaborate with the lawsuit, at the risk of ending up like Judge Garzón if they did not obey.[32]

Other references to Spanish judicial institutions have to do with the degrading treatment that some of the plaintiffs have suffered from some Spanish judges who *grudgingly* collaborated with the Argentine Lawsuit, prior to this internal order. In an interview, one plaintiff described her feelings a few days after having testified in a court in Madrid. It seems that the judge, whom she describes as close to the Popular Party, did not take note of the entire statement she gave, and

Figure 10.2 Plaques in memory of the victims of the 1936 coup and Francoist violence at Boisaca's Cemetery, Santiago de Compostela (Galicia, Spain), 2019. © Histagra Collection / Histagra Research Group.

he humiliated her on different occasions.[33] In this way, past injustices overlap with present ones, producing new processes of re-victimization. Once again, we can observe how the demand for justice is closely intertwined with the demand for recognition, since the response of the Spanish state during all these years has been one of indifference and blocking, if not boycott and delegitimization of the lawsuit: not recognizing the victims as such.

The 'victory' of the cemetery of Guadalajara: The two deaths and the two exhumations of Timoteo Mendieta

If we return to Judge Servini's office in Comodoro Py, on her table we find a framed photo of Ascensión Mendieta, which she keeps with great affection.[34] This plaintiff turned eighty-eight on the plane that took her to Argentina in 2013 to testify before the judge and ask her to exhume the remains of her father, Timoteo Mendieta. Timoteo was a member of the General Union of Workers from Sacedón (Guadalajara) who had fought on the Republican side. As he had not committed any violent crime, he did not think that he would be retaliated against. However, weeks after the war's end, in the spring of 1939, he was taken from his home and imprisoned for months, until one day without prior notice to the family and without trial or due process, he was shot and thrown into a mass grave at the wall of the Guadalajara cemetery, together with twenty other people. Ascensión, who was thirteen years old at the time and the oldest of seven siblings, was the one who opened the door to the Civil Guard the day they took him away.[35]

Since his killing, Timoteo's family knew that he was in one of the graves by the wall of the cemetery, in a remote area and almost adjacent to the cemetery's edge; but they did not know exactly where, nor could they ask the authorities about it. Thus, these illegal and clandestine executions and burials functioned as one of the most powerful and exemplary tools of the dictatorship to engender fear and uncertainty in the population. In addition, some authors speak of *a second death* for these people: first a physical death, and then a social death, since they were also expelled from the community of death[36] in a strongly Catholic culture such as that of Spain.

During the years of the dictatorship, Ascensión, her mother and her sister Paz would take the train or bus from Madrid and 'get off' at the Guadalajara cemetery, on the dates of his birthday, his killing or All Saints' Day. It is not coincidental that it is women who go to the cemetery, since within families they are the ones responsible for the management of family grief and for leading the actions to recover or dignify their relatives.[37] At that time, the Guadalajara cemetery authorities had put up a fence and did not allow relatives to enter or bring flowers, not even on the day that Ascensión got married and her mother tried to leave some there. This discriminatory treatment should be considered in relation to what one first sees, still to this day, at the entrance of the cemetery. Presiding over the enclosure, one suddenly encounters a large cross on a tombstone, shiny and well kept with fresh flowers, dedicated to those 'Fallen for God and for Spain': soldiers, civilians and clergymen on the Francoist side who were retaliated against or killed during the war by the Republican army, who were remembered by a Francoist policy of recognition and memory during all the years of the regime – which has largely continued into the present.[38]

With the arrival of democracy, the authorities removed the cemetery fence, and Ascensión and her family were able to access the wall; they also put up a tombstone where they inscribed the name of Timoteo Mendieta and the phrase: 'Died for democracy and freedom.'[39] However, the possibility of being able to exhume his remains, even though Timoteo was registered in the cemetery records as one of those shot in grave number two along with twenty other people, was unthinkable. They sometimes tried to initiate administrative or judicial procedures to request the exhumation, but it was always in vain – until the opportunity came through the Argentine Lawsuit, which they joined. After several letters rogatory, the Guadalajara court decided to accept the judge's proceedings, and in January 2016 the exhumation work began.[40]

A few months later, through a process of identifying the bodies removed from the grave by DNA, the test of this first exhumation was negative: contrary to the data in the cemetery records, none of the twenty-two mortal remains that had been exhumed corresponded to Timoteo. This negative result of a genetic match led Judge Servini to issue other letters rogatory to exhume the area by other walls of the cemetery that contained the mortal remains of those shot on the same day as the union member. After a series of complex legal difficulties, in May 2017, a second exhumation was carried out by order of the judge. In this exhumation, finally, the remains of Timoteo Mendieta were identified and could be delivered to the family, along with another twenty bodies.

In this way, it was *genetic and forensic evidence* and not other criteria – historiographic, religious, ideological or of another type – that categorized these bodies, producing a truth about the events of the past and pushing the records, documents and historiographic sources or bibliographies aside to a status of less objectivity. Forensics intervened as the main factor in making sense of what was happening in the exhumation.[41] Likewise, the negative result of the first exhumation permitted the recovery of other bodies that, through the work of the ARMH, publicly revealed another twenty stories of people with names and surnames and enabled a search for their family members to return the remains. Of this unexpected consequence of the two exhumations of Timoteo, the lawyer Ana Messuti wrote in *El Diario*:

> Precisely, now, the universe of Timoteo Mendieta is being populated with the names of his fellow companions in the mass grave, and in the neighbouring graves, which were opened to search for him, and we will no longer need to say that there were many Timoteos, because we are learning the names of each man and of each woman, and they can be returned to their families while they still have them.[42]

But let us return to the Guadalajara cemetery. The work of excavating and identifying the remains during the two exhumations was done in an open and public way for those who wanted to know more about the initiative. The ARMH volunteers set up a table with a small awning, and there they received anyone who approached them: people who came to ask about relatives buried in that grave, or who simply came attracted by the media coverage. Meanwhile, Ascensión kept a close eye on everything that happened: sitting in a plastic chair and wrapped in a coat and scarf in the cold January of 2016; or looking impatient and leaning on a bench in May 2017.

During those weeks of daily work, it was evident how the work and processes involved in an exhumation make it a privileged space of memory, where a strong restorative function can be observed. Bergerot explains in this first exhumation how different neighbours shared family stories of repression with their relatives for the first time or listened to technicians recount the traces of violence when they described the work's progress every day,[43] forming intergenerational public encounters. Along these lines, Laura Martín Chiappe points out how the disciplinary power of mass graves around fear and silence is broken by the actions of technicians and families during exhumation, but also by those of participating neighbours.[44] The context of the grave becomes a space of communication in which different stories of repression and pain, absences and resistance, emerge and circulate for the first time. All of this permits a collective conversation about the violent past in Spain; scientific evidence of the violence perpetrated by the regime – in a Spanish context where impunity and denialism still reign in part of society; closure to mourning; or the beginning of new processes of political identification among younger family members.

On 2 July 2017, Ascensión was finally able to bury her father in the Almudena Cemetery, in Madrid, next to his loved ones. That day turned into a major event, in which approximately 500 people arrived to bid a final farewell to Timoteo and show support for the plaintiff. In some way, the reparation became collective: some people expressed to me 'the joy' of feeling that finally there was 'closure to grieving' and that the Argentine Lawsuit, for this alone, had 'been worth it', 'it served a purpose' or it had generated 'a victory'. The feeling of 'reparation' was *shared* among the plaintiffs, moving from an individual reparation to a moral and social reparation, which could *be appropriated* by the others present.

The Argentine Lawsuit has shaped different round-trip journeys between Spain and Argentina that have (re)produced a transnational space of practices and discourses regarding memory and human rights. This has had enormous consequences for the transformation of the repertoires of collective action among the plaintiff associations, their processes of identification as victims and their manners of social representation in Spanish society. Throughout this chapter, an attempt has been made to describe and analyse the logic behind this process from the basis of different physical places that are symbolic enclaves within it: the protests and demonstrations; the testimonies given in judicial headquarters; the exhumations of mass graves. From the courts of Buenos Aires to the walls of the Guadalajara cemetery, passing through the Ronda of the Puerta del Sol square, these places show the ambivalences of the process of constituting the victims of the Franco regime. It is a process that is still open and unfinished. We will have to wait to see what its next scenarios will be.

Notes

1 Isabel Piper-Shafir, Roberto Fernández-Droguett, and Lupicinio Iñiguez-Rueda, 'Psicología Social de la Memoria: Espacios y Políticas del Recuerdo', *Psykhe* 22, no. 2 (2013): 26.
2 Elisabeth Jelin, *State Repression and the Labors of Memory* (Minnesota: University of Minnesota Press, 2003), introduction.
3 Patrick Eser and Stefan Peters, *El atentado de Carrero Blanco como lugar de no memoria* (Madrid: Iberoamericana, 2016), 26-7.
4 Francisco Ferrándiz, 'Unburials, Generals and Phantom Militarism: Engaging with the Spanish Civil War Legay', *Current Anthropology* 60 (2019): 62-76.
5 Pierre Bourdieu, *The Weight of the World: Social Suffering in Contemporary Society* (Stanford, CA: Stanford University Press, 1999), introduction.

6   Marina Montoto, *Un viaje de ida y vuelta: la construcción social de la víctima del franquismo en la Querella Argentina* (Madrid: Universidad Complutense de Madrid, 2018).
7   Francisco Ferrándiz, *El pasado bajo tierra: Exhumaciones contemporáneas de la guerra civil* (Barcelona: Anthropos Editorial, 2014), 13.
8   Paloma Aguilar, *Políticas de la Memoria y Memorias de la Política* (Madrid: Alianza, 2008), 326.
9   Ricard Vinyes, 'La memoria del Estado', in *El Estado y la memoria: gobiernos y ciudadanos frente a los traumas de la Historia*, ed. Ricard Vinyes (Barcelona: RBA, 2009), 25–6.
10 Walter Bernecker, and Sören Brinkmann, *Memorias divididas. Guerra Civil y franquismo en la sociedad y la política españolas (1936–2008)* (Madrid: Editorial Abada, 2009), 204–5.
11 Francisco Ferrándiz, 'De las fosas comunes a los derechos humanos. El descubrimiento de las desapariciones forzadas en la España contemporánea', *Revista Antropología Social* 19 (2010): 163–4; Gabriel Gatti, 'De un continente al otro: el desaparecido transnacional, la cultura humanitaria y las víctimas totales en tiempos de guerra global', *Política y Sociedad* 48, no. 3 (2011): 519–36.
12 Sergio Gálvez Biesca, 'El proceso de recuperación de la "memoria histórica" en España: Una aproximación a los movimientos sociales por la memoria', *International Journal of Iberian Studies* 19 (2006): 25–6.
13 Francisco Ferrándiz, 'Exhuming the Defeated: Civil War Mass Graves in 21st-Century Spain', *American Ethnologist* 40, no. 1 (2013): 40–2.
14 Ana Messuti, *Un deber ineludible. La obligación del Estado de perseguir penalmente los crímenes internacionales* (Buenos Aires: Sociedad Anónima Editora, 2013), introduction.
15 Javier Alvarez Chinchón, 'El tratamiento judicial de los crímenes de la Guerra Civil y el Franquismo en España. Una visión de conjunto desde el Derechos Internacional', *Cuadernos de Derechos humanos Universidad de Deusto* 67 (2012): 76–96.
16 CEAQUA. Available in https://www.ceaqua.org (accessed 30 June 2020).
17 Belen Picazo, 'Estos son los 20 españoles acusados de crímenes en el franquismo a los que busca Interpol', *El Diario*, 12 November 2014.
18 Sergio C. González García, '(Re)apropiación política del espacio: La puerta del Sol, memoria y rebeldía', in *Pasados de violencia política. Memoria, discurso y puesta en escena*, ed. Jean Franços and Mario Martínez Zauner (Madrid: Anexo Editorial, 2016), 257–79.
19 Ulrike Capdepon, 'Del "caso Pinochet" a los desaparecidos de la Guerra Civil: La influencia de los discursos sobre los Derechos Humanos del Cono Sur en el debate español sobre el pasado franquista (1998–2012)' in *Pasados de violencia política.*

Memoria, discurso y puesta en escena, ed. Jean François Macé and Martínez Zauner (Madrid: Anexo Editorial, 2016), 271–2.
20 Marie-Jose Devillard and Alejandro Baer, 'Antropología y derechos humanos: multiculturalismo, retos y resignificaciones', *Revista de Antropología Social* 19 (2010): 35.
21 Sally Engle Merry, 'Transnational Human Rights and Local Activism: Mapping the Middle', *American Anthropologist* 108 (2006): 42.
22 Gabriel Gatti, '"Lo nuestro, como en Argentina". Humanitarian Reason and the Latin Americanization of Victimhood in Spain', *Journal of Latin American Cultural Studies*, 25, no. 1 (2016): 1–19.
23 Manuela Bergerot, 'Porque tenemos memoria, tenemos futuro', in *Construyendo memorias entres generaciones: tender puentes, buscar verdades, reclamar justicia*, ed. Ana Messuti (Madrid: Postmetrópolis, 2019), 59.
24 Ibid., 60.
25 Piper-Shafir, Fernández-Droguett and Iñiguez-Rueda, 'Psicología Social de la Memoria', 26.
26 EFE, Agency, 'Las víctimas del régimen franquista concluyen sus declaraciones ante la jueza argentina', *La Vanguardia*, 7 December 2013.
27 Montoto, *Un viaje de ida y vuelta*, 248.
28 Pierre Bourdieu, 'La fuerza del derecho: elementos para una sociología del campo jurídico', in *Poder, derecho y clases sociales*, ed. Pierre Bourdieu and Gunther Teubner (Bogotá: Siglo del Hombre Editores. Facultad de Derecho de la Universidad de los Andes, 2000), 196–7.
29 Bourdieu, 'New Directions', in *In Other Words: Essays Towards a Reflexive Sociology* (Stanford, CA: Stanford University Press, 1990), 123–40.
30 Luc Boltanski, *Love and Justice as Competences*, English edn (Indianapolis, IN: Wiley, 2012), 266.
31 Alejandro Torrús, 'Los policías a las víctimas: "cuéntaselo a Garzón"', *Público.es*, 10 December 2013.
32 Pédro Águeda, 'La Fiscalía advierte a la jueza Servini de que no puede cuestionar la transición española', *El diario*, 6 October 2016.
33 Montoto, *Un viaje de ida y vuelta*, 244.
34 Cesar G. Calero, 'Nos cuesta horrores seguir investigando los crímenes del franquismo', *Contexto*, 7 August 2018.
35 Katharine Q. Seelye 'Ascensión Mendieta, 93, Dies; Symbol of Justice for Franco Victims', *The New York Times*, 22 September 2019.
36 Ferrándiz, *El pasado bajo tierra*, 25.
37 Zoé De Kerangat and Maria Laura Martin-Chiappe, 'Mujeres en -y en torno a- fosas comunes de la represión franquista en la guerra civil española', in *Mujeres en la guerra civil y la posguerra. Memoria y educación*, ed. Alicia Torija and Jorge Morín (Madrid: Audema, 2019), 265.

38 Jaio Iratxe, 'La Ruta Más larga', blog, 8 November 2018. Available online: http://guerraenlauniversidad.blogspot.com/2018/11/la-ruta-mas-larga.html (accessed 4 July 2020).
39 Montoto, *Un viaje de ida y vuelta*, 245.
40 Ibid., 252.
41 Francisco Ferrándiz and Antonius C. G. M.Robben (eds), *Necropolitics: Mass Graves and Exhumations in the Age of Human Rights* (Philadelphia: University of Pennsylvania Pres, 2017), introduction.
42 Ana Messuti, 'La universalidad de Timoteo Mendieta', *Eldiario.es*, 29 August 2018.
43 Bergerot, *Porque tenemos memoria, tenemos futuro*, 75.
44 Mª Laura Martin-Chiappe, 'De la fosa al cementerio: el complicado camino de la reparación para los represaliados/as por el franquismo', in *Construyendo memorias entres generaciones: tender puentes, buscar verdades, reclamar justicia*, ed. Ana Messuti (Madrid: Postmetrópolis, 2018) 121–58 (p. 148).

Select Bibliography

Anderson, Peter, *The Francoist Military Trials: Terror and Complicity, 1939-1945* (New York: Routledge, 2010).

Anderson, Peter, *Friend or Foe? Occupation, Collaboration and Selective Violence in the Spanish Civil War* (Brighton: Sussex Academic Press, 2017).

Anderson, Peter, and Miguel Ángel Del Arco, eds, *Mass Killings and Violence in Spain, 1936-1952: Grappling with the Past* (New York: Routledge, 2014).

Arco, Miguel Ángel del, Carlos Fuertes, Claudio Hernández, and Jorge Marco, eds, *No solo miedo. Actitudes políticas y opinión popular bajo la dictadura franquista (1936-1977)* (Granada: Comares, 2013).

Babiano, José, Gutmaro Gómez Bravo, Antonio Míguez, and Javier Tébar, *Verdugos impunes. El franquismo y la violación sistémica de los derechos humanos* (Barcelona: Pasado & Presente, 2018).

Baumeister, Martin, and Stefanie Schüler-Springorum, eds, *'If You Tolerate This', The Spanish Civil War in the Age of Total War* (Frankfurt: Campus Verlag, 2008).

Chinchón, Javier, *El tratamiento judicial de los crímenes de la Guerra Civil y el franquismo en España: una visión de conjunto desde el Derecho internacional* (Bilbao: Universidad de Deusto, 2012).

Ealham, Chris, and Michael Richards, eds, *The Splintering of Spain: Cultural History and the Spanish Civil War, 1936-1939* (Cambridge: Cambridge University Press, 2005).

Escudero Alday, Rafael, ed., *Diccionario de memoria histórica. Conceptos contra el olvido* (Madrid: Catarata, 2011).

Fernández Prieto, Lourenzo, and Antonio Míguez Macho, *Golpistas e verdugos de 1936. Historia dun pasado incómodo* (Vigo: Editorial Galaxia, 2018).

Ferrándiz, Francisco, and Antonius C.G.M. Robben, *Necropolitics: Mass Graves and Exhumations in the Age of Human Rights* (Philadelphia: University of Pennsylvania Press, 2015).

Hernández Burgos, Claudio, ed., *Ruptura: The Impact of Nationalism and Extremism on Daily Life in the Spanish Civil War (1936-1939)* (Brighton: Sussex, 2020).

Gómez Bravo, Gutmaro, *El exilio interior. Cárcel y represión en la España franquista, 1939-1950* (Madrid: Taurus, 2008).

Jelin, Elizabeth, *State Repression and the Labors of Memory* (Minneapolis: University of Minnesota Press, 2003).

Jerez-Farrán, Carlos, and Samuel Amago, eds, *Unearthing Franco's Legacy: Mass Graves and the Recovery of Historical Memory in Spain* (Notre Dame: University of Notre Dame Press, 2010).

Leonisio, Rafael, Fernando Molina, and Diego Muro, eds, *ETA's Terrorist Campaign: From Violence to Politics, 1968–2015* (London: Routledge, 2017).

Macé, Jean François, and Mario Martínez Zauner, eds, *Pasados de violencia política. Memoria, discurso y puesta en escena* (Madrid: Anexo Editorial, 2016).

Maddrell, Avril, and James D. Sidaway, eds, *Deathscapes Spaces for Death, Dying, Mourning and Remembrance* (Farnham: Ashgate, 2010).

Michonneau, Stéphane, *'Fue ayer'. Belchite: un pueblo frente a la cuestión del pasado* (Zaragoza: Prensas de la Universidad de Zaragoza, 2017).

Míguez Macho, Antonio, *Genocidal Genealogy of Francoism: Violence, Memory & Impunity* (Brighton: Sussex, 2016).

Mir Curcó, Coxita, and Josep Gelonch Solé, eds, *Duelo y memoria. Espacios para el recuerdo de las víctimas de la represión franquista en perspectiva comparada* (Lleida: Universitat de Lleida, 2013).

Patterson, Ian, *Guernica and Total War* (Cambridge: Harvard University Press, 2007).

Preston, Paul, *The Spanish Holocaust: Inquisition and Extermination in Twentieth-Century Spain* (London: Harper Press, 2012).

Rivera, Antonio, ed., *Nunca hubo dos bandos. Violencia política en el País Vasco 1975–2011* (Granada: Comares, 2019).

Rodrigo, Javier, *Los campos de concentración franquistas. Entre la historia y la memoria* (Madrid: Siete Mares, 2003).

Santidrián Arias, Víctor Manuel, *Diario del soldado republicano Casimiro Jabonero. Campo de prisioneros de Lavacolla, prisión de Santiago de Compostela, 1939–1940* (Santiago de Compostela: Fundación 10 de Marzo, 2004).

Zubiaga, Erik, *La huella del terror franquista en Bizkaia. Jurisdicción militar, políticas de captación y actitudes sociales* (Bilbao: UPV-EHU, 2017)

Index

Boldface locators indicate figures and tables; locators followed by "n." indicate endnotes

act of writing (prisoners)
    act of resistance 155
    graffiti 155
    rehumanization 154
Aguirre, José Antonio 131
Ajuriaguerra, Juan 169
Alexandre Bóveda Foundation 135
Alfonso Daniel Rodríguez Castelao. *See* Castelao
Alltagsgeschichte 106
Alonso, Martín 56, 173
Álvarez, Brasilino 148
Álvarez, Lucía 155
Álvarez Gallego, Xerardo, *Vida, paixon e norte de Alexandre Boveda* 135
Álvarez López, Marcelino 76
Amnesty Law (1977) 157–9, 190, 192
Anderson, Peter 20
anti-Francoism 114, 174
anti-Spain 4, 154, 172
Ánxel Casal library, case 73
Aranguren Ponte, Juan 67
Arc de Triomphe 2
Arco, Miguel Ángel del 16
Ardao Seijido, Juan Antonio 71
Argentina
    human rights organizations in 193
    Memory, Truth and Justice 157
    round-trip journeys 188, 204
Argentine Lawsuit 19–20, 159, 187, 189, 194, 202, 204
    comparative mirror 199
    against Franco-era crimes 187–8
    opportunity of 192–3
    as transnational space of memory 188
Argomoso, parish of 76
Armed Defence of Granada 36
Armenian genocide 9
Armistice Day 3
Assault Guards 28, 31–2, 37

Assmann, Jan 126
Association for the Recovery of Historical Memory (ARMH) 72, 192–3, 203
Asturias, concentration camps 91, 150–1
Auschwitz memorial museum 8
'authentic and imperial Spain' 33
Auxilio Social (Social Assistance) centres 109
Auz Auz, José 56
Azarola, Antonio 49

Badajoz, extermination 127, 135–8
Badajoz massacre 71, 137–8
Baixo Miño region 147–8, 162 n.2
Balkan secession wars 86
Ballesta, José 155, 158, 160–1, 166 n.57
Basque Country 167, 182 n.24
    Álava 168
    Basque nationalism 129, 132, 168–70
    coup, evolution 168
    escalation of terrorism 173
    jurisdictional function 199
    memorials **170**, 175
    political violence in 168, 180
    public memory policies 176
    public space 177
    regional and municipal institutions 175–7
    'the martyrs of the Movement' 169
    war of 1936 168–71
Basque Nationalist Party (PNV) 168, 170–1
Battle of the Ebro 188
Belchite (armed conflict) 128, 138–41
    disaster 139
    Francoist myth of 140
    readaptation of symbol 141
Betriu, José, 'Come closer to our sanctuary' 160

Bilbao
    fall of 169
    National Historical Archive of Euskadi 177
    reminders of war 174
Blanco, Eugenio 151, 161
Blanco, Miguel Ángel 176
Bloch, Jan 8
Boer War 85
Bóveda Iglesias, Alexandre 133–5
Brenan, Gerald 33
Buenos Aires
    Circle of Mothers and Grandmothers 196
    A derradeira leicion 134
    judicial headquarters, role 189
    lawsuit 4591/2010 159, 192
    March of Mothers of Plaza de Mayo 189, 194
    testimonies 197
Buxeiro, Xabier 17

Cabanellas, Miguel 50
Cabezas, Juan Antonio 153
A Caeira, parish of 133
Calvo, Juan 111
Calvo Sotelo, José 67
Campins Aura, Miguel 30–1
Campo da Rata (A Coruña) 73
Campo Robles, Miguel del 31
Camposancos camp (gates of hell) 151
    Cedeira camp to 153
    rehumanization 154
Cañón, Lisandro 20
Carabanchel Prison 188, 191
Carballeira, Johan, memorial **13**
Carballo, Florencio 66
Carballo, Pilar 66
Carlism 168
Casares Quiroga 29–30
case studies
    Badajoz 135–8
    Belchite 138–41
    Guernica 128–32
    Pontevedra 132–5
Castelao 133, 134
    Alba de Groria (1948) 135
    Galicia Martir/Atila in Galicia 134
    Galicianism 133
Castile-La Mancha 90, 156

Castro, Juan 148
Catalan law 159
Catalonia, memorial significance 97
Cenotaph (Whitehall, London) 2
CGT-Memoria 193
Cidrás, Aldara 18
Ciriego cemetery 74
'civic guards' 30
civil government buildings 16–17, 27–9, 39–40, 60
    and surrounding silence 33–4
    volunteers 36
civil government clique. *See* 'Valdés clique'
civil governments (military government) 17, 35, 44 n.50
    coup d'etat and 29–33
    and men in summer (1936) 34–7, **38**, 39–41
    rebel violence 28
civil organization, coordination 48
civil wars 87, 125
climate of terror 5
Code of Military Justice (CMJ) 47, 61 n.6
    declaration of martial law 49
    Ordinary Penal Codes of Military Justice 49
    procedures 51
collective learning, space for 161
collective memory 72, 107, 126, 133, 137, 141, 178, 187
commemorative actions 187
Comodoro Py court 189, 192–3, 196–201
concealment of violence 72
concentration camps 5, 9–10, 18–19, 147, 153–4. *See also specific concentration camps*
    coup plotters 87
    dehumanizing prisoner 89
    forced prison labour (*see* forced prison labour (concentration camps))
    Francoist penitentiary system 88
    inscriptions and drawings (prisoners) 150, **150**, 162
    life span of 90
    prisoners, types 88
    systems 85–7, 149
confinement spaces. *See* sites of confinement
controlled spaces 112–17
Costas, Javier 155

coup d'état 4, 54, 60, 65, 69, 71, 105, 111, 131, 132, 148
  and civil governments 29–33
  memory of victims 69, **200**
  paseos (*see* paseos)
Cuervo, Máximo 133

Dachau (refugee camp) 8–9, 86
dark tourism 12
dates of memory 187
dedicated sites 12, 14
democratic learning 72
denunciation, era of 8–11, 51–2, 109, 189, 193–4
detention centres 18, 86–8, 92–3, 99–101, 102 n.25, 136
Dia de Galiza Martir 135
Díaz Álvarez, José Antonio 75
Díaz y Díaz Villamil, Antonio 69–71
Domínguez, Manuel 149, 152, 160
drawings 19, 147, 161
  prisoners 147–8, **150**, 151–6, **162**
  Spanish War of Independence (Goya) 134
dynamics of coup violence 16, 51, 73, 133, 135, 155–6

economic crisis (2008) 159
El Kenz, David 138
El Prado de Los Remedios 76
'enemies of the regime' 88, 111
Europe
  concentration camps systems 85–7, 97
  defeat of fascism in 9
  democratization 11
  Memorial to the Murdered Jews 14
  memory regime 3
  museumization process 97
Euskadi ta Askatasuna (ETA) 19, 132, 167
  anti-Francoism 174
  contemporary narratives 174–7
  mobilization of citizens against 167
  'new gudaris' 171–4
  'permanent ceasefire of armed activity' 181 n.1
  terrorism (1959–2018) 167, 175, 177, 199
Euskal Memoria 175
executions 40, 65–6, 68, 74, 79, 137–8, 153. *See also* sites of execution

exhumations **15**, 16, 72, 158, 189, 193
  demands for 190
  Law of Historical Memory (2007) 175
  Priaranza del Bierzo (León) 175
  subcontracting human rights 192
  of Timoteo Mendieta 201–4
exploitation 91
  and humiliation 154
  as manual labour 18, 87
extermination camps 8–9, 13, 85, 138. *See also specific extermination camps*
Extremadura 4, 97, 138
extreme right-wing terrorism 167, 175

Faculty of Law (in Granada) 34
Falange 5–7, 32, 36, 54, 59
Falangists **4**, 30, **35**, 37, 69, 111, 116, 130, 136, 149, 169
Falla, Manuel de 41
Fariñas, Elisa 67
Fariñas Reinante, Santiago 67, 69–72, 76
fascism 7, 9, 96, 107, 130, 137–8, 154, 171, 176
Fernández, Antonio 110
Fernández, Miguel Anxo 155, 158
Fernández Montesinos, Manuel 31
Fernández Prieto, Lourenzo 20
Fiesta del Caudillo 59
Finland civil war (1918) 5, 87
First World War 1
  military cemeteries 2
  nationalization 2
Flechas Negras 169
forced prison labour (concentration camps) 89–91
  living conditions of 88
  'Prisoners' Canal' 89
  reconstruction of towns 89, 91
  re-education and re-Christianization 91
  salary 91
  suffering of abuse 88, 92
Fossar de la Pedrera 157
Franco, Francisco 6–7, 49, 88, 90, 140, 152, 157, 187. *See also* Franco regime
Franco-German rivalry 1
Francoist concentration camp 92–6. *See also* Lavacolla concentration camp
'forgetfulness,' promoting 97, 99
  memory and forgetting of 96–9

punishment of defeated 99–101
  sentence reductions 101
Francoist violence 16–18, 106, 108, 156
Franco-Prussian War 1
Franco regime 6–7, 9, 14, 17–19, 28, 30, 66, 67, 72, 87, 100, 158, 167, 169, 173
  Argentine Lawsuit 19–20
  constant resignification 117
  control over morality 114–16
  coup plotters, public rally 110, **110**
  de-Christianization 115
  defeat of fascism 96
  democratic reality 61
  paradigm shift 10
  place of memory 188
  public places and civil government facilities 60
  reappropriation process 189
  redefinition and regeneration 105, 107–8, 112–13, 115
  'scourge of Marxism' 115
  social regeneration 116
  source of legitimacy 47
  space and violence 107–12
  Valley of the Fallen monument 10, 15, 88, 97, 188, 191
  'victim of Francoism' 188, 193, 195, 198
  victims, sculpture in memory of **179, 180**
  voluntary surrender 7
Frederick the Great, statue 2

GAL (1983–1987) 167
Galicia 4, 69, 135, 148. See also specific city in Galicia
Galicianist Party (1931) 133
Galician Statute of Autonomy 59, 133
García, Manuel Guzmán 63 n.35
García de Frutos, Ignacio 70
García Ferreira, Rafael 17
García Lorca, Federico 10, 28, 34, 41, 44 n.44, 70, 73
garrison town (*plaza militar*) 49, 52, 57, 60
Garzón, Baltasar 192–4, 200
'Garzón case' 192
General Directorate of Security 16, 194–5
genocide 85, 157
  Armenian 9
  Indonesia 14
  Jewish 11
  lawsuit 4591/2010 for 159
  Nazi 12
German concentration camps 85
German Condor Legion 128
Gipuzkoa 168–9
Giral, José 29
Glorious National Uprising 30, 32
Gogora 177–8
Gogora Institute for Memory, Coexistence and Human Rights 177
Gomá, Isidro 115
González, Lorena 155
González, Siervo 75
González Espinosa, Antonio 44 n.53
González Pacheco, Antonio 199
Goya masterpieces (Spanish uprising) 2, 134
Granada
  civil governor group (summer of 1936) 28, 34–7, **38**, 39–41
  Faculty of Law 34
  monuments 109
  October (1934) revolution 37
Great War. See First World War
Greece civil war (1946–1950) 86–7
Guadalajara, cemetery 189, 193, 201–4
Guernica, atrocious violence 18–19, 127–32
  Basque nationalism 129, 132
  Carlists, role of 130
  fuero-based traditionalism 130
  Gernika Agreement (2010) 132
guerrilla fighters 85
Gulag (USSR) 86

Halbwachs, Maurice 1–2
Hernández Angosto, Julián 154
Hernández Burgos, Claudio 18
'heroes of Jaca,' monuments 3
'The Heroes of the Alcázar of Toledo' 113, 138
Hervella, Gustavo 20
High Court of Justice (24 October 1936) 50
Himmler 85, 90
'Himno de Riego' (song) 196
Hispanic-Imperial race 140
Historical Memory and Justice 193
Historical Memory Law (2006/2007) 15, 61, 158, 175–6, 191

Hitler 85–6, 99
Holocaust Memorial Museum (Washington, DC) 12
'Holocaust' series (1978) 11
hot terror 30, 169
human rights translators 195

Ibárruri, Dolores. *See* La Pasionaria
illegal detention centres 18
Indonesia, genocide 14
Inspection of Concentration Camps for Prisoners (ICCP) 86–7, 149
institutional denial 15
institutional transition 14
Iparraguirre, José María, *Gernikako Arbola* 129
Italian Legionary Air Force 129
'Italobalbo' 40

Jabonero, Casimiro 93, 95
Jesuit school of Camposancos (A Guarda) 19, 147–52, 156, 160–1. *See also* Camposancos camp (gates of hell)
Jiménez de Parga, Antonio 39
Jiménez de Parga, José 39
Jiménez de Parga, Manuel 39
Joven Hernández, Mariano 34
judicial institution as recognition/grievance 196–201
judicial process 19–20
Junta de Defensa Nacional (Council of National Defence) 50
justification, era of 1–7

La Comuna Association of Former Prisoners and Political Prisoners 193
Lanero Táboas, Daniel 20
La Pasionaria 96, 103 n.33
Lavacolla concentration camp 18, 92, 97, **98**
   diary of Jabonero **93**, 93–4
   financing and manpower, lack of 95
   hygienic conditions 94–5
   work battalion 100
Law of July (1933) 49
León Maestre, Basilio 44 n.53
lieux de memoire 11, 19, 72–5, **74**, 126, 141, 187
living historical archive 161

'Long live Communism' 114
'Long live Spain' 113
López Sánchez, Conchi 17

Madariaga, Julen 172
Madrid 188
   Almudena Cemetery 204
   battalion of workers (reinforcement) 95
   concentration camps 91
   Government of the Community of 194
   horrendous crimes 71
   Modelo prison 137
   'modern Jerusalem' 115
   Puerta del Sol square 189, 194
   Reina Sofía Museum 131
Madrid Metro 91
Mao regime 86
Mao Zedong 196
March of Mothers of Plaza de Mayo 79, 189, 194
Margolles de la Vega, César 76
maritime and land jurisdiction 53–60
   accusation, type 53
   Cádiz 54
   Cartagena maritime department 54–5
   Contramaestre Casado 54
   A Coruña 56, 58
   Ferrol 53–4, 62 n.21
   General Command of the Maritime Department 54
   Lugo and Pontevedra 58–9
   Palace of Justice 56–7
   trials as public events, uses 57
Martín Chiappe, Maria Laura 203
Martínez, Víctor 52–3
Martín Martínez, Joaquín 63 n.35
Maseda, Ramón 63 n.35
mass executions 153
mass violence 3–5, 9–10, 14, 65
   civil government buildings 17
   civil governments 28, 41
   memory of 12
Mazariegos, Francisco 63 n.35
Memorial Centre for Terrorism Victims (CMVT) 177–9
'Memorial Democrático' 97, 159
memorials/monuments 2, 8–9, 12–14, 19, 73–4, 127, 156, 158, 160, 174–5. *See also specific memorials/monuments*

Basque fighters 175
exhibition 75
'fallen and martyrs of the Crusade' 109
neighbours 'killed by Francoism' **78**
plaque **74**
'a reminder of Marxist barbarism' 109
memory 1, 9, 16, 127, 155, 196. *See also* sites of memory
   conflicting management of 177–80
   era of 11–16, **13**
   of exclusion 5
   historical memory 15, 66, 73, 99, 138, 178, 189–92
   and human rights 204
   protagonists of 3
   re-elaboration of 187
   regime 3, 8–9, 11, 14
   of singularity 127
   social movements of 9, 158, 175, **191**
   of wartime suffering 125
memory alephs 125, 132, 135
   new map of 141–2
   and unspeakable 125–7, **128**
Méndez, Diego 88
Mendieta, Ascensión 201–4
Mendieta, Timoteo 201–4
Mendizábal's confiscation 148
Messuti, Ana 195
   El Diario 203
military lawsuits/justice 47
   coup plotters 49
   legal domination, spaces of 53–60
   legal *inventio* 47–53
   military trials sites and legal spectacle 60–1
   pretrial proceedings 52
   proclamations of martial law (*see* 'proclamations of martial law')
military organization 48
military trials 7, 17, 48, 53–4, 56–7, 59–61
military uprising 65, 68, 172
Miranda de Ebro concentration camp 10
Mola Vidal, Emilio 48
   coup plot 48
   Instrucciones reservadas 48
Molina Fajardo, Eduardo, *Los ultimos dias de Garcia Lorca* 33
monarchist Alfonsism 168
Mondoñedo (Galicia)
   memorial plaque (coup plotters) **74**

municipal warehouses 76
residents killed 76, 82 n.36
sites of death 76
sites of memory 75
Montoto, Marina 19
'moral sanitation policy' 115
Moreda Rodríguez, Antonio 67
Moreno, Eduardo. *See* Pertur
Morgade, Iria 19
Mount Intxorta (Elgeta, Gipuzkoa) 171
Muñecas Aguilar, Jesús 199
Municipal Boards of Sanitation and Good Customs 116
municipal prison 70, 76, 92
Museum of Modern Art (New York) 131

National Confederation of Labour (CNT) 149
'national crusade' 138
National High Court 189, 196–201
National Historical Archive (Euskadi) 177
Native Americans 14
Nazi extermination camps 9, 13
Nazi genocide 12
Nazism 7
necropolitics 125
Negrín, Juan 130–1
'NEITHER FORGET NOR FORGIVE' (slogan) 195
Nelson's Column 2
Nénard, François-Xavier 138
Nestares Cuéllar, José 31, 40
Network of Memory Spaces 159
Neves, Mário 135
'New State' 29, 105, 118
Nora, Pierre 126, 188
   événement monstrueux 129
   lieux de memoire 11–12, 72–4, 126, 141, 187
notitia criminis 51
Noya, Juan 148, 152–3, 157, 160
Noya, Manuel 149–50, 152
Nuremberg Laws 7

oblivion 138
occasions prison labour 40, 91
Oliveira, José 153–4
Onaindia, Mario 173
Ordóñez, Gregorio 177
orthophoto technique 33

Otegi, Arnaldo 177
overgeneralization 106, 119 n.5
O Vicedo, commemorative plaques 75

Palacios, Honorino 160
para-police terrorism 167, 175
Pardines, José 172
Paris International Exposition 130
paseados 66, 69, 71, 73
paseos 10, 17, 51, 65
    absences and tributes 71–6
    definition and typology 66–71
    Díaz y Díaz Villamil case 70
    and executions 66
    Fariñas case 69–70
    and memory policies 77–9
'patriotic aims' 114
'patriotic militias' 36
Paz, Graciano 75
Peña Lemona (Biscay) 171
penitentiary system 87–8, 99, 149
Penón, Agustín 40
Pérez, Eduardo 151
Pérez Carballo, Francisco 56
'Perico el Cafetero' 116
perpetrator memory site 138
Pertur 175
Peter the Great, statue 2
physical violence 107–9, 112, 117. *See also* sites of violence
    perpetration 16
    prolongation 17
Picasso, Pablo, *Guernica* 130–1, 134, 171
places of non-memory 187
Plaza de la Memoria 178
Political Responsibilities Law (1939) 7
political violence 19, 168, 178, 180, 188
Pontevedra, omnipresent violence 127, 132–5
pre-revolutionary violence 67
Priaranza del Bierzo (León, 2000) 175
Primo de Rivera, José Antonio 5–6, 173. *See also* Falange
    assassination 109
    tomb of 6, **6**
Prisoners' Canal (Lower Guadalquivir Canal) 89, 188
prisoners of war (POWs) 86, 88–9
Proclamation of A Coruña 49–50
Proclamation of Santa Cruz de Tenerife 49

'proclamations of martial law' 31, 49
    Council of National Defence 50
    crimes 49
    decrees and laws 50
    garrison town (*plaza militar*) 49, 52
    inverting justice, process 51
    military coup power 49
    publicity 51
    'rebellious' behaviour 50
'*Proxecto Nomes e Voces*' 96
'public amorality' 115
Public Order Court (TOP) 199
public policies of memory 65, 73, 76–8, 168
    modus operandi 78, **78**
    during Spanish transition 156–9
public spaces 57, 107, 110, 113, 116, 122 n.43, 169, 174, 195
    Francoist symbolism 61, 159, 176
    resignification of 6, **191**

Queipo de Llano 31, 44 n.53
querella argentina. *See* Argentine Lawsuit

Ranz Alonso, Eduardo 197
'rebel,' concept of 50
rebel illegality 51
reconciliation 173, 178, 190
    struggles for historical memory 189–92
red barbarism 111, 140
redefined spaces 112–17
'Redemption of Sentences through Work' scheme 87
Red Finns 9
red terror 137
regime of justification 3
reparation 198, 204
Republican law 65
Requetés 169
Restoration (1875–1930) 29
reverse justice 51
re-victimization 201
revolutionary environment 113
Ribadeo (Galicia) 67
    killing residents of 69–71, 75–6, **77**
    lieu de memoire 75
    municipal warehouses 76
Rodríguez, Manuel 75
Román Sánchez, César Manuel 20

Ronda de la Dignidad (Sol) 189, 193–6
   anti-austerity 15-M 'Indignados' camp 196
   reappropriation 194
   re-elaboration of human rights 196
Ruiz Giménez, Joaquín 34
Ruíz Vilaplana, Antonio 68
Russia civil war (1917–1923) 86–7

Salazar dictatorship 136
Salcedo Molinuevo, Enrique 56
San Amaro cemetery (Pontevedra) 135
Sánchez, Antonio 113
Sánchez 'El Charro,' Julián 55
San Esteban de las Cruces cemetery (Oviedo) 73
San Simón islands 132–3
Santa Isabel barracks 92, 96
Santa María de Oia (Oia), monastery 19, 147–52
   exhibition of 156
   inscriptions and drawings (prisoners) **150**, **162**
Santiago de Compostela (Galicia) 96, 99
   Boisaca's Cemetery **200**
   confinement spaces 92
   'Cross of the Fallen' in **6**
San Vicente, parish of 76
'the scene of the crime' 15
'Sección Femenina' (public rally) **128**
Second World War 1, 67, 85–6, 96, 140
sentencing site 55, **55**, 57, **58**, 78
Serrano Súñer, Ramón 51, 114
Servini, Judge 196–7, 199, 201–2
Sestás cemetery 149, 152, 155, 158
significative entity 127
Silva, Emilio 76
sites of burial 10, 78, 107, 153
sites of business 12
sites of confinement 10, 54, 56, 75–6, 79, 88, 92, 101, 108, 125, 148, 150, 171.
   See also Santiago de Compostela (Galicia)
sites of death 27–8, 70, 76
sites of denial 12, 14, 15, 73, 158
sites of execution 10, 36, 40, 97, 107, 154, 171
sites of memory 8, 12, 14, 18, 73–5, 126, 156, 187–9, 194
   conservation of 159
   memory alephs and 126–7
   policy of choosing 79
   prisoner drawings as 152–6
   public policies on 78
   treatment of 14, 19, 147
   types 12, 75
'Sites of Memory of State Terrorism' 157
sites of morbid fascination 12
sites of social control 106, 109
   post-war communities as 117–18
sites of torture 16, 148
sites of violence 10, 16, 18–19, 27, 73, 75, 106, 108, 147, 149, 155, 159, 161, 171
   humiliation and explicit punishment 110
   mediation 111–12
   protection and resignification 156–7
   'punishment communities' 111
   victims and executioners 112
   victors and regime supporters 110
Slepoy, Carlos 195
social control 18, 106, 112, 114, 116, 169. *See also* sites of social control
   overgeneralization 106, 119 n.5
social memory 132, 187
social mobilization 190
social regeneration 116
social space 188–9
society as whole 112–13, 116, 179, 190
space(s)
   defining 105
   groups, victims 75
   legal domination 53–60
   of reparation 161
   struggle 112–17
   and violence 107–12
'Spain of Victory' 114
Spanish Civil War (1936-1939) 3–5, 18, 27, 70, 72, 86, 89, 106, 136, 141, 167–71, 188, 190
   daily post-war reality 113
   exhumation 72
   as human and fratricidal drama 190
   new map of 142
   public policies 177
Spanish Patriots 36
Spanish War of Independence, Goya's drawings 134
spatial representativeness 127
spatial twist 106

spatial violence 108–9
Stalin, Joseph 196
State Coordinator of Support for the Argentine Lawsuit (CEAQUA) 193
statues 2, 7, 191, 194. *See also* memorials/monuments
Steer, George L. 171
struggle, spaces of 112–17
Suárez Ferrín, Alfredo 63 n.35
subcontracting human rights, model 192
Supreme Council of Military Justice (5 September 1939) 50
symbolic spaces 198

Taboada, Leovigildo 63 n.35
Talón, Vicente 128
Tercio Mora-Figueroa (Cádiz), case 30
territorial planning 48–9
Third Reich 99
Third Republic 86
Topographie des Terrors 12–13
Torres Martínez, César 30
torture 40, 148, 199. *See also* sites of torture
Transition 11, 14–15, 19, 156–60, 173, 188–90, 193, 199
Treblinka extermination camp 8

usucaption 7
Uzelai, José María 131

'Valdés clique' 37, 39
Valdés Guzmán, José 32, 34, 36–7, 39–40
Valencian Community 90, 159
Valery Karpim 155
Valladolid, sites of executions 107
Valley of the Fallen project 6, 10–11, 15, 88, 97, 188, 191
Velasco Simarro, Nicolás 37
Vendôme Column 2
Ventas Prison 188
victimization processes 178
Vitoria massacre (3 March 1976) 188

Whitaker, John T. 137
Wyden, Peter 137

'XXV Years of Peace' campaign 138

Yad Vashem memorial complex 8
Yagüe, Juan 136–7
'Year of Victory' 47

Zubiaga, Erik 19

www.ingramcontent.com/pod-product-compliance
Lightning Source LLC
Chambersburg PA
CBHW062219300426
44115CB00012BA/2135